A WAR BORN FAMILY

A War Born Family

*African American Adoption in the
Wake of the Korean War*

Kori A. Graves

NEW YORK UNIVERSITY PRESS
New York

NEW YORK UNIVERSITY PRESS
New York
www.nyupress.org

A portion of chapter 5 was previously published as Graves, Kori A., "Amerasian Children, Hybrid Superiority, and Pearl S. Buck's Transracial and Transnational Adoption Activism" in *Pennsylvania Magazine of History and Biography* 143, no. 2 (2019): 177–209.

References to Internet websites (URLs) were accurate at the time of writing. Neither the author nor New York University Press is responsible for URLs that may have expired or changed since the manuscript was prepared.

Library of Congress Cataloging-in-Publication Data
Names: Graves, Kori A., author.
Title: A war born family : African American adoption in the wake of the Korean War / Kori A. Graves.
Description: New York : New York University Press | Includes bibliographical references and index.
Identifiers: LCCN 2019008917 | ISBN 9781479872329 (cl : alk. paper)
Subjects: LCSH: Interracial adoption—United States—History—20th century. | Intercountry adoption—United States—History—20th century. | Intercountry adoption—Korea (South)—History—20th century. | Racially mixed children—Korea (South) | African American parents. | African American families. | Korean War, 1950-1953—Children.
Classification: LCC HV875.64 .G73 2019 | DDC 362.734089/05960730957—dc23
LC record available at https://lccn.loc.gov/2019008917

Manufactured in the United States of America

10 9 8 7 6 5 4 3 2 1

Also available as an ebook

CONTENTS

Introduction

When the African American magazine *Ebony* published "How to Adopt Korean Babies" in September 1955, its descriptions of the Korean black children in need of adoptive families caught the attention of many of the magazine's readers and child welfare officials throughout the United States. Calling them "the least loved boys and girls in Korea," the article suggested that Korean black children might not survive if they remained in that nation. Although all Koreans experienced extreme privations as a result of the Korean War (1950–1953), mixed-race children and their mothers suffered additional hardships. Many Koreans considered racial purity to be an essential aspect of their national identity, and they ostracized children fathered by white or black American soldiers. Mixed-race children were also stateless because they could not claim membership in the patrilineal family systems that defined citizenship and belonging in Korea. These circumstances led *Ebony*'s editor and staff to encourage the magazine's readers to learn more about the nascent Korean adoption process to determine whether they could adopt one of the estimated 300 Korean black children available to "qualified American families virtually for the asking."[1]

"How to Adopt Korean Babies" was not the first time *Ebony* had attempted to inspire members of its largely African American audience to become adoptive parents. Since the late 1940s, the magazine had published articles telling readers why they should and how they could adopt children in the United States and mixed-race children of African American soldiers born in countries throughout Western Europe and in Japan. Articles like "How to Adopt Korean Babies" also appeared in African American magazines and newspapers across the country. They caused an untold number of people to adopt informally or work with public child welfare organizations and private adoption agencies to complete formal, legal adoptions. However, in the early 1950s, African Americans faced barriers to formal adoption because of the ways segregation and racial inequality influenced domestic and transnational adoption practices.

Officials with International Social Service (ISS) also wanted to facilitate adoptions of Korean black children. But they knew that African Americans often encountered discrimination when they attempted to adopt children through agencies in the United States. Founded in 1924 under the auspices of the Young Women's Christian Association (YWCA), ISS was an international social welfare organization that negotiated social welfare concerns across national boundaries. Called International Migration Service until 1946, ISS had its headquarters in Geneva, Switzerland and a network of branches located in the United States, Japan, and several Western European nations by the early 1950s. When *Ebony* published "How to Adopt Korean Babies," ISS staff had already encountered difficulties coordinating services for the growing number of Americans interested in adopting a Korean child. While ISS welcomed the black press's efforts to recruit adoptive parents, officials understood that arranging transnational placements between the United States and Korea would present many challenges. ISS America Branch director, William T. Kirk, indirectly addressed this issue when he wrote to *Ebony*'s editor, John H. Johnson. He complimented the magazine on its explanation of the political significance of US-Korean adoption and its inclusion of step-by-step instructions for prospective adoptive families. Kirk reported that the article had already inspired a number of African Americans to contact ISS. He also affirmed ISS's commitment to encouraging child welfare agencies to assist African American families that qualified to adopt a Korean child.[2]

The same day that Kirk sent his letter to *Ebony*, ISS America Branch assistant director, Susan T. Pettiss, sent a press release to the directors of state departments of child welfare around the United States to tell them about "How to Adopt Korean Babies." Pettiss echoed Kirk's praise for the article's depiction of the dire circumstances in Korea, and she asked that agencies work with African American families to place Korean black children. But Pettiss did not stop there. Aware of the chronic need for African Americans to adopt the European children fathered by African American soldiers during and after World War II, she asked that agencies help identify suitable families for these children too. Pettiss acknowledged that her request might create new challenges for agencies already struggling to identify adoptive families for African American children in the United States. However, she suggested that the right African American couples for GI babies were not the same as couples that would pursue a domestic adoption. To identify such couples, she encouraged agencies to be on the lookout for people who were motivated by the humanitarian aspect of transnational adoptions. Pettiss ended her press release by advising officials to show compassion toward the African American families that expressed a desire to adopt a Korean black child.[3] With these measures, Kirk and Pettiss hoped they could help implement a transnational adoption strategy that would assure "the most secure future possible" for Korean black children.[4]

Throughout the 1950s and 1960s, an array of adoption advocates joined the black press and child welfare professionals in efforts to define what constituted a secure future for Korean black children. As the above exchanges between *Ebony*, ISS, and child welfare agencies throughout the United States suggest, child welfare professionals and nonprofessionals understood that America's race problems would inform whatever plans they attempted to make for Korean black children. Thus, advocates of US-Korean adoption would devise numerous, and at times competing strategies to accommodate African American and mixed-race children in the United States and mixed-race Korean GI children. Initially, child welfare professionals and nonprofessionals agreed that African American couples or interracial couples—those that included an African American and white spouse or a spouse(s) of mixed-race heritage—were the clients best suited to adopt Korean black children. However, by the late 1960s, African American and interracial couples became less relevant in Korean adoption, while white families' participation in adoptions involving Korean children and nonwhite children in the United States increased. *A War Born Family* tells the story of the evolution of African Americans' adoptions of Korean children to explain how and why this method of family formation changed so drastically in the 1950s and 1960s.

The first time I encountered stories about efforts of the black press to recruit African American adoptive families, I was conducting research on the popular representations of African American families in 1940s and 1950s magazines like *Ebony*. At that time, I had a superficial awareness of African Americans' transnational adoptions of the so-called brown babies of Germany because of the work of scholars like Brenda Gayle Plummer and Heide Fehrenbach.[5] But there was not a considerable body of scholarship on African Americans' adoptions of other brown babies—the children of black soldiers and women in Japan and countries throughout Western Europe—born during and after World War II. There was even less written about African Americans' adoptions of Korean children. What I did find indicated that the dearth of historical analysis into this topic was related to the fact that efforts to create US-Korean adoption programs involving African American adoptive couples had largely failed. According to Michael Cullen Green, "in contrast to African American endeavors to assist European brown babies . . . no sustained campaigns arose for the support of biracial children in Asia." Green further explains that this difference existed because African Americans faced legal, economic, and cultural barriers that made adoptions of Korean black children harder to complete than adoptions of mixed-race children born in European countries. Consequently, the "Cold War imperatives that encouraged cultural celebrations of the adoption of Asian orphans and abandoned white-Asian children . . . did not extend to Afro-Asians."[6]

Green's conclusions intrigued me. What were the legal, economic, and cultural barriers that limited African Americans' adoptions? How had some African Americans overcome these barriers to adopt Korean children? What happened to Korean black children once transnational adoption efforts for them failed? Had African Americans simply "lost interest" in Korean black children, as Green suggests?[7] My search for answers to these questions led me to evaluate the ways the black press, adoptive families, and child welfare professionals and nonprofessionals characterized the political and symbolic significance of African Americans' adoption experiences during the first two decades of US-Korean adoption. I found that some in these groups emphasized the child rescue aspect of African Americans' Korean transnational adoptions. Others equated African Americans' informal and formal adoptions of Korean children with broader efforts to advance racial equality. A few promoted reevaluations of long-standing negative characterizations of African American men and women, interracial adoptive families, and mixed-race children. Among child welfare professionals, these changes were most evident in the ways some incorporated African American families into their new definitions of suitable adoptive families. Whereas social workers routinely denied African American couples' adoption bids if they were older than forty or if they included a wife who worked outside of the home, some adapted prevailing adoption standards to place Korean black children. This book therefore explores the ways the Cold War and struggles for civil rights in the United States influenced many of these transformations. I argue that the ideals and rhetoric of Cold War civil rights that facilitated adoptions of Korean black children increasingly benefited white adoptive families more than African American adoptive families. This shift was the result of white and black adoption advocates' efforts to institute reforms by characterizing transracial and transnational placements as liberal, antiracist endeavors.

"African Americans Adopt?": Locating African Americans in Histories of US Adoption

One of the first questions people asked me when I explained that I was writing a history about the African American families who adopted Korean children was "African Americans adopt?." Given the ways that white families figure so prominently in popular representations of transracial and transnational adoption, this response is understandable. Contemporary accounts of white celebrities' and noncelebrities' adoptions of Native American, African American, Asian, and African children often present these stories as examples of a redemptive kind of color-blind love that transcends familial concerns. In other words, many depictions suggest that white families involved in transracial and transnational adoptions are not just rescuing children who might otherwise experience homelessness, violence, or even death. They are also intervening in complicated domestic and foreign affairs. It is certain that love and the desire to parent have inspired many people to create families across national borders and culturally constructed (yet meaningful) lines of race. But such adoptions have also raised troubling legal and ethical questions about this method of family formation. As sociologist Sara K. Dorow posits, "transracial, transnational adoptive kinship might just as readily transform as reproduce forms of injustice, might just as easily forge new cultural politics as ignore the constraints of existing ones."[8]

Indeed, early critics of transracial and transnational adoptions worked to highlight the ways cultural, economic, political, and social inequalities made it difficult for people in marginalized communities and war-torn countries to keep their children. Throughout the 1960s and 1970s, activists and social workers in the United States and Canada were among the most vocal and visible opponents of white families' adoptions of African American, Native American, African Canadian, and Canadian First Nations children. To many people in these communities, transracial adoptions amounted to "the theft of children and an attack on minority communities."[9] During the 1980s and 1990s, a number of the children caught up in the waves of adoptions from countries including Argentina, El Salvador, and Guatemala were, in fact, the "disappeared" victims of civil wars and politically motivated kidnappings.[10] But efforts to expand private adoption programs that largely catered to white families in the United States persisted in spite of activists' attempts to expose the atrocities that fed both legal and illegal, profit-driven adoption industries throughout Latin America. Thus, events like the National Association of Black Social Workers' condemnation of transracial adoptions of black children 1972, the passage of the Indian Child Welfare Act in 1978, and the activism of mothers of disappeared children and their allies in Latin America have highlighted the ways that some transracial and transnational adoptions were the result of and resulted in exploitation, coercion, and violence—not *rescue*.

The field of critical adoption studies has expanded as a result of interdisciplinary scholarship that interrogates the kinds of paradoxes that transracial and transnational adoptions have created.[11] In this context, Korean transnational adoption has generated considerable attention from adoptees, adoptive parents, scholars, and those scholars who are themselves adoptees or adoptive parents. Their work has uncovered the ways that ideas about adoption as rescue masks the neocolonial political entanglements and market relations that are also a part of the Korean story.[12] These investigations have replaced questions about the humanitarian and color-blind aspects of Korean transnational adoption with questions about the "broader socioeconomic and social welfare failures that produce the conditions of the adoption economy."[13] Because white, affluent families in Western nations have been the largest group to adopt Korean children, assessments of their activities have also attracted more critical scrutiny.

Thus, efforts to correct what have been, at times, simplistic explanations for white adoptive parents' motives have revealed what Dong Soo Kim describes as "discrepancies in their altruism, if not hypocrisies, in that their concern and love for poor homeless children were color-biased and somewhat romanticized."[14] This scholarship has answered and raised important questions about the reasons ideas such as *color-blind love* and *adoption as rescue* grossly mischaracterize the complicated political, social, economic, religious, and emotional factors that shaped the origins and evolution of Korean transnational adoption. However, emphasizing how and why these ideas evolved to explain white families' roles in Korean transnational adoption (and other episodes of transracial, transnational adoption) obscures the history of African Americans' participation in these practices, which is the focus of my work.

One reason it is difficult for many people to imagine African Americans as adopters of children is that their experiences can be difficult to locate in the records that detail the development of US and transnational adoption. When Massachusetts lawmakers passed the nation's first modern law establishing that state's minimum requirements for adoption in 1851, most African American children were slaves.[15] Religious leaders, benevolent reformers, and child welfare professionals had white orphans and displaced immigrant children in mind when they devised the "placing out" strategies that were the precursors to adoption and foster care in the late nineteenth and early twentieth centuries.[16] Even though the families who boarded and adopted during these decades often wanted children (not babies) to provide labor, the institutions that arranged such placements rarely accommodated African American children.[17] In the early 1920s, Progressive Era reformers and social welfare policymakers planned that mothers' pension programs would benefit "deserving" white mothers and their children.[18] In the 1920s and 1930s, social workers were particularly concerned about white babies, birth mothers, and adoptive couples when they endeavored to regulate the black and grey market adoptions many people associated with baby farms and baby selling.[19] Throughout the 1930s, 1940s, and 1950s, child welfare professionals affiliated with the US Children's Bureau (USCB) and the Child Welfare League of America (CWLA) promoted adoption standards to ostensibly protect all children, birth parents, and adoptive parents from the risks associated with placements brokered by volunteers, physicians, or lawyers.[20] But most of the agencies that implemented these measures did not arrange adoptions for African American clients.[21]

Throughout the late 1940s and the 1950s, many white social workers considered adoption to be a remedy for two issues hindering the development of healthy domesticity in white communities, namely infertile couples and unmarried, pregnant women. Often using coercive and punitive tactics, social workers encouraged white, unmarried birth mothers to relinquish their children.[22] For the most part, white social workers did not emphasize adoption to address issues of infertility or unmarried pregnancy affecting African American communities. Even though some African American social workers fought to increase adoption services for black clients during this time, few agencies did. Karen Balcom explains the results of such neglect in her study of cross-border adoptions between the United States and Canada, noting that "mixed-race or non-white children were shadows at the edges of adoptability, since relatively few social agencies in Canada or the United States provided adoption services" to minority clients.[23] Consequently, the number of adoptions involving white clients grew at an unprecedented rate during the 1950s and 1960s, while members of minority communities continued to struggle to gain access to professional adoption services.[24]

African Americans adapted to these exclusions by devising formal and informal strategies to care for orphaned and displaced children. Beginning in the late nineteenth century, African American churches, benevolent organizations, and women's clubs took leading roles in efforts to sponsor facilities for children in need.[25] Although African Americans established few orphanages, black child welfare professionals and nonprofessionals created kindergartens and day nurseries, which, despite their names, sometimes provided full-time care for abandoned children.[26] Throughout the first half of the twentieth century, informal arrangements between family members, friends, and neighbors that included short-term or long-term child care were common practices.[27] African Americans did complete formal adoptions by working with the few public and private agencies that provided adoption services to minority clients. After World War II, some completed transnational adoptions of brown babies, often through private agencies or programs.[28] But these efforts took place largely outside of the institutions that regulated adoptive placements by the middle of the twentieth century. As this limited overview suggests, the individuals and institutions that shaped the legal and cultural contours of adoption in America rarely considered the needs or desires of African American clients.[29]

However, changes associated with the Cold War and the Civil Rights Movement produced episodes when agencies did prioritize African Americans, causing their adoption experiences to become more visible in institutional settings. The Cold War inspired an untold number of black and white Americans to embrace family life and reimagine domestic spaces as refuges from the instabilities that were a product of the nuclear age.[30] Indeed, in one of only a few histories to compare the postwar adoption patterns of white and African American working-class couples, Sarah Potter shows that African Americans pursued adoptions because, like many of their white counterparts, they embraced a "powerful ideology that depict[ed] family membership as essential to happiness and fulfillment."[31] The Civil Rights Movement increased peoples' awareness of the ways African Americans were resisting their exclusion from many of the nation's institutions, including its child welfare institutions. In this context, some agencies became more attentive to African Americans' requests for adoption services, in part, because child welfare officials were beginning to understand the social and political import of their efforts. But most of the projects that agencies designed to recruit African American adoptive families experienced limited success. Thus, histories that consider African Americans' domestic adoption experiences during the 1950s and 1960s largely emphasize the failures of efforts to address racial inequality in adoption service delivery.[32] These failures are part of the origins story of African Americans' resistance to transracial adoption, which gained national attention in the 1970s.

The agencies that began experimenting with transracial placements of African American children in the 1950s did so out of desperation when they could not place children with families that shared the same racial background.[33] In fact, this was the circumstance that motivated the African American social worker who facilitated the first recorded "intentional" transracial adoption of an African American child by a white family in Minneapolis, Minnesota in 1948.[34] Although the number of transracial adoptions involving African American and black-white mixed-race children remained relatively low throughout the 1950s and 1960s, the National Association of Black Social Workers' (NABSW) criticism of the practice became a flashpoint for debates over the morality and efficacy of this type of transracial placement. The NABSW officially condemned transracial adoptions at its 1972 conference, "Diversity: Cohesion or Chaos—Mobilization for Survival." The presentations at that conference highlighted the organization's concern that racial inequality in social service delivery harmed black communities. The two addresses on the issue of transracial adoption were unequivocal in their rejection of such placements, and black social worker Audrey T. Russell's speech made the provocative charge that it was "a practice of genocide." This statement and her shocking comparison of transracial adoptions to the Nazis' use of gas chambers in their atrocious attempt to exterminate Jews during World War II attracted a lot of media attention.[35]

Adoption scholars including Laura Briggs and E. Wayne Carp note that these controversial statements were indicative of the growing influence of black nationalism that was shaping many African Americans' assessments of the failures of the nation's institutions to achieve full racial equality.[36] These statements were also effective in the short run. The number of white families adopting black children declined from a peak of more than two thousand in 1971 to 831 in 1975. While opponents of transracial adoption likely considered this transition a positive trend, the NABSW's condemnation ignored divisions within black communities concerning transracial adoption. Ellen Herman describes that it also "encouraged the simplistic view that African Americans were monolithically opposed to transracial adoptions at a time when blacks were almost surely more tolerant of interracial families than whites."[37] And she is correct. Some African Americans had supported and continued to support adoptions that placed African American children with white families as a more desirable outcome than allowing children to languish in foster care or in other institutional settings. African Americans' ideas about transracial adoption were also much more varied than the NABSW's statement indicates because of the ways some had participated in and advocated for transracial and transnational adoptions in the 1950s and the 1960s. Thus, *A War Born Family* attempts to fill a gap in the literature that discusses African Americans' adoption experiences by exploring the ways their support of and involvement in Korean adoption helped define the contours of the early years of that episode of transracial, transnational child placement.

African Americans, Transnational Adoption, and Transformations of Race and Rescue

African Americans moved in and out of Korean transnational adoption schemes as the practice expanded from an emergency measure to accommodate the needs of Korean War orphans and mixed-race Korean GI babies into more formalized systems to coordinate adoptions of poor and displaced Korean children. Even though there were no Korean laws or clearly defined policies regulating out-of-country placements, black and white soldiers and volunteers affiliated with the sectarian and nonsectarian aid agencies in Korea began pursuing adoptions as a form of rescue before the Korean War ended.[38] After the war, ideas about adoption, race, and rescue took on new meanings as Americans adopted more mixed-race Korean children fathered by American soldiers. Notions of color-blind love took root among many white adoptive families as they began thinking about Korean-white babies as their responsibility because they were the children of white American soldiers. However, scholars have noted that color blindness actually meant the erasure of mixed-race children's Korean-ness by some white child welfare professionals and white adoptive families who believed that "Korean-white children were whitened—redeemed—by the presence of white blood."[39] Because such ideas have obscured how this construction of race reproduced racial inequality, Catherine Ceniza Choy cautions that we cannot ignore the complicated ways that ideas about "race and rescue" have shaped Americans' perceptions of and participation in transnational adoption.[40] Choy and other scholars in the fields of Asian American Studies and Adoption Studies have paid particular attention to these themes as they relate to white adoptive families and their Asian adopted children.[41] Since a similar reformulation of Korean black children's identities took place in the black press and among some African American adopting parents, this book considers how and why ideas about Korean transnational adoption, race, and rescue evolved in black communities.

Throughout the 1950s and 1960s, African Americans' ideas about foreign-born, mixed-race children changed as they participated in what Rachel Rains Winslow calls the "remapping of children's racial identities."[42] For example, although African Americans would play a larger role in the adoptions of World War II brown babies than in any other transnational adoption effort, a number of issues made this outcome seem unlikely in the immediate aftermath of the war. Chief among them was the fact that some African Americans did not identify brown babies as kin or consider the mixed-race children of foreign women to be the responsibility of African American communities.[43] Instead, they associated these children with their mothers' racial and national identities. Consequently, advocates of African Americans' adoptions of World War II brown babies stressed that these adoptions promoted racial solidarity, and they emphasized the ways that mixed-race children suffered ostracism because of their African American heritage. This strategy helped inspire African American families to see brown babies as members of the black community.[44]

Because comparable cultural messages influenced African Americans' ideas about Korean transnational adoption, their efforts to incorporate Korean black children into black communities also involved a reimagining of the children's racial identities. There are few records produced by African American adoptive families themselves that describe the meanings they ascribed to their Korean black children's mixed-race identities. Therefore, to assess the diverse ways African Americans negotiated questions of identity, I rely heavily on reports in the black press and social workers' case notes from the records of ISS that relay the comments of African American adoptive families. These sources show that in some instances, African Americans applied the logic of the one-drop rule and erased or ignored the children's Korean identities. Other times, adoptive parents seemed to embrace their children's mixed-racial heritage. This response was evident in families that included adoptive parents who were themselves mixed-race. African American and mixed-race parents also revealed the complex meanings of skin color in black communities when they indicated color or skin complexion preferences. No matter how they defined Korean black children's color or racial identity, African Americans understood that their involvement in Korean transnational adoption was based on cultural perceptions of the children's blackness and how it connected them to black communities.

Adoption scholars have described how and why religion, liberalism, humanitarianism, and, to a degree, race influenced the growth of Korean transnational adoption among white families in the United States.[45] While these factors also played a role in African Americans' adoptions of Korean children, my work demonstrates that race was the primary factor that shaped their adoption experiences. The professionals and nonprofessionals who arranged Korean transnational adoptions attempted to adhere to the principle of race matching when placing children fathered by US soldiers. Matching was a strategy that many agencies in the States used to pair children and families based on specialists' determinations of their religious, racial, and, as best as could be determined, intellectual sameness.[46] In adoptions involving mixed-race Korean children, matching meant that agencies attempted to pair each child with a family that shared the racial identity of the child's GI father. This approach initially made African Americans integral to Korean transnational adoption efforts.

However, because racial inequality and segregation informed how agencies selected adoptive parents for both US and US-Korean placements, African Americans faced barriers to Korean adoptions in much the same way that they did in domestic adoptions. Therefore, I evaluate how race and the notion of rescue encouraged public and private agencies and organizations including ISS, USCB, and CWLA to facilitate African Americans' adoptions of Korean black children. The reforms these agencies promoted made it possible for social workers to approve African American couples that would have been, and in some cases had been, judged unsuitable for a domestic placement. Since many of these reforms addressed the ways agencies evaluated African Americans' conformity to the nuclear family model, I also assess the changes officials made in their appraisals of gender and the gender division of productive and reproductive labor in black families.

These shifts were possible, in large part, because of the Cold War imperatives *and* civil rights ideals that shaped people's understandings of African Americans' practical and symbolic roles in Korean transnational adoption. Indeed, the individuals and organizations that fought for reforms by linking African Americans' efforts to care for and adopt Korean children with their struggles to achieve racial equality often utilized a strategy consistent with what Mary L. Dudziak has called Cold War civil rights.[47] Practitioners of Cold War civil rights mobilized international critiques of US race relations to compel US political leaders to address domestic civil rights issues. Some leaders began to associate efforts to end racial discrimination with "international priorities" because they were anxious about the nation's ability to direct world affairs.[48] Cold War struggles between the United States and the Soviet Union realigned US foreign policy and domestic race relations as these nations jockeyed for influence over the destinies of newly independent nations in Africa and Asia.[49] In the United States, poorly conceived strategies to extend democracy and limit the spread of communism set the stage for domestic unrest, costly wars, nuclear proliferation, and global instability. The failures of US military and foreign policy to resolve international conflicts like the Korean War did further damage to the nation's reputation around the world. In this context, marches, demonstrations, and protests that revealed the brutality and inhumanity of racism in the United States helped bring about many of the most celebrated victories of the modern Civil Rights Movement. But this strategy had very real limits because it did not require comprehensive reform of institutional racism. Political leaders "did not have to solve the US racial problem; they only had to manage the way the world perceived it."[50]

Efforts to increase support for African Americans' adoptions that mobilized Cold War anxieties and civil rights ideals similarly failed to produce comprehensive reforms in adoption policies. To demonstrate the limits of Cold War civil rights in child welfare, this book evaluates the parallels between the strategies of the National Urban League's Project in Foster Care and Adoption with those of agencies that facilitated African Americans' adoptions of Korean black children. When it began in 1953, the League's project was the most ambitious effort spearheaded by African Americans to increase adoptions of minority children. League records indicate that adoption agencies and child welfare organizations were not immune to the changes that the Cold War and civil rights activism inspired, even though the reforms that resulted were uneven and inconsistent. They further show the similarities between the rhetoric of civil rights activists who fought for issues including school desegregation and the rhetoric of individuals fighting for African Americans' greater access to adoption services. Although Ellen Herman has observed that most people and organizations fighting for civil rights did not "consider the family a key locus of struggle over racial equality," officials with the National Urban League did.[51] Evaluating these episodes of adoption reform in tandem shows that many adoptive families also saw a connection between their struggles to adopt and struggles for civil rights.

The Cold War and the Civil Rights Movement also shaped white families' participation in transracial and transnational adoptions in the 1950s and the 1960s. But, questions about the extent to which these events influenced Americans' early transnational adoptions have led to different conclusions. Rachel Rains Winslow has offered compelling arguments suggesting that white, middle-class couples' interest in transracial and transnational adoptions spurred the growth of these placements and not just a "particular Cold War response to civil rights pressures and the large number of American-fathered children."[52] A number of adoption scholars have, however, chronicled the ways that both the Cold War and the Civil Rights Movement inspired changes in immigration laws, adoption policies, and popular representations of Korean children that led more white families to pursue Korean trinational adoption.[53] These changes were necessary. Dating back to the nineteenth century, anti-Asian sentiment and anti-Asian legislation reinforced negative stereotypes about Asians and beliefs that they could not assimilate into American culture or society.[54] Thus, the media and sectarian and non-sectarian aid organizations encouraged adoptions by emphasizing the assimilability of Korean children. Some efforts to increase adoptions also exploited Cold War anxieties by suggesting that adoptions of Korean children saved them from communism and disproved American racism. This book evaluates how novelist and adoption reformer Pearl S. Buck combined both strategies to attract white adoptive families to transracial and transnational adoption. My approach does not discount the ways that love and benevolence influenced white families' desires to participate in transracial and transnational adoption. But it does suggest that the powerful legacies of racism and colonialism did shape how white families understood their adoptions of nonwhite children. Consequently, Buck's work demonstrates why some adoption advocates believed it was necessary to emphasize the ways that supporting and adopting Korean children—and in Buck's case mixed-race children of Asian descent in the United States and Korea—advanced the goals of the Cold War and evinced the civil rights ideals of racial harmony.

African Americans' roles in the development of Korean transnational adoption would largely be forgotten as the practice grew from an emergency solution to Korea's orphan crisis into the first large-scale, transnational adoption project of the twentieth century. This book uncovers the diverse manifestations of inequality that simultaneously made Americans believe that Korean transnational adoption was necessary and created categories of adoptees and adoptive families that were more vulnerable than others. Evaluating how and why African Americans participated in the rescue of Korean children adds to our understanding of the significance of race in the growth of this adoption stream and affirms SooJin Pate's observation that "the genealogies of Korean adoption are multiple and varied."[55] Although US-Korean adoptions were ostensibly about the rescue of vulnerable children, they also revealed the contested meanings of identity, citizenship, and belonging for the children, birth mothers, and prospective adoptive parents involved in numerous adoption schemes. For African Americans, these contests could not be separated from their struggles to obtain equality in all aspects of their lives.

A War Born Family evaluates how and why African Americans' participation in US-Korean adoption evolved from the beginning of the Korean War to the late 1960s. Instead of following a linear chronology, the five chapters of this book follow complimentary narratives that overlap chronologically. Each chapter explores how different individuals and groups understood African Americans' roles in adoption as a form of rescue, and how adoption policies and practices affected plans to create a secure future for Korean black children. The first two chapters consider how the struggle for racial equality in the military and US child welfare institutions informed African Americans' participation in US and Korean child welfare schemes as well as the first Korean transnational adoptions. Chapter 1 analyzes African American soldiers' roles in wartime child-centered humanitarianism that became the basis of the adoptions that would take place after the Korean War. The black press made stories about African American soldiers' care of Korean children an element of its aggressive promotion of military desegregation. But these stories took on new meanings once the army desegregated and black soldiers continued to face discrimination and the criticisms of some white politicians, military officials, soldiers, and members of the mainstream press. Throughout the war, members of these communities continually questioned African American soldiers' bravery and fitness to serve. The black press countered with stories of African American soldiers' honorable service that included examples of their informal and formal adoptions of Korean children. But these stories also revealed the ways African American soldiers exploited vulnerable Korean women and fathered the Korean black children that would become the focus of the first US-Korean adoption programs.

As Korean transnational adoption expanded in the 1950s, a number of officials with US and international child welfare organizations debated the need to reform policies that limited African Americans' US and Korean adoptions. These debates emerged at the same time that officials with the National Urban League (NUL) intensified their efforts to increase reforms to facilitate African Americans' efforts to adopt in the United States. Chapter 2 examines the ways the NUL's fight for domestic adoption reform identified the institutional inequalities that limited African Americans' involvement in US, and by extension, transnational child welfare schemes. When the League began its Project in Foster Care and Adoption in 1953, it promoted an integrationist civil rights agenda to accomplish comprehensive, nationwide reform in child welfare agencies. League officials also proposed reforms in adoption policies to address the ways that racial inequality influenced adoption practice. Few white adoption agencies implemented the comprehensive reforms League officials encouraged. Further, White Citizens' Councils mobilized a number of strategies to stop the League's efforts that paralleled segregationists' efforts to slow the pace of integration in education. Segregationists successfully increased cultural and institution barriers to adoption reforms using racist and anticommunist rhetoric to attack the League's mission and League officials. However, the limited successes of the League's project revealed the ways that some agencies responded to civil rights ideals to pursue interracial cooperation and assist African American adoptive families.

The last three chapters chronicle the evolution of African Americans' roles in Korean transnational adoption through an assessment of the strategies and programs that people associated with the military, and sectarian and nonsectarian organizations devised to address the child welfare crisis in Korea. Chapter 3 describes the competing strategies that child welfare professionals and nonprofessionals implemented to facilitate US-Korean adoptions for Korean GI children. Soldiers' and civilians' efforts to adopt Korean children in the immediate aftermath of the war exacerbated tensions between child welfare professionals and nonprofessionals who disagreed about the policies that should regulate Korean transnational adoption. Professionals who attempted to strengthen regulations to assure that mixed-race Korean children had the same protections as children adopted in the United States increasingly identified African American families associated with the US military as ideal adoptive families. These families benefited from their affiliation with the US military, which made it possible for many to conform to the gender conventions characteristic of the nuclear family model. However, reports of the brutal circumstances that shaped the lives of Korean black children and their mothers led nonprofessionals to work to reduce the regulations that they believed limited adoptions and increased these children's vulnerability.

Chapter 4 evaluates the ways that some US adoption agencies revised their definitions of ideal adoptive families to increase placements of Korean black children with families not affiliated with the military. Often these couples could not meet the standards agencies typically applied when evaluating prospective adoptive families. The case notes of social workers employed by agencies affiliated with ISS reveal two striking patterns among families that were not affiliated with the military but successfully adopted Korean black children. First, they included a number of interracial couples. Second, these couples usually included wives who worked outside of their homes. These patterns disrupted race and gender conventions that were central to the burgeoning nuclear family ideal, and they demonstrate how racial inequality shaped African American family life. Social workers' interactions with such families caused a number to appreciate that they represented recognizable patterns in communities of color, where working wives and interracial intimacies existed on a spectrum of familiar family types. But the accommodations some social workers made to increase adoptions of Korean black children were not sufficient to meet the needs of this population. Paradoxically, by the 1960s, a small number of white families who adopted Korean black children began to benefit from the accommodations social workers made to assist African American and interracial adoptive couples. A few also associated their actions with the efforts to increase racial equality that characterized civil rights activism for two decades after World War II. Consequently, some child welfare professionals and members of the press would begin to describe white families' participation in this type of transracial and transnational adoption as liberal and antiracist.

The successes of early US-Korean adoptions influenced changes in policies and popular representations of transracial and transnational adoption that expanded the roles of white families in the care of vulnerable children of color in the United States and abroad. Chapter 5 explores this shift by describing novelist Pearl S. Buck's involvement in US and Korean adoption reform in the 1950s and 1960s. Buck's institution-building and rhetorical reframing of transracial families illustrates the ways the ideals of color-blind love and racial equality drew white families to transracial and transnational adoption at the height of the Civil Rights Movement. As an adoptive mother of mixed-race children, cofounder of the Welcome House Adoption Agency, and founder of the Pearl S. Buck International Foundation, Buck was able to fashion an institutional framework and controversial rescue narrative that appealed to white adoptive parents who were trying to make sense of domestic racial inequality and global Cold War conflicts. Although Buck was a vocal supporter of civil rights and an advocate of African Americans' Korean adoptions, her work ultimately reinforced the idea that white families, as adopters and supporters of her child welfare facilities, could provide the most secure future possible for mixed-race children in the United States and South Korea.

1

African American Soldiers and the Origins of Korean Transnational Adoption

In February 1953, Captain Sylvester Booker became the first African American to bring a Korean child to the United States for adoption. Captain Booker's effort to adopt Rhee Song Wu made him a member of a small but growing number of Westerners who attempted to rescue children they believed to be war orphans during the Korean War. When Booker began his 18-month-long bureaucratic struggle to adopt Rhee, the child was not officially an orphan because his mother was alive. But Booker claimed that Rhee's mother wanted him to adopt her son. According to him, she had even signed papers to that effect because she believed Rhee would have a better life in the United States.[1] Booker agreed. He was confident that he could provide Rhee "a good home, excellent schooling, and an opportunity to make himself a first-rate citizen."[2] But getting Rhee to the United States was not easy. Booker had to request that the US Congress pass a private law that would bypass immigration restrictions that imposed limits on the number of visas available to citizens of Asian nations. Although Booker was in Korea when he began investigating ways to adopt Rhee, he was not able to secure the necessary paperwork to take Rhee with him when his tour ended. However, on July 9, 1952, Congress passed Private Law 82–801, "An Act for the Relief of Rhee Song Wu," and less than a year later, Rhee was on his way to live with Bookers.[3]

The media coverage of the Booker adoption presented the story as a triumph of humanitarianism. Articles about their separation and reunion appeared in African American and white newspapers from 1952 to 1954. Most publications only alluded to the tragedies Rhee experienced before he left Korea or the circumstances that would set the stage for the unprecedented growth of transnational adoptions involving Korean children in the postwar years.[4] Instead, articles described Rhee as a charming and spunky youngster who was "not afraid of anything except little girls."[5] Many publications also characterized Booker as an accomplished and caring medic who attended to Rhee's injured hand and then "took the waif into his camp, fed him, clothed him, taught him to speak English and, in the process, came to love him as a son."[6] Several pieces did not make Booker's race a central element of the story. In fact, the Congressional Record of Booker's case and a number of the white publications such as the *Los Angeles Times* did not reference his race at all. Even when articles mentioned that Booker was an African American, most publications emphasized the ways he was an exemplary American who would be able to raise Rhee to be the same.[7] In the decades after the Korean War, many African American soldiers would join Captain Booker and attempt to adopt Korean children. Much like Booker, the experiences they had and the circumstances they encountered while serving in Korea inspired this response. This chapter evaluates those circumstances to demonstrate how they became the roots of Korean transnational adoption for black soldiers.

During the Korean War, black soldiers devised many formal and informal ways to assist the Korean children they encountered. These efforts often began with small gestures of charity that grew to become more long-term commitments of care. This form of benevolence attracted considerable attention because it made sense in the context of a war that brought men from wealthy nations into contact with impoverished children in a war-torn country. Discussions of soldiers' kindness toward children also served multiple political and social purposes. As SooJin Pate describes, during and after the war "military humanitarianism became the primary tool in which to assuage the image of the United States as colonizer and occupier . . . [and] the phenomenon of GIs as humanitarians became the strategy in which to do so."[8] Political leaders, military officials, and members of the media emphasized how all soldiers' efforts to aid Korean children were politically and culturally significant to US foreign relations. Yet, the black press's emphasis on the "American" qualities of the black soldiers who provided care for Korean children was consequential because of the civil rights struggles that embroiled many African Americans in efforts to redefine the terms of their citizenship.[9]

Throughout the Korean War, the black press mobilized depictions of compassionate African American soldiers as part of a larger campaign to bolster appeals for racial equality in the US military and society. In this context, the cultural and political significance of black soldiers' child-focused charity evolved as the goals of the Civil Rights Movement shifted. This chapter evaluates how civil rights struggles shaped popular characterizations of African American soldiers' child-focused charity as well as their social and sexual relations with Korean women during the Korean War. Ideas presented in African American newspapers, and especially the *Afro-American*, are central to this analysis. In most cases, stories in the black press about African American soldiers' humanitarian activities were overwhelmingly positive. These assessments helped counter the criticisms of black soldiers' conduct on and off the battlefield that followed them throughout the conflict. But soldiers' actions in Korean communities had many far-reaching negative effects because they took place within a web of intricate political and social relations. While some soldiers sacrificed to provided material aid to some Korean children, they also engaged in the very martial activities that decimated Korean communities. Similarly, black soldiers' social and sexual relations with Korean women contributed to community instability, and the children born as a result of these relationships suffered because of the war *and* because they were mixed-race. The black press was largely uncritical of black soldiers' roles in these destructive aspects of the war, which obscured the ways some African American men were complicit in the violence and exploitation that harmed Korean women and the Korean children they aided, fathered, and would adopt. Instead, the black press developed narratives that highlighted themes of rescue and responsibility that influenced African Americans' wartime ideas about Korean children.[10]

Scholarship exploring the contradictory nature of soldiers' military humanitarianism during the Korean War has focused largely on the behaviors of white soldiers.[11] A few scholars of African American history have attempted to make sense of black soldiers' child-centric benevolence by situating their Korean War experiences in the genealogy of the Civil Rights Movement.[12] Indeed, such histories explore the ways soldiers and civil rights activists characterized African American men's military service as a leading wedge in the fight to dismantle segregation in the military and US society. However, ideas about gender, and not just race, defined African American soldiers' experiences and assessments of their conduct. Consequently, many activists prioritized the defense of black manhood, because "the link between valorous military service and civil rights was so tight . . . that many critics feared admission to black faltering would only damage their claims to full civil rights as well as the inherent assertion of equal manhood."[13] This chapter builds on these assessments to evaluate what scholar Katharine H. S. Moon calls the "people-to people" strand of US-Korean relations that influenced black men's military service, roles in wartime Korean child welfare, relationships with Korean women, and involvement in early Korean transnational adoptions.[14]

African American Soldiers in Korea's Military and Child Welfare Crises

African American soldiers were among the first United Nations (UN) troops to fight in the conflict that began after the June 25, 1950 melee at the 38th parallel between the Korean People's Army (KPA) and the army of the Republic of Korea (ROK). Immediately after the KPA began its invasion of South Korea, the UN Security Council condemned North Korean leaders for orchestrating the attack. Within days, US president Harry Truman ordered air strikes to slow the advance of the KPA in South Korea. These measures were insufficient to stop North Korean troops and by June 29, they had routed ROK forces in Seoul and taken control of South Korea's capital city. The retreat of the army of the ROK, South Korean president Syngman Rhee, and other political officials revealed that ROK troops were not equipped to fight a full-scale ground war. Advised by his Secretary of State, Dean Acheson, that Korea was strategically significant in the fight against the spread of communism, President Truman ordered combat troops into the conflict in early July. Although civil rights activists had been agitating for years for the desegregation of the armed forces, Truman sent a segregated army to Korea to take part in what he called a police action.

Members of the all-black Twenty-Fourth Infantry Regiment traveled to Korea the second week of July 1950 and immediately observed the deprivation that affected many Korean children. A number of veterans who served with the Twenty-Fourth had vivid memories of the stark environments they encountered in the early days of the conflict. Decades after the war, these men could still describe the chaos that characterized the troop mobilization from Japan, where they had been members of the occupation forces in that nation. Many recalled traveling for more than twelve hours on poorly provisioned, non-military vessels that smelled of fish and fertilizer. After landing in Pusan, a port city on the peninsula's southeastern coast, some had to unload equipment alongside Korean dockworkers that seemed reluctant to assist them. A few veterans recalled the smell of what they learned to euphemistically call the honey wagons, which were carts of human waste Koreans used to fertilize crops. The heat of summer would have accentuated the smells and the discomfort these tired and hungry soldiers felt as they boarded the trains or trucks that took some to Yecheon and others to Kumchon, where they attempted to stop the advancing KPA forces.[15]

In spite of this unpleasantness and uncertainty, the great need they witnessed surprised these soldiers, and some responded with small acts of kindness. Sharing their food or other supplies with Korean children began for some soldiers as soon as they landed in Korea. In his memoir describing the time he spent as a white officer of an all-black platoon in Korea, Lieutenant Colonel Lyle Rishell recounted how he attempted to help a Korean child he encountered during his first night on the peninsula. Touched by the tattered appearance of one Korean boy, Rishell spent the evening hemming an old pair of pajamas to give to the youngster. That same night, Rishell observed a number of his men sharing their meager rations with the children they met near the Port of Pusan, whose circumstances would only worsen as the war continued.[16]

The first US soldiers in Korea had received the requisite amount of basic training, but it did not prepare them for the privations they would observe and experience. Nor did it equip them to wage a full-scale war against the well-trained KPA forces. After World War II, the US government had drastically cut the size of the military and reduced military expenditures. As a result of the postwar demobilization, army enlistments dropped from just over eight million men in 1945 to around six hundred thousand men when the Korean War began. The regiments that made up the occupying forces in Japan were not operating at full strength, and replacements sent to fill these units often had minimal basic training and limited infantry training. For African American soldiers, the army's pattern of assigning black soldiers to service units compounded the situation. As veteran Julius Becton Jr. remembered, prior to going to Korea his unit was under strength, so commanders filled its ranks with men from service units who had little if any infantry training. Regardless of the amount or type of training soldiers had received, they quickly learned that they would have to adapt to fight in Korea's mountainous terrain against troops using guerilla tactics.[17]

The KPA's ranks included seasoned soldiers who had fought alongside Chinese communists during China's civil war. These men were combat ready. The KPA also had Russian artillery and tanks. By the fall of 1950, it had control over much of the southern half of the peninsula. Although US political and military leaders had expected a quick and decisive victory, the KPA and guerilla fighters overwhelmed UN troops, and defeat seemed imminent. According to historian Bruce Cumings, US casualties in the first three months of the war amounted to 2,954 dead in addition to "13,659 wounded, and 3,877 missing in action."[18] The casualty rates of African American soldiers were high. After just six weeks in combat, 1,235 of the Twenty-Fourth Infantry Regiment's 3,157 servicemen in Korea had died.[19] The carnage of the war was stunning for soldiers who had expected to be home by Christmas. Veterans like Charles Berry remembered the shock of seeing the dead bodies of the hundreds of soldiers he had to transport from the front lines.[20]

US troop casualties did not compare with Korean losses. Ground combat, US aerial bombings, and UN soldiers' systematic burning of villages left much of Korea in ruins and disrupted the lives of millions of civilians. In a number of cases, UN soldiers responded with violence to perceived and real threats from civilians, including children, who seemed to support the KPA or the guerilla fighters who hid in civilian communities. Charles Rangel, a Korean War veteran who later became a member of the US House of Representatives, remembered other soldiers warning him that people who appeared to be noncombatants could be the enemy.[21] The guerilla tactics of KPA forces and the support they had from Korean villagers surprised UN troops and made UN forces suspicious of Korean soldiers and civilians alike. Reports of attacks by civilians who appeared to be peaceably fleeing war zones encouraged military officials and soldiers to resort to brutal tactics that included burning villages and, in some cases, mass murder. In their chilling account of one of the confirmed mass murders carried out by US troops in

Korea, Charles J. Hanley, Martha Mendoza, and Choe Sang-Hun chronicle the events that led soldiers to kill more than 400 women, children, and elderly Koreans at No Gun Ri.[22] Although government and military officials attempted to cover up these war crimes, it was not uncommon for soldiers to talk about and plan for smaller-scale acts of violence against Korean civilians.[23]

Violence against combatants and civilians contributed to the staggeringly high rate of Korean casualties in the first year of the war. Between June and October 1950, more than 110,000 South Koreans died, 106,000 sustained injuries, and another 57,000 went missing. Scholars do not have precise figures of the number of North Korean losses, but it is certain that the 50,000 acknowledged by the North Korean government represents the low end of estimated casualties for that nation. The fighting between the KPA and UN troops also left hundreds of thousands of civilians homeless, and reports of the dire circumstances of the orphaned Korean children and the children who were among the injured and homeless quickly circulated in the United States.[24]

Numerous articles in mainstream newspapers heralded the professionals and volunteers who scrambled to get needed supplies to Korea. Major newspapers like the *Boston Globe* and *Los Angeles Times* ran stories about the growing refugee crisis and the efforts of international organizations to address the needs of Korean children.[25] For months, the *New York Times* described the negotiations that resulted in the UN's commitment of millions of dollars in aid for Korean children. The *New York Times* also reported on the numerous aid organizations that quickly collected food, money, clothing, and medical supplies. When organizations mobilized to provide aid to Koreans displaced by the war, efforts on behalf of children received widespread attention and support. While the large donations from international organizations were vital, they did not overshadow the charity of average citizens in the United States. The stories of suffering children inspired Americans from all walks of life to coordinate or contribute to various relief projects. Many people likely agreed with the sentiments of the twelve-year-old student in a summer program in Brooklyn, New York, who explained the motivation behind his class' clothing drive. They gave because "the kids in Korea are dying like ants . . . there's no reason they shouldn't live just as nice as we do."[26]

The circumstances of Korea's children also prompted many UN soldiers to devise their own strategies to relieve the suffering around them. Some became directly involved in Korean children's lives. A number of children whose families died or disappeared would attach themselves to an individual soldier or an entire unit where soldiers took on roles as unofficial guardians and caregivers. Acclaimed journalist Nora Waln's description of the circumstances of several of these children certainly applied to hundreds of other Korean children affected by the war. Her article, "Our Softhearted Warriors in Korea," in the September 1950 edition of the *Saturday Evening Post* described the story of a boy simply called Kim, who came to the attention of an army sergeant when he found the boy hiding under a bush near a combat zone. The sergeant decided to share what he had with Kim, who was "ragged and dirty [but] no filthier than his hosts." Kim then became the unit's mascot and unofficial spotter, helping this group of soldiers locate fresh water and evade North Korean troops. According to Waln, the death of the sergeant devastated the boy. She witnessed the funeral of this sergeant and attempted to comfort Kim, who lingered by the sergeant's grave. Although members of the sergeant's unit pledged to care for Kim, two navy chaplains Waln encountered wondered what he, and other mascots like him, would do after the men "went into barracks for the winter."[27]

Waln's descriptions of other mascots and the soldiers who cared for them reveal that soldiers were talking about adopting these boys and bringing them to the United States in the first months of the conflict. Waln reported that a soldier who was fond of one mascot he called Dickie declared, "I'm taking him home to Texas. I'm a lawyer. Dickie is going to live in Texas if it takes a special act of Congress to get him in."[28] This Texan was correct about needing to get an Act of Congress to bring Dickie to the States because, as Waln noted, US immigration laws limited migrations from Asian nations. The Immigration Act of 1924 had introduced a national origins quota system that limited the number of visas available to any given nation to 2 percent of the number of people from that nation that were included in the 1890 US census. The officials who crafted the 1924 Act wanted to stem the tide of immigration from Eastern and Southern European countries that had brought millions of people to the United States between the 1880s and the 1920s. However, it also included provisions that virtually ended immigration from Asian nations. Consequently, when soldiers began investigating ways to bring Korean children to the United States during the war, they had to navigate immigration restrictions. Even the small allotments that the 1924 Act should have provided many Asian nations were void because the Act introduced prohibitions on immigration for individuals classified as "ineligible for citizenship," which Asians were and would be until the McCarran-Walter Act of 1952 eliminated the national origins quota system and bans on Asian naturalization.[29]

Despite these restrictions, and the lack of a legal framework for transnational adoptions from Korea, there is evidence that some Americans did bring Korean children to the United States during the war years.[30] The *Pacific Stars and Stripes*, the daily newspaper covering the US military in Asia, reported on one such case when it described the efforts of soldiers like Chaplain Ray D. Seals, an army captain who adopted a Korean child whom he sent to live in Los Angeles in 1951.[31] These people likely used the strategy the lawyer/soldier attached to Dickie mentioned and that Captain Booker used when he brought Rhee to the States before the war ended in 1953. With the help of a member of Congress, they obtained a private act to change the Korean child's legal status from "inadmissible alien" to that of a "natural born alien child" of the person bringing them to the United States. In Booker's case, California senator William F. Knowland sponsored the bill that changed Rhee's status. In all cases where Congress passed a private law of this nature, the law allowed the child to enter on a non-quota visa, but this status did not make the child a legally adopted citizen of the United States. It is certain that some of the families that brought Korean children to the United States during the war (and after) did not realize that they needed to get their adopted child naturalized or, in some cases, that they needed to complete a legal adoption. Although the carnage soldiers observed certainly stirred their impulse to rescue Korean children, taking them from Korea in this manner made the children's legal status in the United States precarious. However, during the war, stories about soldiers' relationships with mascots and their efforts to meet Korean children's day-to-day needs were more common than stories about their attempts to take them to America.[32]

As the war progressed, mascots like Kim became fixtures around the camps and barracks of UN troops. Mascots were overwhelmingly boys, but there are indications that soldiers also used the term when describing young girls affiliated with a unit. This was the case for two such mascots described in the May 14, 1951 *Pacific Stars and Stripes* article, "Rugged GIs Weep as 'Mascots' Depart."[33] The article mentions two female mascots among the twenty-four children between the ages of six and sixteen who were on their way to an orphanage. Relationships that developed between soldiers and children like the ones described in the article led to some of the early official and unofficial adoptions. But most mascots performed odd jobs in exchange for basic provisions of clothing, food, and protection. Some mascots who learned English served as interpreters and others engaged in more dangerous tasks as scouts for troops. Mascots also worked as spies for the United States, became unofficial members of the military, and a few became "fully fledged members of the US Army."[34]

Soldiers' care for mascots garnered considerable attention because of the sentimental, and in some cases familial, nature of these relationships.[35] Soldiers fed mascots and some also made room for the children to live in the camps with their unit. When they were unable to provide shelter for their mascots, some soldiers took up collections to pay for the child's education or arranged to pay for care in an orphanage. Sometimes soldiers made a pact that the last man in a unit would try to adopt their mascot when that soldier's tour of duty ended.[36] The arrangements soldiers made to care for mascots allowed some to form and express emotional attachments that provided a temporary escape from the dehumanizing aspects of the war. But their care of mascots also replicated the colonial imbalance of power that structured US-Korean relations and created the conditions for exploitation.[37] The way soldiers dressed their mascots is suggestive in this regard.[38]

Soldiers frequently dressed their mascots in military uniforms or, as Waln noticed in "Rugged GIs Weep," in cowboy outfits. Soldiers performed these acts as gestures to demonstrate a Korean child's fictive membership in their units. However, given that black men were largely excluded from the popular representations of both icons in the 1950s and 1960s, their participation in the practice of dressing mascots as soldiers and cowboys is suggestive.[39] Certainly some African American soldiers dressed their mascots this way because of contemporary depictions of these icons as quintessential American heroes. Yet, these celebrated symbols of American masculinity were historically agents of US imperialism and neocolonialism. Consequently, African American soldiers' involvement in America's wars revealed the ways members of an oppressed group could also become oppressors. Nonetheless, the black press published stories about and images of soldiers and their mascots because these men's actions served symbolic and political purposes.[40]

The political import of African American soldiers' benevolence toward Korean children was evident in the early coverage of the war. During the Korean War, black journalists were on the front lines with soldiers, and their reporting served a number of purposes. Journalists kept stateside African Americans abreast of developments in Korea. Additionally, they chronicled the lives of solders in ways that created a counternarrative to military officials' and political leaders' negative assessments of black men's military service. Journalists were also explicit about their political agendas. They were advancing claims on civil rights through stories of soldiers' honorable service. Consequently, the record they created of African American soldiers' encounters with Korean children depicted black men as good soldiers and conscientious humanitarians.

The black press published notices and stories about African American soldiers' care of mascots throughout the war. One of the first mentions of this kind of relationship was more of an endorsement of military integration than a celebration of troop charity. In the winter of 1950, the *Baltimore Afro-American* ran a short piece describing the duties of a black quarter master, Lieutenant Albert C. Brooks, noting that he had "adopted" a young Korean boy he called Butch. In the article, Brooks explained how he found Butch hungry, "shivering and dirty" outside of the big warehouse that held supplies for the Eighth Army. From this warehouse, Brooks oversaw an integrated group of men who together provided food for more than 15,000 soldiers and civilians in the areas north of Seoul. When Butch showed up, Brooks and his men decided to feed him too. Unaware of whether Butch had any family or where he was from, Brooks became the boy's unofficial guardian. The men in Brooks's unit had an army uniform altered to fit Butch, and he became the "mascot" of the warehouse. The few English words and phrases Butch could speak and understand—"mi rifle, carbine, 45., candy" and "go wash your face"—indicate the nature of his interactions with the soldiers. They also suggest the kinds of violence he had observed. As SooJin Pate explains, mascots' familiarity with weapons "reveal how gun violence ha[d] become naturalized among male orphans because of what they witnessed from the war."[41] Although the article emphasized the message that black and white soldiers could work together and, more important, that black men could supervise white soldiers without incident, it also hinted at the complicated role African American soldiers would play in the developing Korean child welfare crisis.[42]

Instances of African American soldiers managing men and caring for children were good press for advocates of racial equality who were pushing for the full integration of the military. But violent realities also structured soldiers' interactions with Korean children. Veterans Charles Berry and William Harvey remembered that their units learned to be wary of children because soldiers had heard rumors about children carrying out surprise attacks on behalf of the KPA. During his tour in Korea, Berry drove supply trucks from Pusan to troops in combat. He resorted to telling his men to shoot any child who approached the truck after learning of a young boy who allegedly used two grenades to carry out an ambush that killed at least one unsuspecting soldier. While he recalled his superiors telling the soldiers to be nice to the children, Berry believed that his life and the lives of the men in his unit were worth more than that of a Korean child who posed a threat to UN soldiers.[43] Although soldiers often responded compassionately to the countless number of children like Kim and Butch, they also used deadly force in encounters with children they suspected of assisting KPA troops and guerilla fighters. Many soldiers considered such callous assessments and actions to be an unfortunate but necessary consequence of war. Some also recognized that soldiers on both sides of the conflict exploited displaced children. But the media coverage of soldiers' interactions with children largely focused on their benevolence.

As early as the fall of 1950, *Pacific Stars and Stripes* began publishing articles about soldiers' humanitarian work on behalf of Korean children. The paper featured stories about soldiers who sponsored children in existing orphanages with names like "Friendship Home" and "Happy Mountain." Reporters even spotlighted the work of men like Captain Charles C. Blake, the African American "flying chaplain" for the Seventy-Ninth Ordnance Battalion. Blake, who had degrees from Boston College and Jackson Theological Seminary, ministered to the needs of African American soldiers and helped organize and support orphanages.[44] With each piece about military personnel like Captain Blake building orphanages and schools, coordinating "operations" to raise money for food and school supplies, and collecting thousands of dollars to provide medical care for severely injured children, *Pacific Stars and Stripes* bolstered the image of the UN soldier as a sympathetic figure. As one 1952 article about soldiers' donations to the Korean Children Amputee Fund noted, "the United Nations soldier, who in combat bayonets, bludgeons, dynamites, and shells the Communist aggressor in Korea, is the same humanitarian who is helping the defenseless sufferers of Korean fighting."[45] These articles were effective propaganda that underscored the compassion and generosity of soldiers from the United States and the nations that made up the UN coalition forces. However, the stories also revealed the ways that violence and inequality shaped US-Korean relations. As Eleana Kim notes, the "Janus-faced nature of the American military occupation—exploitative and humanitarian—has characterized the neocolonial relationship between America and Korea since the 1950s."[46]

The *Pacific Stars and Stripes* did not mention the racial makeup of the units it featured when discussing humanitarian activities. The paper avoided discussing race or the activities of African American soldiers except when reporting on matters like military integration or the race-baiting tactics used by North Korean interrogators in prisoner of war camps. Nonetheless, it is certain that African American servicemen like Chaplain Blake participated in many of the charity and fund-raising ventures the paper highlighted. Photographs in *Pacific Stars and Stripes* do show African American soldiers working on behalf of Korean children. They provide some evidence of these men's involvement with displaced children and orphans. But segregation structured all aspects of black soldiers' wartime experiences as well as the media's coverage of their activities. Consequently, neither the mainstream white press nor the *Pacific Stars and Stripes* devoted considerable attention to African American soldiers' specific responses to Korea's child welfare crisis. In contrast, the black press included stories about African American soldiers' humanitarianism in its coverage of the war to emphasize celebrated aspects of black men's military service.[47]

African American newspapers made the exploits of the all-black Twenty-Fourth Infantry Regiment and other African American soldiers headline news soon after they landed in Pusan. Although President Truman's Executive Order 9981 called for the elimination of racial discrimination in the armed services in 1948, the army followed a plan of gradual integration of troops during the Korean War. Thus, the black press stressed the importance of African American men's wartime service to efforts to dismantle racial inequality in the military and US society. When the Twenty-Fourth retook Yecheon on July 19, 1950, the *New York Amsterdam News* stressed that the integration of the military was "one of the goals toward which democracy in America has been moving." The article also cheered the "heroism, daring and excellent fighting qualities" of African American soldiers.[48] Although the victory at Yecheon would prove to be of minor strategic significance, it was the first major victory for the Twenty-Fourth. Christine Knauer explains that the victory caused President Truman, members of Congress, and white journalists to comment on the bravery of the all-black unit.[49] The *Afro-American* acknowledged the important work of black men in the ambulance companies, engineering battalions, housekeeping, and other service units that supported all troops in Korea and made the victory possible.[50] The *Chicago Defender* highlighted the many ways black soldiers were "playing leading roles" in the war by fighting and doing the important work of building bridges and transporting needed supplies to troops all along the front lines.[51] The *Amsterdam News* also pointed out the symbolic nature of African American soldiers' performance in newly integrated units as they prepared to "fight for democracy and a free world."[52] Finally, these pieces enumerated the many reasons black communities should be proud of African American soldiers. Soldiers' care of Korean children was one of those reasons, and the *Afro-American*, in particular, highlighted this aspect of African American men's service in Korea.[53]

The *Afro-American* in Korea

During the Korean War, the work of exposing patterns of discrimination eclipsed all other objectives for African American correspondents embedded with the troops. Although most black publications advocated for African American soldiers, some newspapers, including the *California Eagle*, and a number of African American civil rights leaders opposed the war.[54] Civil rights and labor activists A. Philip Randolph and Grant Reynolds supported the Korean War, believing that black men's service would advance civil rights goals. This position was a departure from their earlier work with fellow activist Bayard Rustin. Throughout the second half of the 1940s, Randolph, Reynolds, and Rustin had encouraged African Americans to resist service in the segregated military. During the war, several African American civil rights activists continued to oppose black men's involvement in the Korean War, including W.E.B. Du Bois, Paul Robeson, Bayard Rustin, and George Schuyler.[55] But weeklies like the *Afro-American* supported the war and vigorously defended African American soldiers. Indeed, this paper was the first to have an accredited black correspondent in Korea when James L. Hicks left to cover the war in July 1950. Hicks chronicled the war for the *Afro*'s chain of papers, and his status was a victory for the organization. Prior to the Korean War, the army had been reluctant to give black correspondents access to soldiers on the front lines. Editors of the *Afro-American* took advantage of the opportunity to have journalists in the field during the Korean War, and, unlike any other black newspaper, they kept reporters in Korea until the end of the war.[56]

Established in Baltimore, Maryland in 1892 by minister, journalist, and equal rights activist, William Alexander, the *Afro-American* was one of the leading and longest-running black newspapers in existence by the 1950s. Under the direction of John H. Murphy Sr., who purchased the paper in 1897, the *Afro-American* became one of the largest black newspapers on the East Coast and one of a small number that, for a time, could boast an all-black editorial, reporting, and production staff. The paper's success was due in part to its owners' ambitious business model. They expanded sales into markets beyond the Baltimore/Washington, DC area by establishing bureaus in New York, Philadelphia, and Richmond, in addition to establishing many distribution offices along the East Coast and in the Midwest. Under the leadership of Carl Murphy, one of John Murphy Sr.'s sons, the paper's circulation among black newspapers was second only to that of the *Pittsburgh Courier* by the late 1940s.[57]

From its inception, editors of the *Afro-American* made challenging segregation and injustice one of the paper's main objectives. The staff worked tirelessly to expose the myriad ways inequality left black people vulnerable and limited their institutions. Until the 1930s and 1940s, the paper supported the notion that advancement in black institutions was the most effective way to achieve racial equality. How-ever, as the late Hayward Farrar explained, throughout the 1940s the editors became more insistent that integration was the only way African Americans would secure equal status with whites. They also continued to demand "the best possible position for blacks within a segregated so-ciety."[58] Although Farrar called this accommodation a "strange duality in the newspaper's advocacy," it allowed editors of the *Afro-American* to be pragmatic and to endorse the tactics that seemed likely to serve the multiple interests of African American communities.[59] This strategy was also evident in the paper's evolving position on the desegregation of the armed forces. Editors who had pushed for African American soldiers to have more opportunities in segregated units during World War I be-came unapologetic apostles of integration by World War II. Like many civil rights leaders who advocated for military integration, the staff of the *Afro-American* often framed black soldiers' successes as crucial steps in the fight to achieve racial equality for all African Americans. James Hicks's coverage of the war stayed true to that tradition.

Hicks arrived in Korea within weeks of the Twenty-Fourth Infan-try Regiment's victory at Yecheon, and he spent the next four months posting harrowing descriptions of battles and colorful accounts of the day-to-day challenges of life in Korea. A veteran of World War II, Hicks had worked for the War Department's Bureau of Public Relations and the Negro Newspaper Publishers Association (NNPA) before joining the staff of the *Afro-American*. Hicks understood the difficulties African American soldiers faced in the segregated army, and he was committed to presenting them in the best possible light. He often emphasized the bravery of combat and noncombat personnel. For one piece, he followed a determined Captain Sylvester Booker—the man who would become the first African American to adopt a Korean War orphan—as he gave smallpox vaccinations to members of the 159th Field Artillery Division that was fighting North Korean forces at the Haman-Masan front. In articles and in his column, "Up Front with Hicks," he promoted the full integration of the military by describing the ways segregation hurt the armed services as a whole. The *Afro-American* also relied on the report-ing of its Far East correspondent and soldier Bradford T. Laws, and NNPA pool correspondent Milton A. Smith. Along with Hicks, these men simultaneously humanized and lionized African American soldiers by making their daily activities, triumphs, and struggles the subject of national news. They also stressed the ways soldiers' struggles for equality in Korea were related to African Americans' fight for civil rights in the United States.[60]

During Hicks's four-month tenure in Korea and for many months after his return to the States, the *Afro-American* included short descriptions of black soldiers' efforts on behalf of Korean children. The few references the paper ran during that time period were like the short notice about Sergeant Johnnie Autrey and Sung Manpak, a ten-year-old Korean youngster he was taking care of and teaching English. The *Afro-American* told their story with a photo and caption that showed Autrey holding a piece of paper and kneeling in front of Manpak. In the picture, Manpak is dressed in a military uniform that someone altered to fit him, and he seems to be squelching a smile as he salutes Autrey. The caption accompanying the photo explains that Autrey, who worked in a mess hall, had been feeding and taking care of Manpak since August 1950. It is impossible to know how many encounters turned into relationships like that of Captain Booker and Rhee, or Lieutenant Brooks and Butch, or Sergeant Autry and Manpak. Still, these few examples served the paper's goal of positively depicting African American soldiers' combat and noncombat activities. Such stories also offered a marked contrast to articles about UN troop losses to the combined Chinese and North Korean troops and courts martials of black soldiers that became characteristic of the paper's coverage of the war during the fall of 1950.[61]

Throughout August and September 1950, the *Afro-American* published lengthy lists of casualties that were sobering reminders of the losses black units endured as UN troops struggled to maintain a defensive perimeter around Pusan. The paper attempted to balance stories about the human costs of the war with coverage of the gradual progress of integration throughout the armed services. But the tone of correspondents' coverage was bleak until the September 15 amphibious landing of UN forces at Incheon that forced KPA forces to fight on two fronts. Hailed by many as a risky but brilliant operation planned by General Douglas MacArthur, the landing at Incheon gave UN forces their first major strategic advantage. The next day, the *Afro-American* printed Hicks's article reporting that the invasion at Incheon had inspired members of the Twenty-Fourth Infantry Regiment. According to Hicks, the win encouraged the men to hope that the successful attack was a sign that the war would end soon.[62]

In the following weeks, UN forces were able to retake territory the KPA had occupied in South Korea and they gained temporary control over Seoul in September 1950. By the end of September, UN troops were back at the 38th parallel and ready to reestablish the line of containment. But political and military leaders in the United States and members of the UN decided to abandon plans to contain communism in North Korea in favor of a plan to defeat communism in North Korea. On October 7, 1950, members of the UN General Assembly passed a resolution authorizing UN troops to cross the 38th parallel and pursue KPA forces into North Korea. UN and US officials agreed to this strategy of rollback, believing that a decisive victory would set the stage for the reunification of Korea. The Chinese entrance into the war in support of North Korea in mid-October frustrated these plans.[63]

The combined KPA and Chinese People's Volunteer Army (PVA) forces overwhelmed UN forces and forced them to retreat south in late November. After the PVA and KPA forces recaptured North Korea, they moved into position to retake Seoul. According to Bruce Cumings, the KPA's retreat in the early weeks of October was a trap to lure UN troops away from their supply lines and make them vulnerable to attack in the harsh winter months.[64] This plan worked. By the end of December 1950, it was clear that rollback had failed.[65] The *Afro-American* chronicled the experiences of the black soldiers who attempted to hold ground in places like Chosin and along the Chongchon River in the fall of 1950. These articles were full of declarations of the men's bravery and critiques of the army's lack of supplies, which made the losses inevitable.[66] The soldiers who fought at Chosin encountered what some described as terrifyingly relentless and deadly combat. Charles Berry, Charles Brooks, and Joseph Crawford all talked about the carnage and the cold of the days they spent in Chosin. Berry jokingly referred to himself and the other UN soldiers who fought in the area as the "frozen Chosin." He also recalled, "the Chinese just wave after wave come over they [*sic*] own dead. Just a human sea of humans and the bombardment of body parts falling all over on your stuff."[67] Just as soldiers had struggled in the heat of the summer months, many complained that they were not equipped for the bitter cold of winter in Korea. Brooks remembered it being so cold that his weapon froze.[68] Crawford suffered frostbite in his hands and feet that continued to affect him five decades after the war.[69] Many of the soldiers who endured the bitter, below-zero temperatures of the winter of 1951 abandoned hope that the so-called police action was nearing an end. For some, the dawning awareness of their vulnerability intensified as the army sent new recruits to replace the growing number of dead, missing, and injured soldiers.[70]

UN forces sustained heavy casualties as they retreated back across the 38th parallel. Carnage on and off of the battlefield during the fall of 1950 and the winter of 1951 caused many African American soldiers to struggle with their role in the war and the harm they caused Koreans. In his frank and compelling memoir about the time he spent in Korea, Curtis James Morrow described the day he did not kill a young boy as one of the most memorable of his tour. When Morrow arrived in Korea in December 1950, he was only seventeen years old and eager to see action on the battlefield. On his first patrol, he approached a bridge and suspected that someone or something was under it. Instead of throwing the grenade he was holding, Morrow chose to throw a rock, which saved the life of a boy hiding under the bridge with his ox. Morrow's platoon was able to connect this eleven-year-old with a group of Korean laborers who worked with the battalion, which provided the boy a measure of safety.[71]

Countless other young people did not fare as well, and the memory of those children haunted Morrow. His description of the circumstances of one little girl in particular reveals his discomfort with the knowledge that he hurt children. After destroying a village in a battle, Morrow's unit passed a young girl on the road. She was alone and trying to eat the inside of a cornstalk. He knew that it was likely that he or someone in his unit had killed her family. Morrow felt responsible for her suffering, but he could not stop to help this child because his unit was pursuing North Korean troops. His limited ability to assist the many Koreans he encountered caused Morrow to reject the idea articulated by some of his friends in the United States that he was a hero. He could not forget the images of these abandoned children, and other children whose suffering he observed; they lived in his nightmares. These experiences caused Morrow to discourage others from joining the military.[72]

Michael C. Green, Christine Knauer, and Kimberly Phillips have discussed the ways the violence black men experienced and caused in

Korea motivated some to question their participation in the war. These scholars note that many black soldiers resented fighting to supposedly protect democracy for Koreans when African Americans did not enjoy the full rights or protections of democracy in the military or US society. Like Morrow, some of these men wondered why they were fighting Koreans when no Korean had done anything to violate their civil rights. However, black soldiers had suffered indignities at the hands of many of the white soldiers and superiors for whom they were supposed to provide support and fight alongside. According to Phillips, these contradictions produced a "collective critical consciousness" among black soldiers that led many to engage in antiwar and civil rights activism.[73] Some even developed a sense of solidarity with Koreans because they saw similarities in the global inequalities that led to the Korean War and the racial oppression that African Americans experienced in the United States. For some activists, "domestic and international issues of race fused, as people attempted to make sense of and explain the war on the Asian peninsula."[74] But Phillips, Knauer, and Green agree that some black civil rights activists and intellectuals overstated the extent to which sentiments of solidarity influenced African Americans' responses to Koreans during the war.[75]

Indeed, ideas about African Americans' solidarity with Asians and other oppressed peoples around the globe were more pronounced in the years before World War II. In the early twentieth century, a number of African American intellectuals and members of the black press constructed a critique of colonialism that drew on the idea that blacks and Asians shared a history of oppression, which created opportunities for alliances to resist white supremacy and European domination. Hence, leading civil rights activists had promoted a pan-African, pan-Asian anticolonial movement as a component of their activism for African Americans' rights in the United States. African American activists W.E.B. Du Bois, Ralph Bunche, and Paul Robeson were among the civil rights leaders who "created a universalist vision of a genuinely democratic world" and displayed a "fluid understanding of unity" that exceeded notions of exclusively race-based activism.[76] Du Bois, in particular, articulated a version of Afro-Orientalism that scholar Bill V. Mullen characterizes as "a counterdiscourse that at times shares with its dominant namesake certain features but primarily constitutes an independent critical trajectory of thought on the practice and ideological of Orientalism in the Western World."[77] For Du Bois, Africans and African Americans' unity with Asians would lead to the demise of racial oppression and produce "global liberation."[78] Although Du Bois's writings and ideas at times essentialized Asian peoples and denied the exploitative potential of Asians' participation in colonialism as colonizers, his belief that Asian liberation was the leading wedge in struggles for worldwide black liberation influenced African American intellectuals and the black press.[79]

The black press had also taken a leading role in promoting a universalist anticolonial struggle, and many black journalists and intellectuals had originally described the US instigation of Cold War antagonism as another example of the nation's imperialism. But the black press and a number of black civil rights leaders changed their positions on the Cold War in 1947, when President Truman issued the Truman Doctrine and introduced the Marshall Plan for European Recovery. After 1947, liberal African American activists increasingly began to identify with the nation's stance against the Soviet Union and communism. Civil rights organizations also became targets of red baiting, which stifled activists' critiques of US Cold War policies. Instead, "the criticism of American foreign policy that had been an integral part of the politics of the African diaspora fell beyond the bounds of legitimate dissent, and the broad anticolonial alliances of the 1940s were among the earliest casualties of the Cold War."[80] Thus, by the late 1940s, many leading black newspapers and liberal civil rights activists saw the separation between the struggles for US civil rights and anticolonial struggles in Africa and Asia as the most promising route to achieving racial equality in the United States. Although African American civil rights activists on the left, like Du Bois and Robeson, continued to promote universalist anticolonial activism throughout the 1950s, many activists and average African Americans embraced domestic civil rights.[81]

Michael C. Green has argued that many black soldiers identified more readily with their status as Americans and that they did not display a sense of solidarity with Koreans. In his assessment, black soldiers' embrace of US imperialist and racist attitudes toward Asians led many to discriminate against and some to brutalize the Korean civilians they encountered. In other words, these men did not respond to Korean civilians out of any sense of a shared experience of racial oppression.

However, a consideration of African American soldiers' methods of caring for Korean children reveals their diverse responses to the complex systems of oppression that produced varying degrees of advantage and disadvantage in the United States and Korea. When black soldiers coordinated activities to assist Korean children, they demonstrated an awareness of both the limitations of their rights as citizens and the benefits their status as Americans garnered in Korea and other nations devastated by wars.[82]

The *Afro-American* gave more attention to these issues and black soldiers' efforts on behalf of Korean children after Ralph Matthews arrived in Korea in July 1951. Before his assignment in Korea, Matthews had worked his way up from reporter in the 1920s and 1930s to editor of the *Afro-American*'s Washington bureau in the 1940s. His skill and versatility when reporting on topics ranging from celebrity news in Hollywood to lynching in the South solidified his reputation as a leading journalist. His commitment to the fight for racial equality was evident in his writings and activism, which won Matthews the regard of members of the black press and the trust of the *Afro-American*'s readership. On one occasion, Matthews demonstrated his willingness to put his safety at risk to force the issue of integration. His legal challenge of a Virginia law requiring African Americans to sit in segregated train cars led to the ruling that identified that Virginia statute as unconstitutional. Like his counterparts at the *Afro-American*, Matthews was also an advocate for the integration of the military. His colleagues found Matthews to be a "witty and acerbic man" who did not hesitate to express skepticism or irreverence when covering sensitive issues. This penchant was evident in his early writings about the Korean War. However, Matthews's stories about Korean children displayed a compassion, sensitivity, and perspective on the war that his colleagues at the *Afro-American* could not match.[83]

One of Matthews's first pieces opened with a critical assessment of Seoul. His complaints about the smells of death and decay that enveloped the city were reminiscent of James Hicks's reaction to the country a year earlier. Hicks had called Korea "the most dirty, the most stinking, the most filthy place on God's earth," and complained about Korea's lack of basic conveniences.[84] Matthews encountered similar challenges, but he understood them to be the consequence of the war. Additionally, he was not negative about all of his experiences in Seoul. Matthews described his interactions with the few civilians in the desolate city as pleasant, and the tone of his article softened even more when he commented on the "half naked boys [who] shine correspondents' shoes" but refused payment for their efforts. The short article ended with an optimistic assessment of both the city's recovery and the continued integration of the air force.[85]

Matthews prominently featured the children of Seoul in his moving articles and sketches that ran concurrently on September 1, 1951. In "Korean War National Tragedy," he reminded *Afro-American* readers that "it is the children who suffer most." Matthews was moved by the resilience of the unaccompanied young boys who lived in abject poverty and begged for food or offered to shine shoes in exchange for food. These same children impressed Matthews with the games they made up and how they played in the sewers and on the tops of mountains of garbage. He was certain the devastation in Seoul eclipsed the adversity any of his readers had encountered when trying to assist poor families in the United States. Thus, Matthews applauded the soldiers who allowed the shoeshine boys to polish their dusty boots and paid the children with food when they could. A sketch of his, called "GIs Have Big Hearts," depicts one of these moments by showing a soldier carrying a young child, holding the hand of another, and walking with three more children who wanted "Chop Chop"—food.[86]

More reflective in "A Rejuvenated Metropolis," Matthews revealed his own discomfort with the agony of refugees returning to Seoul after UN forces lost and then regained control of that city in January and March 1951 respectively. He was overwhelmed by scenes of families in the streets building shelters out of discarded materials, barely clothed women trying to make and sell food, and swollen-bellied, half-dressed children playing mumblety-peg with stones. These conditions caused him to feel remorse for the part the United States played in providing the weapons of warfare that destroyed the city and its people. Matthews attempted to convey why the loss of Seoul meant the loss of the nation's political and cultural center by comparing the city to New York, London, and Paris. It is possible he imagined that, in the long run, the United States would attempt to atone for its part in the war by supplying much of the aid Korea would need to rebuild. But during the war, Matthews observed incidents of servicemen assuming that responsibility. He made the most of opportunities to talk about the sacrifices of some African American soldiers to provide a small measure of relief for Korea's children. Matthews certainly knew that soldiers confronted worse scenarios than he encountered in Seoul, and some probably felt the same culpability that caused him to pray for a "loaves and fishes" miracle to feed Korea's starving children.[87]

The poverty Matthews described that shaped the lives of Korean children also appalled many African American soldiers. Veterans like Curtis Morrow, Alfred Simpson, and Richard Smith commented on the extreme depravation of Korean civilians that they observed. Simpson explained that he had never seen anything like the devastation of Korea. The things Korean children did and ate in order to survive stunned Smith. Many of the soldiers who devised strategies to assist and later adopt Korean children were reacting to these privations. Some likely understood and resented the inherent contradictions of what veteran Eugene Hill Jr. remembered as fighting to liberate others knowing that he was not liberated.[88] But this awareness did not necessarily lead them to participate in organized and sustained activism in the United States or in Korea. Instead, some black soldiers used their status as Americans to assist Korean children because they reasoned that the racial oppression African Americans faced in the States was unlike the postcolonial postwar oppression Koreans were enduring. Indeed, in the early 1950s, some in the black community saw improvements in African American soldiers' status as evidence that pressure from civil rights activism was working. A number also hoped the integration of the military was a harbinger for changes in other US institutions that would lead to greater equality for larger segments of the population.[89]

Efforts to integrate all branches of the military and eliminate barriers to African Americans' opportunities received greater support during the Korean War, but this struggle remained controversial. Southern politicians and some members of the white mass media remained critical of African American soldiers throughout the war. As the army moved toward full integration, segregationists resisted the policy changes that would ostensibly give black men equal opportunities in the military. When integration became inevitable, opponents adopted the argument that desegregation was proof of African American soldiers' inferiority and inability to perform well on their own. Supporters of integration countered that African American soldiers had performed much like their white counterparts under similar circumstances. Thus, integration was recognition of their equality. Although the army's courts martial of black soldiers and investigations of the all-black Twenty-Fourth Infantry Regiment suggested that some military officials also saw problems with the segregated units, it moved forward with plans to desegregate. In July 1951, as peace talks began in Kaesong and then moved to Panmunjom, the army announced plans to eliminate the remaining all-black units to begin the integration of all but a few units of the Eighth Army.[90]

African American soldiers had mixed feelings about the news of the army's plans to deactivate the all-black units. Some also questioned whether the army would fulfill its commitment to a 12 percent quota of black men in combat units by the end of 1951. Veterans including Charles Berry, Joseph Crawford, and William Knox remembered being apprehensive about the desegregation of the army because of the support and comradeship they had experienced in all-black units, which they considered to be an important part of their military experience. Members of the 376th Engineer Construction Battalion expressed support for the plan but resented that they would be absorbed into white units instead of white soldiers being brought into their regiment.[91] While many black newspapers made note of soldiers' feelings, a number celebrated the announcement of the army's plan. Integration, and the dismantling of the all-black units, also led all-black newspapers except the *Afro-American* to reduce their coverage of the Korean War. Many black newspapers had made the desegregation of the military their primary focus, and they interpreted these changes as promising signs that the army was committed to greater equality.[92] By the summer of 1951, Ralph Matthews was the only accredited black correspondent reporting on the war from Korea, and he chronicled the progress of integration in all branches of the military. But readers of the *Afro-American* also learned of African American soldiers' growing involvement in child-centered humanitarianism through his coverage of servicemen's efforts to do more than provide food and shelter for displaced Korean children.

In December 1951, one of Matthews's dispatches focused on soldiers' efforts to eliminate an unexpected way the military's presence put Korean children's lives in peril. Members of the 376th Engineer Construction Battalion tried to address one tragic consequence that resulted from their close proximity to a settlement of Korean families when they built a playground near their camp. These men used scrapped supplies and the skills they routinely applied when building structures for the military to construct what they hoped would be a relatively safe space for children. They hoped the playground would reduce the number of automotive accidents that resulted in children's injuries and deaths. This intervention was a short-term solution that could not undo or even address the larger consequences of the war. But it provided a temporary reprieve for the families living in that area, along with some soldiers who admitted that they also enjoyed being in the playground.[93]

Matthews and the African American soldiers featured in his articles knew that building playgrounds, giving beggar children food and money, and caring for mascots would not help Korean children in the long run. Consequently, many of these soldiers worked to support South Korea's growing orphan population. The Korean War dramatically increased the number of Korean children in orphanages. According to SooJin Pate, prior to World War II there were around 2,000 orphans in Korea as a result of Japanese colonization. That number would climb to 7,000 by 1950. When the Korean War ended, the number of orphans in South Korea had reached 40,000 and by 1954, "there were over 400 registered orphanages in South Korea housing 50,936 children."[94] African American soldiers helped build some of these orphanages and many financially supported facilities in Korea and Japan. In both nations, African American soldiers saw how far their limited resources could go toward the purchase of simple meals and clothes for children. These men were among the thousands who worked through the Armed Forces Assistance to Korea to build hundreds of orphanages in the immediate aftermath of the Korean War. Estimates suggest that by the mid-1950s, soldiers had "contributed an additional $2 million in the form of cash and materials toward the support of orphanages . . . [and] Orphanage administrators reported that over 90 percent of their aid came directly from American servicemen, which kept their orphanages running."[95] Although soldiers' support of orphanages would decline after the war, during the war, many soldiers made small sacrifices to provide these basic necessities to the children.[96] After the war, soldiers would become more involved in the care of mixed-race Korean children, but during the war, black and white soldiers were supporting Korean children like Kim, Butch, and Manpak.[97]

In November 1951, the *Afro-American* featured the story of Corporal Lionel C. Barrows Jr., who coordinated donations for an orphanage near Seoul. A member of the public information section of the Twenty-Fifth Division, Barrows solicited donations to raise money for Korea's orphans. The soldiers of the Eighty-Ninth Tank Battalion responded. In a matter of weeks, they collected US$1,575.00 or 9,000,000 won, plus a large quantity of candy and chocolate rations. When a member of the Eighty-Ninth explained that giving made the men "feel like real big-time philanthropists," he articulated the sentiments of many soldiers who supported orphans in Korea and Japan. Simply put, giving made them feel good. Matthews knew that this type of giving also made the soldiers look good, and he placed their humanitarianism in the long tradition of African Americans' civic activism. He underscored this connection by comparing Lionel Barrows Jr. to his father, Lionel C. Barrows Sr., a former member of the Harlem branch of the NAACP.[98] Matthews's endeavors to present African American soldiers as hometown heroes helping to save Korean orphans had clear political implications.

In one of his last dispatches from Korea, Matthews encouraged readers of the *Afro-American* to display their civic charity by donating to agencies that were helping Korean children during the Christmas season of 1951. Matthews was certain that the problems in Korea were far worse than any he had ever encountered in the United States. He explained that South Korea's emergency hospitals, civilian aid stations, Red Cross posts, and refugee camps were already beyond their capacity. These circumstances caused him to encourage readers to send donations to help Koreans. Matthews had observed children who were "not only homeless, orphaned and clothesless [but also] mutilated, suffering from loss of arms, legs, one or the other or both." This was the case of a young beggar boy in Taegu whom Matthews gave some coins. Matthews recounted that he did not realize that there was something unusual about the child until he ran away with his treasure. It was only then that Matthews found out that the boy had suffered severe frostbite, which required the amputation of both of his feet. Below this article, the *Afro-American* printed a picture Matthews had taken of another young Korean boy dressed in altered military clothing, standing in front of a military jeep, and smiling. The heading above the picture read, "Think of Christmas and Him."[99]

After Matthews returned to the United States in December 1951, the *Afro-American* began reducing its coverage of soldiers' experiences in Korea and the needs of vulnerable Korean civilians. In the last nineteen months of the war, the paper only mentioned the war in a small number of articles and letters to the editor from soldiers in Korea requesting mail from people back home. One of the last articles about the need for humanitarian aid to assist Koreans, titled "Relief Packages Can Be Sent to Korea," ran in the *Afro* magazine in February 1952. It included instructions for readers who wanted to send food or cloth care packages directly to Korean civilians. The article encouraged people to send whole powdered milk, chocolate, wheat flour, sugar, and dried fruit in food packages. It also instructed that cloth packages should include fabric or manufactured clothes, shoes, and coats for children, women, and men. The newly established Board of Missions and Church Extensions of the Methodist Church organized this initiative to connect people in the United States with leaders of both Methodist and Presbyterian seminaries and missions in the Korean cities of Pusan, Seoul, Taejon, and Chungju. Articles like this indicate the limited role the *Afro-American* imagined black people would play in ongoing humanitarian work on behalf of Korean civilians. But the issues that motivated black soldiers' child-centric humanitarianism in Korea evolved because of the relationships many of these men had with Korean women and the children born of these encounters. The *Afro-American* chronicled many of the troubling aspects of these relationships and the ways they influenced the origins of African Americans' Korean transnational adoptions.[100]

African American Soldiers, Korean Women, and the Roots of Korean Transnational Adoption

At the same time that some African American soldiers were working to help displaced Korean children, black men were also fathering mixed-race Korean children whose births revealed the ways soldiers directly affected social relations and family life in Korea. During the Korean War, African American soldiers' social and sexual relationships with Korea women existed on a continuum between humanitarian benevolence and violent exploitation. However, when describing their sexual interactions, the black press routinely deemphasized the exploitation that characterized many of these relationships. A few articles hinted at the violent realities that led some Korean women to enter sex work or pursue a more long-term arrangement with a soldier. In memoirs and interviews, soldiers often recounted the ways they attempted to make informal and formal arrangements with Korean women. A few of these men were quite candid about their efforts to pay for dances or sex with women they met in and around their encampments, at dance halls, and at brothels. Less often, black soldiers described the challenges they faced when they tried to date or marry a Korean woman. African American soldiers' wartime interactions with Korean women illustrate the ways global inequalities created opportunities for men from all walks of life to participate in behaviors that increased the oppression of the least powerful victims of war. These relationships also expose the ways war amplified the power imbalance that existed between men and women, which heightened Korean women's vulnerability to domestic violence and sexual exploitation.

Scholars including Hosu Kim, Katharine H. S. Moon, C. Sarah Soh, and Ji-Yeon Yuh have described the evolving cultural and political consequences of Korean women's social and sexual subjugation. Evaluating the periods before, during, and following the Korean War, they have described the ways that colonization and war exaggerated gender and class inequalities and created the conditions for expansions in formal and informal sex industries. During Japan's colonization of Korea (1910–1945), an elaborate sex slavery system took shape and expanded in the 1930s to provide "comfort" to men in the Japanese military. Estimates suggest that between 50,000 to 200,000 women became comfort women and worked in the network of comfort stations in China, Japan, and other Asian nations in Japan's empire. A significant percentage of the women who became comfort women were Koreans whom Japanese officials—often with the assistance of Korean men and women—abducted, coerced, purchased, or tricked into serving in comfort stations.[101]

According to C. Sarah Soh, the four phases of military prostitution in Korea that began after World War II bore some resemblance to the Japanese system that exploited the comfort women. The first phase of camp or *kijich'on* prostitution in Korea began in 1945 when the United States and Soviet Union split the nation at the 38th parallel, and the US Army Military Government in Korea took control of the southern half of the country. Once in power, the military government dismantled the licensed system of prostitution that regulated women's sex work in Japanese comfort stations. This did not end women's sexual exploitation. Instead, military prostitution evolved during the early and late periods of US occupation.[102] Indeed, in her description of the early period, Katharine H. S. Moon notes that between 1945 and 1946, "prostitution took place in US military barracks . . . and in shabby makeshift dwellings called panjatjp (literally, houses made of boards)."[103] The last three years of the US occupation saw an expansion in the private commercial sex industry that grew around American bases until the United States began its withdrawal from South Korea after the creation of the ROK in 1948.

The second phase of camp prostitution began after UN troops entered the Korean War.[104] During this phase, the expansion of recreational opportunities for soldiers drew more women into Korea's formal and informal sex industries. Korean women who became sex workers suffered severe physical and emotional abuse in addition to punishing ostracism. This form of mistreatment was especially pronounced for women associated with African American soldiers because "Koreans had learned and imitated racist language and behavior towards blacks from the white soldiers in Korea since the mid-1940s."[105] But the Korean War made it possible for many black soldiers, like their white counterparts, to take advantage of the political, economic, and cultural instability that historically drew women into formal and informal sex work in war-torn countries. Consequently, some of these men also judged Korean women harshly. Journalists and correspondents with the *Afro-American* unintentionally produced a record of the troubling ideas and histories that structured African American soldiers' interactions with Korean women while writing about these men's experiences in the war. The stories and images of African American soldiers' social and sexual activities in Korea additionally reveal the real and imagined place of women and sex in the lives of black servicemen.[106]

Even before he went to Korea, Ralph Matthews had strong opinions about the importance of sex to soldiers and the challenges servicemen in Korea would face when they attempted to satisfy their social and sexual desires. His August 1950 article, "How Sex Demoralized Our Army in Korea," explained his theory that soldiers in Korea had fewer opportunities to solicit sex than soldiers in any other nation where the United States had troops, which severely depressed morale. Matthews encouraged African American men to hope they received duty assignments in Japan, where there were ample "brothels, cabarets and even theaters where a lonesome soldier can enjoy female companionship." He attributed the absence of such recreational venues to Koreans' desire to protect their daughters from sexual advances from American men who would exploit but not marry Korean women. Matthews also concluded that soldiers' insults offended Koreans, and he cited white soldiers' tendency to call Koreans disparaging racist names to prove his point. He confidently (but prematurely) asserted that a person would have trouble turning "up any brown babies or white babies with almond eyes . . . [because] prostitution is almost nil in Korea."[107]

Matthews was wrong on several counts. The records of the Eighth Army Adjunct General show that the army had to establish procedures for soldiers wishing to marry Korean women as early as November 1951.[108] However, military officials had already created numerous barriers to prohibit marriages between African American soldiers and Korean women by that time.[109] Even though Congress had passed the 1947 amendment to the 1945 War Brides Act to eliminate the racial restrictions that barred war brides from Asian nations, the military maintained a marriage policy that was "manifestly and systematically biased against interracial couples."[110] A soldier wishing to marry a Korean woman had to get permission from his unit commander. Such approval was unlikely, since most military officials vehemently opposed interracial marriages. Consequently, only eleven Korean wives of US soldiers immigrated to the United States in 1951, and only one of these women was married to an African American soldier.[111]

Matthews's suggestion that African American soldiers were more racially sensitive and refrained from using disparaging language when talking to and about Koreans was also incorrect. As mentioned earlier, black intellectuals and civil rights activists had mobilized the idea of Afro-Asian solidarity strategically. But both the black press and African American soldiers demonstrated racism and insensitivity toward Koreans.[112] The births of mixed-race Korean children that increased as the war progressed would show that he was also mistaken in his assessment that few "brown babies" would be born. Although his conclusions were faulty, Matthews's comments say a great deal about the mentality of many men and soldiers who assumed that access to sexual partners, whether they were girlfriends or prostitutes, should be a part of the experience of serving in Korea.[113] Black newspapers including the *Afro-American* helped perpetuate this idea in articles that characterized "commercialized sex as both acceptable and necessary for the effective deployment of American military power, at least in Asia."[114]

A month after Matthews's "How Sex Demoralized Our Army in Korea" appeared in the *Afro-American*, the paper published a compelling photograph portending changes in Korea that would nullify many of Matthews's assertions. "Weary GIs Do Pusan Stomp" shows two African American soldiers each dancing with a Korean woman wearing a traditional Korean dress. The men tower over their Korean dance partners, which adds to the awkward appearance of their embraces. The picture's caption explains that the tired men paid three thousand won, the equivalent of $1.65, to get "two bottles of cider and one bottle of Korean wine" and dance partners at the Metropolitan Dance Hall in Pusan. The picture does not capture the face of the woman in the background of the picture, but the face of the woman in the foreground is expressionless and striking for that reason. Scenes like this one would become more common in Pusan and Seoul as the number of dance halls, clubs, and sporting houses in South Korea grew to accommodate UN soldiers.[115]

One contradiction that emerged early in the war was the tendency of some men to complain about the lack of opportunities to interact with Korean women, even as others criticized the women they did encounter. Soldiers like Joseph Crawford, who arrived in Korea in the early months of the war, likely would have agreed with Matthews's assessment concerning women in Korea and Japan. Crawford remembered that he had "no fun in Korea" but he enjoyed his rest and recuperation in Japan.[116] The observations of war correspondent James Hicks suggest other reasons soldiers preferred the company of Japanese women. In one of his first articles about the war, James Hicks included wildly disparaging comments about Korean women that said more about his expectations than about the people he described. After enumerating the conditions that made his transition to life in Korea very difficult, he launched into a diatribe against Korean women that evoked Western and racist standards of beauty.

Hicks made fun of Koreans' clothing and was bothered that women did not wear brassieres. He also disliked the way Korean women styled their hair and seemed disappointed that there were "no blondes in Korea." Hicks was highly critical of the unsanitary habits he observed and claimed that, "Korean women, judged by the standards of the worst slums in America, would still appear to be unclean. It's hard to put your finger on what it is." His comments underscore the ways that many African Americans did not consider their struggles against racism to be the same as Koreans' struggles against neocolonialism. To the contrary, they suggest that he was complicit in the cultural oppression of Koreans, and Korean women in particular. In this way, the ideas Hicks mobilized were a form of orientalism. Hicks could show contempt for Korean women because, on some level, he agreed with the criteria embraced by the emerging US middle class that labeled Asians as inferior exotics and narrowly defined a woman's value. This kind of assessment was also evidence that some African Americans espoused similar ideas about how women should look and act that many white Americans used when criticizing black women. Although Hicks did not go into an explicit critique of Korean women's sexuality, that topic became a central theme in articles by other writers about Korean women and their encounters with African American soldiers.[117]

Other journalists who covered the war with Hicks used their criticisms of Korean women's appearances to construct a hierarchy of sexual desirability that explains, in part, some soldiers' attitudes toward women in the United States, Japan, and Korea. Milton A. Smith, a correspondent with the NNPA, cited what he considered to be Korean women's unappealing traits to explain why many servicemen were not fraternizing in Korea in his article, "Korean Belles 'No Trouble', Says Smith: VD Rate, Garlic Help Keep GIs 'Straight.'" To assure women in the United States of soldiers' fidelity, Smith suggested that most African American men were not attracted to Korean women because the women smelled of garlic and could potentially spread a venereal disease. Smith did admit that some soldiers were not so put off by these issues that they did not have sex with Korean women or go to Korea's few dance halls and sporting rooms. However, he believed that morality and other logistical challenges kept them from establishing long-term relationships, and this was the salient point of his argument.[118]

To prove his point, Smith included comments from soldiers he polled to explain their feelings about Korean women. These men rather crudely identified characteristics of Korean women that they claimed diminished any inclination they had to cheat on their wives or girlfriends back home. But Smith and the soldiers he interviewed acknowledged that their responses might be different if the women they encountered in Korea were more like the women in Japan. Accordingly, soldiers claimed to engage in a variety of relationships with Japanese women that fell into several categories, including prostitution, dating, traditional Japanese marriage, and legal marriage recognized by the US government. Throughout the Korean War, African American soldiers who wanted to recreate in settings that were or just seemed more like dating went to Japan.

Smith used "Korean Belles" to weigh in on a heated debate that the *Afro-American* had instigated with a series of articles by Hicks that described African American soldiers' supposed preference for Japanese women. In the article, "Japanese or American Girls: Which? Why?," Hicks reported that African American soldiers were attracted to Japanese women because they were submissive and knew how to make men feel appreciated.[119] Additionally, these soldiers believed the African American women who worked with the Department of Army Civilians in Japan were too independent. According to Hicks, these soldiers were not interested in women who often had degrees in social work and seemed too bookish.[120] One stateside veteran added his opinion to the debate in his letter to the editors of the *Afro-American* by charging that "compared to Asiatic women, ours are brassy, shallow, empty-headed and conceited." This veteran encouraged any man who wanted "to find a true understanding and affectionate gal" to go to Japan.[121] In other letters to the editor on this topic, some soldiers challenged Hicks's characterizations of their preferences.[122] However, they did not object because Hicks's claims were incorrect, but because he left out the stories of men who attempted to marry their Japanese girlfriends.[123]

Soldiers may have preferred the diversions they found in Japan, but the stories some black men told about the sexual encounters they or other servicemen had with Korean women suggest how eagerly they pursued such opportunities. James Bishop recalled a time when KPA soldiers ambushed him and some men in his unit after they sneaked across the Main Line of Resistance to "visit the girls." Eugene Hill Jr. laughed as he described an encounter he witnessed between a soldier and a Korean woman while serving at an ammunition dump near Sinanju. A fire and explosion in a shed near the artillery disrupted the activities of the soldier and the Korean woman he was having sex with in a tent near the bunker. According to Hill, the explosion blew the half-naked soldier off of the woman, who ran away in fear. In his memoir, Curtis Morrow also captured the tragedy and uncomfortable humor that surrounded soldiers' pursuits of sex in Korea. Having heard that there was "a beautiful whore . . . selling [sex] in the F Company area," Morrow was stunned when, after waiting in line for his turn, he discovered a woman on a bed disrobed from the waist down whose face bore the telltale signs of abuse. Morrow's buddies laughed as he explained that he could not have sex with the woman but paid her a dollar anyway. He then left the tent pretending that he had enjoyed the experience. Morrow could only "smile sadly" at the memory of that encounter.[124]

James Harp's justification for his behaviors most poignantly illustrates the painful logic behind these activities. He explained that one of the first things he did after arriving for duty in Japan, the Philippines, and South Korea was "find me a girl, you know a woman. A man, you gotta have a woman, that's why a woman was made, for man in my opinion. So, I had my share. They were young women, some of 'em were girls, most of them were women."[125] These attitudes flourished in Asia, in part, because military officials did not police intimacies between African American soldiers and Asian women to the same degree that they attempted to limit black men's interactions with European women. Segregationist attitudes structured the army's official policies and unofficial practices regarding fraternization. While military officials sometimes encouraged—or ignored—soldiers' efforts to meet their sexual needs, they were most troubled by intimacies between black soldiers and European women. Their attempts to regulate these behaviors frequently led to trouble. Some veterans who spent time in Europe before serving in the Korean War remembered that officials set limits on their mobility to keep them from meeting European women. Lawrence Penny Baltimore recalled that his white superiors made the town near their base off limits to African American soldiers when he was serving in Italy after World War II. This rule led to confrontations between black soldiers and the military police because soldiers often broke the rule.[126] In cases involving German women, US officials' "disapproval of both interracial sexual liaisons and the presence of black women [in Germany] illustrates how official thinking about race and sex contradicted itself" and made German women vulnerable to sexual exploitation.[127]

During the Korean War, officials made decisions about troop mobilization that reflected their unease with interracial intimacies in the European theater. Therefore, the US military sent more African American soldiers to Japan, Korea, and the Philippines than to Europe because they felt relationships between black men and Asian women posed less of a threat to the racial hierarchy that mattered most to white officials, soldiers, and civilians. In fact, African American soldiers' sexual activities with girlfriends or prostitutes in Japan and Korea affirmed gender hierarchies and did not disrupt the racial hierarchies because entertainment districts and clubs remained segregated.[128] Black soldiers were aware of this bias. James Bishop remembered being puzzled the day his superiors gave the men in his camp their assignments and he noticed that all the men in line to go to Europe were white. When he asked why there were no African American soldiers in that line, his commander replied that black men were "leaving too many black babies over there."[129] The military's position and policies structuring fraternization "reaffirmed racial hierarchy, but [they] also allowed black men to participate in the domination of Japanese and Korean women."[130] This type of crude prioritization indicated the level of disregard military officials had for both Japanese and Korean women, and for the children soldiers would father with women in these nations.[131]

Reporters with the *Afro-American* demonstrated little concern for the exploitation Korean women experienced as a result of the military's presence. Instead, the paper devoted more attention to telling sordid stories about the dangers soldiers faced as a result of intimacies with Japanese and Korean women. One month after the paper ran "Korean Belles," it published J. P. Spivey's response to Milton A. Smith's observations. Spivey was a corporal with the Medical Detachment of the Sixtieth General Depot, and he alleged that African American soldiers *were* attracted to Korean women and cited the high venereal disease rate in Korea as proof of that fact. Spivey explained that "where sex is concerned, garlic or no garlic, it still goes on." He was certain the African American soldiers were "in there pitching" as much as their white counterparts. Spivey conceded that some soldiers did show restraint to prevent "their bodies from being contaminated with disease," but he ended his article with the assertion that many more men were less cautious.[132]

When Ralph Matthews was reporting on the war from Korea, concerns over the spread of venereal diseases and increased drug abuse among soldiers led to greater scrutiny of the Korean women working in that nation's growing formal sex industry. Matthews hinted at this issue in his scathing critique of the crime and poverty of Pusan in "Corrupt GIs Divert Food, Clothes." Matthews noted that children as young as six years old knew how to ask GIs in English if they wanted directions to a brothel. Although he focused most of the article on describing civilians' criminal behaviors that targeted soldiers and military warehouses, Matthews also mentioned that the owners of the dance halls filled their businesses with beautiful young women to satisfy soldiers' social and sexual desires. But the biggest issue Matthews identified with these arrangements was that they created problems for the medics who tried to treat both the women and soldiers infected with VD.[133] Indeed, as Katharine H. S. Moon describes, in the decades after the Korean War, the US military and the Korean government would orchestrate a VD Clean-Up campaign that downplayed the violence and exploitation military prostitutes experienced.[134]

The *Afro-American* included several of Matthews's sketches depicting life in Pusan with this article, including one of an attractive woman beckoning an African American soldier into a dance hall. There are two women in the sketch—one woman in the foreground with the soldier and another in the background standing under the words "Dance Hall." Both are dressed in revealing, knee-length Western evening dresses that accentuate the contours of their bodies. Matthews's sketch presents a striking contrast to the "Pusan Stomp" photograph mentioned above that showed two traditionally clad Korean women dancing with African American soldiers. These representations demonstrate how quickly prostitution in Korea transformed to support the fantasies of young men. The expansion and transformation of the sites where soldiers could solicit sex from Korean women became the basis for the *kijich'on* Rest and Recuperation system that would expand in the postwar years.[135] During the war, some men sought companionship, sex, alcohol, and drugs in the dance halls to distract themselves from the boredom or violence or fear they experienced, and the formal and informal sex trade accommodated these desires. Consequently, as Matthews's commentary suggests, the exploitation of Korean women was a secondary matter to the men reporting on the war.[136]

The personal tragedies that shaped wartime encounters between soldiers and Korean women rarely made it into Matthews's articles, but in a few of them he did show an awareness of the challenges Korean women faced. One article about the military's response to soldiers' struggles with drug addiction mentioned some reasons Korean women became trapped in sex work. Matthews interviewed a military police officer in Kobe, Japan, who described his strategy for spotting heroin addicts and men in danger of becoming addicts. The MP explained that he arrested soldiers associating with sex workers who had bruises on their arms that indicated the use of heroin. Although soldiers had access to a range of intoxicating substances, heroin was the drug journalists associated with dance halls and sex workers. The MP expressed sympathy for the young women because he knew they were victims and often addicts themselves. He believed that these women owed money to the people running the dance halls, and they received credit for each soldier they introduced to heroin. The MP was proud of the work he did to interrupt the cycle of addiction among soldiers, but there was no such effort to help the Korean women he also encountered.[137] Indeed, the people who ran the dance halls and brothels made drugs and alcohol available to sex workers, and addiction became a lifelong problem for some of the women trapped in Korea's evolving sex industry.[138]

It is telling that a number of Matthews's sketches of Korean men, women, and, to a lesser degree, children mark them as vulnerable, dangerous, or sinister. Matthews's images reinforced stereotypes about Asians that represented a form of orientalism popular in the United States and, as the earlier discussion of James Hicks's attitudes toward Koreans suggests, among African Americans. Although he showed sympathy to many of the Koreans he wrote about, Matthews participated in the cultural reproduction of messages about Koreans' otherness that many Americans had used to justify their oppression. His depictions of the Korean seductress and the Asian drug peddler were also reminiscent of nineteenth- and early twentieth-century depictions of Chinese migrants in the United States. These earlier representations traded in similarly racist and politically motivated stereotypes by associating Chinese communities with opium dealing and prostitution. Such ideas fed anti-Asian racism and led to immigration exclusions and limitations that first targeted Chinese laborers in the nineteenth century, then Japanese laborers and the small number of migrants from Korea and the Philippines in the early twentieth century. They also informed the ways Americans, including African Americans, thought about the inequalities that shaped US-Korea relations and the policies that would inform Korean transnational adoptions.[139]

It is unlikely that the circumstances of Korean sex workers or Korea's looming GI baby crisis were on the minds of representatives of the United Nations Command, the North Korean Army (KPA), and the Chinese People's Volunteer Army (PVA) who signed the armistice that ended the fighting of the Korean War on June 27, 1953. When representatives of the United Nations Command, the KPA, and the PVA agreed to the ceasefire, many in the United States recognized that the settlement fell far short of the nation's goal of an unconditional surrender or the elimination of the communist threat in Korea. Instead, the absence of a clear victory for either side meant that the end of fighting ironically resulted in the establishment of the Demilitarized Zone (DMZ) near the 38th parallel that divided North and South Korea when the war began. The anticlimactic end to the destructive conflict was not lost on African American communities. Still, some celebrated the integration of troops during the war as the greatest victory the nation could claim. The *Amsterdam News* announced the end of the conflict in the article, "Korean War Brought Soldiers New Deal," which surprisingly characterized the integration of troops in Korea as relatively easy. Alex L. Wilson of the *Chicago Defender* described troop integration as "another milestone in the forward march of the Negro and other minorities toward complete integration in the democratic way of life." The *Afro-American* called the story of the army's integration in Korea as the most "important . . . [and] encouraging" of the war. When editors with the paper tallied up their scorecard of the conflict, they acknowledged the many losses but identified integration as the outcome democracy-loving Americans would "rejoice over . . . [more] than in the actual truce settlement." In spite of optimistic assessments like these, the integration of troops in Korea did not bring about an end to the beliefs, behaviors, or institutional practices that perpetuated racial inequality in the military or in the institutions that would attempt to resolve Korea's mixed-race GI baby crisis in the decades to come.[140]

Much like their white counterparts, African American soldiers' participation in child-centered humanitarianism evolved as the war and the needs of Korean children grew. When the Korean War began, the violence of the conflict shocked UN soldiers who thought they would be participating in a manageable police action. The scale of soldier and civilian casualties drew international attention and stimulated widespread humanitarian aid from organizations and individuals who often prioritized the care of Korea's vulnerable children. Throughout the war, soldiers' charity on behalf of Korean children became significant in discussions about the benefits of democracy to international affairs. But segregation and racial inequality structured African Americans' experiences and informed perceptions of black soldiers' involvement in wartime humanitarianism.

The black press made African American soldiers' child-centered humanitarianism an element of efforts to eliminate segregation by linking soldiers' distinguished activities to claims that African Americans deserved equal treatment in US society and US institutions. This formula worked when it described the ways soldiers fed poor children and assisted orphans. But soldiers also engaged in activities that contributed to the Korean child welfare crisis, and these consequences were most evident when Korean women gave birth to mixed-race GI babies. Although inequality and abuse often structured encounters between African American soldiers and Korean women, the black press minimized the exploitative nature of these relationships in order to reinforce the positive image of African American soldiers and promote racial equality in the military. The official integration of troops in Korea encouraged many African Americans to feel optimistic about the course of civil rights struggles, but racial inequality continued to structure soldiers' experiences and would inform the strategies individuals and institutions devised to assist the Korean children fathered by black soldiers. African Americans interested in adopting one of these children would have to contend with racial inequality in the US child welfare agencies that would implement policies to facilitate US-Korean adoptions. Chapter 2 evaluates the National Urban League's efforts to reform these agencies. The League's initiatives to increase domestic adoptions by and for African Americans would reveal the intractable nature of ideas about family and race that affected African Americans' abilities to adopt children in the United States and would affect their efforts to adopt Korean black children after the Korean War.

2

The National Urban League and the Fight for
US Adoption Reform

In 1953, when Captain Sylvester Booker became the first African American to adopt a Korean child, the National Urban League (NUL) began a program to increase domestic adoptions involving African Americans. NUL officials called it the Project in Foster Care and Adoption Services. The NUL started this program after officials with League branches across the country reported that African Americans faced challenges when they attempted to complete legal adoptions. Formal adoptions were uncommon among African Americans because there were few African American adoption agencies and few African American social workers employed by agencies that coordinated adoptions. For these reasons, black clients had to work with organizations that historically prioritized the needs of white clients. Often these agencies would either refuse to extend adoption services to African Americans or they would impose standards that did not take into account the ways racial inequality affected black applicants. The NUL endeavored to change these outcomes with a strategy that called for the integration of adoption agencies' leadership and staff, as well as comprehensive changes in adoption policies to give families and children of color equal access to adoption services. NUL officials believed that the implementation of this type of adoption reform would increase the chances that African Americans could provide families for the black and mixed-race children routinely underserved by US child welfare systems.

The NUL's program did not directly address questions about Korean transnational adoption, but the reforms it promoted would influence African Americans' transnational adoption experiences. The issues that shaped and limited African Americans' adoptions in the United States also proved limiting when some African Americans attempted to complete a transnational adoption. Indeed, many of the agencies that coordinated US domestic adoptions would also facilitate US-Korean adoptions. As US-Korean adoptions increased and became more regulated in the 1950s and 1960s, most families interested in adopting a Korean child would have to work with a domestic agency. These families would not be like Captain Booker, who initially navigated both immigration and military bureaucracy without the assistance of an official adoption agency when he brought his Korean adopted son to the States. Therefore, understanding the issues that motivated NUL officials to promote adoption reform is integral to understanding African Americans' adoptions of Korean black children.

It is not a coincidence that the League initiated its program in adoption and foster care during the same years that a number of adoption and child welfare agencies worked to increase African Americans' participation in Korean transnational adoption. During the 1950s, the dual influences of Cold War anxiety and civil rights fervor were transforming the landscape of US and transnational adoption in unpredictable but related ways. For the first time, the placement of children with any measure of African American ancestry, whether born in the United States or abroad, was becoming a priority for some white adoption and child welfare officials. This response was a consequence of social and political changes taking place in the United States and in nations with growing populations of GI children. As chapters 3 and 4 will demonstrate, the concern that segregation and institutional racism limited adoptions of Korean black children did motivate some agencies to change how they evaluated African American and interracial adoptive families. Successful agencies encouraged case-by-case accommodations for families that could provide a secure future for a Korean black child, in part because officials understood that racial inequality damaged the nation's reputation around the world. But this chapter explores the reasons most agencies in the United States remained resistant, in practice if not in policy, to instituting comprehensive adoption reforms.

Scholars including Laura Briggs, Donna Franklin, Ellen Herman, and Rickie Solinger have identified the domestic and international consequences of the persistence of racial inequality in adoption service delivery. Their assessments chronicle the many ways institutional racism allowed some child welfare officials to define certain nonwhite families and children as being largely outside of the category of "adoptable" from the 1950s to the end of the twentieth century. Consequently, in both the

US and international contexts, adoption agencies' promotion of white adoptive couples' interests frequently undermined efforts to address the reasons that certain families of color, poor communities, and industrializing nations struggled to keep their children. My analysis of the NUL's adoption project builds on these foundations to explore the reasons the League's sweeping reform agenda, which included the promotion of transracial adoption as an antiracist endeavor, fell short of its goal to eliminate racial inequality in adoption service delivery. We begin here with a description of the origins of the NUL's adoption project and move into an evaluation of its strategies to increase both the adoptions of children of color and the opportunities for African American communities to keep their children. I argue that the League attempted to redefine the relationship between adoption agencies and communities of color by identifying adoption processes for white children in the United States and the nation's children of color as complimentary and not competitive endeavors. However, in the absence of national adoption reform, foster care emerged as a leading solution to the perennial shortage of approved African American adoptive families for America's black and mixed-race children.[1]

The National Urban League Interprets African Americans' Adoption Crisis

In 1953, the NUL launched the Project in Foster Care and Adoption Services to increase foster and adoptive placements for children of color throughout the United States. When NUL executives began the program, they revised the organization's tradition of using "investigation and diplomatic persuasion" to resolve community problems.[2] From its inception in 1910, the NUL functioned as a social work organization. Many of the League's officials had backgrounds in the burgeoning fields of sociology and social work, and they agreed that the NUL should leave political and legal activism to organizations such as the National Association for the Advancement of Colored People (NAACP).[3] Throughout the League's history, its officials and staff employed the methods and skills of professional social workers to assist African Americans with housing, labor, and other social challenges associated with urban life. Instead of creating new agencies to confront or replace existing institutions that were not assisting black clients, League administrators tried to bring about reform in agencies already set up to handle all manner of day-to-day challenges. League staff did advocate for social justice, but they also attempted to avoid tactics that unions or other established social agencies might consider too aggressive, political, or radical. Often, League officials would encourage individuals to transform personal behaviors before considering direct confrontations in the workplace or other settings. They believed in "the capacity of respectable behavior to undermine race prejudice."[4] The NUL tried to resolve social problems by networking to provide alternative opportunities for individuals who found themselves in circumstances that could lead to confrontations.[5]

The NUL took a new approach to reform when it created the national program to increase foster care and adoption services for communities of color. The League was an interracial organization and its officials "countered separatism with integrationist ideology" and usually avoided initiatives that supported the creation of segregated agencies or endorsed segregation in service delivery.[6] Into the 1950s, NUL officials attempted to stay true to the organizations' social service roots and mission to avoid "direct action" and instead to "reform existing governmental and some nongovernmental structures."[7] This is one reason a few League officials initially had questions about establishing a program that focused exclusively on the needs of black and mixed-race children. They preferred to get established adoption agencies to implement reforms that would accommodate nonwhite clients. However, some League executives believed that there were not enough agencies willing to make adjustments to their adoption requirements to assist members of nonwhite communities.[8]

Before embarking on this new direction, League officials coordinated studies to ascertain the reasons for the low number of African American formal adoptions. Based on the results of their investigations, League staff believed adoption agencies needed to develop more flexible selection guidelines and to create community-based programming. Staff at the national office and branches throughout the country also lobbied against what they considered to be unrealistic standards that put the "Negro adopted or foster child under better home conditions than the average 'non-neglected' children enjoy."[9] In other words, they wanted agencies to recognize that stable African American families might not have the same characteristics as the ideal white adoptive family. The records of the US Children's Bureau include references to agencies that were experimenting with new methods of attracting and retaining African American clients in the late 1940s and early 1950s. The agencies that the Children's Bureau staff frequently recommended to African Americans asking for help adopting a child included the Children's Home Society of New Jersey in Trenton, Sheltering Arms Children's Service in New York, Spence-Chapin Adoption Service in New York, the Child Placing and Adoption Committee in New York, Child Welfare in Hartford, Connecticut, and the Children's Aid Society of Pennsylvania in Philadelphia. League executives replicated some of the strategies of these successful programs as they emphasized the importance of African American child welfare professionals in efforts to reach African American clients.[10]

The national branch of the Urban League began the foster care and adoption project to expand on the work of League branches that had tried on their own to develop a comprehensive approach to minority child placement at the local level. The number of displaced children of color was on the rise in urban areas throughout the country, and League officials were aware that many white social workers avoided efforts to assist this population. Many white, professionally trained social workers had little experience recruiting African American families. As a result, child welfare advocates identified a disturbing trend. A relatively small but growing number of children of color requiring social workers' assistance remained institutionalized longer than their white counterparts. In some cases, officials with white child welfare organizations contacted the League to find out how they could coordinate foster care and adoption services for children of color. But League staff frequently complained that most white organizations were unresponsive to the needs of African American communities.[11]

Critiques of the responses of white social workers and child welfare officials to African American clients were not new. As early as 1931, social science researchers had noticed the need to improve the training of white social workers assigned to African American clients. Bertha C. Reynolds, a research assistant with New York's Institute for Child Guidance, identified three main problems in her clinics serving African American patrons. First, in interview settings with white social workers, African Americans were more likely to provide incomplete or inaccurate histories that included information they assumed the caseworker wanted to hear. Second, Reynolds noted that African Americans were suspicious of caseworkers and routinely missed scheduled appointments. Third, African Americans often seemed to ignore treatment plans. Reynolds surmised that the reasons for the last two problems were related to the clients' lack of resources or inability to access the resources they needed. The solution Reynolds recommended required caseworkers to recognize the diversity among African American clients and create individualized treatment plans to meet client needs. Offering an assessment that challenged standard institutional interpretations of African Americans, Reynolds encouraged caseworkers to see that most of the behaviors that made African Americans challenging clients were related to social constraints and not innate inferiority.[12]

Leora L. Conner also called on social workers to pay attention to the social constraints that shaped African Americans' lives to help these professionals develop viable treatment plans. Conner, who represented the Family Welfare Society of Memphis, Tennessee, identified critical differences that would place African Americans at a clear social disadvantage and make them unique consumers of social welfare resources. Focusing on the disparities in housing and employment that often necessitated African American women's labor outside of their homes, Conner recommended reform in policies to address the special needs of these families. She argued that, in many cases, the low wages an African American man earned made it necessary for an African American woman to enter paid labor, often "in domestic service necessitating long hours away from her family." While Conner repeated Reynolds's admonition that caseworkers evaluate African American clients on an individualized basis, she took her critique of child welfare professionals a step further. She concluded that the real problem of service provision for African American clients went deeper than a need for simple procedural reform. She was certain that social workers had to recognize that "intellectual acceptance is not enough, so too we must live democracy."[13]

Many of the issues Reynolds and Conner described in the 1930s and 1940s motivated officials with the Children's Aid Society of Pennsylvania to initiate the Seybert program in the 1950s. The Seybert program was a project the Society initiated to increase adoptive and foster care placements for African American children in 1951. Funds from the Adam and Maria Sara Seybert Institution for Poor Boys and Girls covered the expenses of the two-year program, which NUL officials identified as a promising model for their adoption program. Based on assessments of the problems they faced reaching families in the black community, Children's Aid Society officials began by revamping the agency's organizational structure. Walter P. Townsend, general secretary of the Children's Aid Society, explained that he realized there were few African American applicants because the agency had not made the necessary efforts to reach members of the black community. Townsend was also aware that most African American clients had little confidence that the Society was committed to serving children of color or African American prospective adoptive parents. Additionally, he lamented that the Children's Aid Society "had no real working relationship with the Negro group in the community," as he critiqued the agency's lack of African American staff or board members.[14]

Architects of the Seybert program outlined a three-step approach to locate potential adoptive parents and engender ties with African American communities. First, they identified a member of the staff to serve as a liaison to the black community and publicize the Society's needs and intentions. This involved a change in hiring practices and led to the selection of an African American board member and staff member who worked with all clients regardless of race. Officials with the Society considered these additions important because of the networks African American staff brought to the agency. They also imagined that contact with African American colleagues would give white staff opportunities to learn more about African American communities and culture. Townsend believed that the "day-to-day" interactions would educate white "case workers about the particular pressures Negroes encounter." Society officials also believed that the interactions white staff would have with African Americans who were their professional equals would be the most effective way to dispel stereotypes that informed some white social workers' negative ideas about black clients.[15]

The second step involved Society staff working with African American professionals and community leaders who could endorse the adoption program. This strategy relied on a publicity campaign in local African American weekly newspapers and the recruitment of supporters among black "school principals, lawyers, physicians, [and] social workers." The agency hoped these contacts would generate support among African American professionals, the group the Children's Aid Society had the most trouble recruiting. Townsend confessed that few professional families adopted from his agency, even though he believed the children available for adoption would excel in such homes. He remained impressed with the African American families who did apply to adopt through the Society, noting that they came from all segments of the community. He was excited about the prospect of attracting more "quality" families from a range of economic and social categories through the publicity campaign. Townsend was confident that African Americans had much to offer the Society because of the cultural and social tools African Americans possessed and had historically used to deal with community problems.[16]

The final step in the Seybert plan brought African American families throughout the community together at public meetings where they learned more about the Society's adoption and foster care options. The agency's goal was to help African Americans appreciate the value of the professional approach to placements and the protections social work standards provided families and children. Townsend was aware of and complimented African Americans' long tradition of informally caring for displaced children, but this practice meant that many were not familiar with the benefits of legal adoptions arranged by professional social workers. Child welfare professionals like Townsend believed that that adoptions that did not involve "careful study" put children, birth parents, and adoptive parents in jeopardy.[17] Thus, social workers, in conjunction with physicians and psychologists, made evaluating perspective adoptive children and parents a routine part of the professional adoption process. They also emphasized systematic documentation and record keeping as an element of casework that would allow child welfare professionals to assess and then recommend a course of action for each individual, family, or case. These specialists often used scientific validation to determine which couples and children were best suited for adoption. Scientific validation included the use of tools such as intelligence quotient tests (IQ tests), developmental assessments, home studies, and matching.[18] While it is unclear the extent to which Society officials used assessment tools like IQ tests, they did employ home studies and matching to place children.

African Americans responded favorably to the innovations of the Seybert program, and Townsend reported a significant increase in the number of inquiries the Society received as a result of the first stage of the project. As Society staff members followed the three-step approach to finding families for children of color, they also experienced notable increases in African Americans' application completion rates. In its first two years, the number of African American adoption placements in Philadelphia rose from four to thirty-five. Regarding the families who adopted through the Society, Townsend happily reported that "these families may be seen as representatives of the good, solid middle-class that falls between the Negro professional and the large group of un-skilled laborers." Ultimately, the Seybert strategy reformed the Children's Aid Society's administration, staff, and procedures to meet the needs of African American children. Officials with the NUL subsequently pat-terned some but not all of the League's foster care and adoption program after the Seybert project.[19]

NUL staff combined the tactics used by the Children's Aid Soci-ety of Pennsylvania and the strategies of League branches around the country to develop its national foster care and adoption project. Prior to the formation of the League's project, a few of its branches had at-tempted to coordinate with national agencies including the Children's Bureau to promote changes in adoption service delivery in local child welfare agencies. For example, officials with the League's Kansas City branch made recommendations to the Children's Bureau in 1951 calling for better service to African American families. Kansas City League of-ficials accused the Children's Bureau of not doing enough to ensure that adoption agencies provided African American clients the same level of service that they gave to white clients. They complained that adoption agencies insisted on standards that many prospective adoptive African American parents could not meet. But they also noted that too many adoption agencies failed to assist the African American families who were financially and emotionally capable of parenting an adopted child. Consequently, they encouraged the Children's Bureau to employ more "qualified Negro case workers" who could better interpret the needs of African American clients.[20]

Kansas League officials were particularly concerned that most Afri-can American unmarried mothers were not able to relinquish a child for adoption or gain access to the maternity homes that were available to their white counterparts. Many child welfare professionals saw an unmarried mother's stint in a maternity home as an important part of the adoption process. Officials of these residential facilities often coordinated with social workers and adoption agencies to standardize the process of transferring a baby from its birth mother to adoptive parents. While they did not require women to relinquish their children for adoption, many emphasized adoption as the choice that was in the best interest of the child and the birth mother. These facilities often used coercive tactics to convince unmarried mothers to relinquish a child, and some agencies provided their services for free only to women who agreed to give up their child. For many birth mothers, the experience of being secreted away to a maternity home and then forced to give up a child was painful and not what they wanted. But some birth mothers and/or their families did want these services, and social workers with the Kansas City League believed that there were not enough facilities to provide these services to African American unmarried mothers. According to Rickie Solinger, in 1951, the year officials with the Kansas City League contacted the Children's Bureau with the above concerns, few maternity homes sponsored by white organizations admitted African American women, and there were only seven African American maternity homes in the United States.[21] Kansas City League officials saw a direct link between these numbers and the low number of completed adoptions among African Americans, and they highlighted these issues to officials with the Children's Bureau.

Officials with the Children's Bureau were also aware of the struggles African Americans faced when pursuing adoption services because of the many letters they received from black women who wanted to adopt. The records of the Children's Bureau contain a number of compelling letters from African Americans who needed help navigating the bureaucracy of adoption. The letter writers were always women, and some letters were from women who wanted to adopt because they were infertile. Other women wrote in response to an article in a magazine or local newspaper that described the need for African American adoptive families. In 1949, the publication of one such article in the African American popular magazine *Ebony* led many women to write to the Children's Bureau. Mrs. Albert Bashfield was one of these women. She wrote to say she wanted "to help my race" by adopting an orphan. Mrs. Bashfield made this assertion because the article had emphasized the problems many child welfare agencies faced because there were not enough African American families approved to adopt the black children who needed placement.[22]

The interest the article generated revealed that African Americans had limited formal adoption options. In her replies to families who wrote asking for help, Mildred Arnold, director of the Children's Bureau Division of Social Welfare, encouraged them to contact their state department of child welfare. Months after the Children's Bureau stopped receiving letters that referenced the *Ebony* article, Arnold and other Children's Bureau staff directed African American families to contact one of a few agencies they knew of that coordinated placements across state lines. Children's Bureau staff explained that most agencies only placed children within their state, but the shortage of homes for African American children caused a few to work with families in other states. In her correspondence with other Children's Bureau staff, Arnold suggested that they develop a strategy to reach African American prospective adoptive families because the responses to the *Ebony* article indicated "there are families in the Negro group who desire to adopt children." Arnold admitted that agencies frequently identified the challenges they encountered when trying to locate African American adoptive families as a "racial problem." However, the responses to the *Ebony* article caused her to conclude that agencies were not doing enough to provide adoption services to African American clients.[23]

Urban League officials in cities like Denver, Colorado; Little Rock, Arkansas; Los Angeles, California; Milwaukee, Wisconsin; and Pittsburg, Pennsylvania that tried to coordinate with local adoption agencies would have agreed with Arnold's assessment. League staff in these areas reported that local agencies repeatedly sought their assistance with adoption and foster care placements for children of color. In one case, a white representative of a local agency complained that none of the families they were "forced to use" should receive a child. The social worker in this example felt that the African American families suffered from economic and emotional deficiencies that caused her to question the families' motives for trying to become foster parents. This social worker did concede that her agency might be predisposed to misinterpret the challenges African Americans faced, which motivated her to contact the Urban League for assistance. League staff interpreted this to mean that agencies were not equipped to fairly assess African American homes or the circumstances that shaped many African Americans' economic circumstances. League staff explained that, for many families, the shift from rural to urban communities created economic and social challenges that limited the resources in African American communities. Interactions like these caused staff members with local League branches to push for a national project to address the inadequate foster care and adoption services African American clients received from state and local child welfare agencies.[24]

When the League began the national project in 1953, community services director, Nelson C. Jackson, expressed regret that the agency had to promote separate services for minority children. Jackson was a professional social worker who had graduated from the Atlanta University School of Social Work in 1929. He then completed graduate work at Rutgers University and the University of Michigan. Before becoming the League's community services director, Jackson held a number of positions that exposed him to the casework needs and challenges of diverse populations. He had been the Boys' Worker at New York City's Utopia Neighborhood House, a supervisor with the Bureau of Transients in Alabama and later New Jersey, and the Southern field director of the League's Atlanta, Georgia branch. In the fall of 1936, Jackson joined the faculty of the Atlanta University School of Social Work, which earned him the distinction of being the first alumnus of the program to become a full-time faculty member. Jackson's academic credentials and fieldwork experience made it possible for him to see the disadvantages segregation created for social workers and their clients. He conceded, however, that designing a program specifically for children of color was necessary. But he also believed it "ran counter to democratic practices which hold that there should be no distinction on the part of needs of clients by agencies."[25]

The new program introduced an innovative approach to foster care and adoption services that emphasized the significance of African Americans' participation in domestic child welfare schemes. The League encouraged placement policies that recognized both the constraints of African Americans' lives and the contributions African American communities made to child rescue efforts. Through programs that defined the care of children of color as the responsibility of all child welfare agencies and a vital component of a democratic nation, the League created a national, inter-agency coalition to meet the needs of hard-to-place children of color. By the 1950s, child welfare communities were reevaluating what it meant for a child to be unadoptable or hard to place.[26] While these categories could include older children, children of color, or children with congenital or developmental disabilities, League officials believed that their project would dismiss any doubts about the adoptability of children of color.[27]

The League's involvement in the foster care and adoption fields represented a new direction for its branches that were traditionally invested in developing community-based social service programs. League branches had an established history of assisting African American families, but League administrators designed most of these programs to address education, employment, and housing challenges. From the 1910s to the 1930s, League branches had mothers' clubs to teach African Americans the latest trends in homemaking and nutrition. The League sponsored Big Brothers and Big Sisters programs, boys' and girls' clubs, and summer camps for boys between the ages of twelve and sixteen. The League also established emergency programs to assist families on a short-term basis. These initiatives used the skills of African American social workers to coordinate agency responses on behalf of African American communities. Because foster care and adoption services were almost exclusively white arenas, the League required a new level of agency response to assist white social workers who dealt with African American families. Although the League attempted to place African American social workers in adoption agencies to mediate these interactions, this was not always possible. As an alternative, the League had to rely on its research, publicity, and coordination procedures to prepare African American clients and white social workers to navigate the foster care and adoption systems together.[28]

The League used its resources to connect interested families with adoption agencies equipped to handle the professional and legal aspects of child placement. League officials resisted suggestions that the organization's staff should take the leading role in establishing adoptive services for minority children. Instead, using a model the League called the interpretive approach, staffers established effective "interpretation" or communication networks between agencies and their target communities. This approach was fundamental to the organization's social service programs. League founders designed the organization to coordinate between established agencies, and until the 1950s, the League avoided direct service projects. Instead, the organization's staff attempted to provide research and support to established agencies that, for whatever reasons, resisted extending services to African Americans. If an agency remained reluctant to work with African Americans, the League would create an alternative program and then try to turn it over to another agency.[29]

In the area of foster care and adoption, the League designed the interpretive approach to counter two issues that limited African Americans' participation in adoption. First, it encouraged local agencies to commit to serving minority populations, and then they could reach out to local communities to provide homes for children. League staff pursued this first level of interpretation because many agencies chose to close cases that involved African Americans instead of working to find homes for minority children. For example, in 1955, officials with one agency were "aghast at the idea" of meeting the needs of children of color because they believed it would deplete their finances. The League addressed this concern by providing staff that would provide short-term assistance to help cash-strapped agencies. League officials also coordinated efforts to obtain funds from government and charitable organizations to meet long-term staffing needs.[30]

To promote the interpretive approach, Nelson C. Jackson contacted local and national child welfare agencies to solicit their advice and assistance. When Jackson met with Mildred Arnold, Annie Lee Sandusky, I. Evelyn Smith, and Alice Scott of the Children's Bureau, they expressed enthusiasm for the project but also voiced concerns about the agencies the League officials were willing to work with to place children. The Children's Bureau team wondered if there might be confusion regarding which agencies provided what services, and how the League would advise clients. They wanted Jackson to make sure that League branches understood their role as a referral service and not a placement service so that African American clients received the right information and guidance. In his report about this meeting, Jackson noted that the Children's

Bureau team strongly recommended that the League create pamphlets to publicize the program, and that the pamphlets emphasize the need for foster home services in addition to information about adoption.[31]

The Children's Bureau staff's recommendations grew out of their awareness that professional social workers had complained of the challenges associated with locating suitable African American adoptive families for children in the United States throughout the 1940s and 1950s. These conversations resulted in lengthy debates to determine what strategies would lead to more completed adoptions. Several articles in the social work journal *Child Welfare* encouraged social workers to be sensitive to the fact that some of the differences they observed in African American families might be the result of segregation and discrimination. Annie Lee Davis Sandusky was one of a small number of African American social workers employed by a predominantly white agency who stressed the need for a greater sensitivity to such differences. Sandusky, who held several leadership positions during her long career at the Children's Bureau, emphasized the importance of having the support and involvement of the black press, prominent African American leaders, and the mainstream white press to support outreach efforts. Sandusky acknowledged that "the physical and psychological separation of the Negro community from the larger community" created divisions that social workers struggled to bridge. Specifically, she identified the problems associated with the low economic status of many African Americans as a leading cause of failed adoptions. Sandusky noted that economic insufficiency forced many African Americans to live in substandard housing and experience community disorganization, which became a significant obstacle in adoption completions. In spite of these problems, many African American couples continued to pursue adoption. This pattern reassured Sandusky. It also inspired her optimistic assertion that professional social workers would learn to reach these families, an opinion the Urban League officials shared and worked to facilitate.[32]

After meeting with the Children's Bureau team, Jackson met with representatives from the Child Welfare League of America, Family Service Association of America, and Community Chests and Councils of America. He hoped to get their support for the project that incorporated many of the elements Annie Lee Davis Sandusky had described. Following up on ideas presented at one of these meetings, Michael Schapiro, director of the Child Welfare League of America's adoption project, shared some of his agency's strategies in a brief correspondence. Schapiro explained that the Child Welfare League of America planned to use funds from the Heinz Foundation and the Benjamin Rosenthal Foundation to tackle the growing adoption problem his organization encountered. The Child Welfare League of America recognized that there were not enough agencies to accommodate the estimated 25,000 children who lost parents due to death or desertion or the estimated 130,000 children of unmarried mothers. Schapiro and his colleagues proposed a study of this problem by experts in several fields who would evaluate adoption laws and practices to determine what standards were necessary. Although Schapiro expressed interest in the Urban League's focus on "Negro children," he made no specific commitment to the program at that time.[33]

In addition to their outreach efforts, the League received requests from local child welfare agencies asking for assistance to place children of color who were in their care. Ashby B. Gaskins, Child Service Division Committee chair for the Hennepin County Welfare Board in Minnesota, contacted the League to request information about the challenges other states faced and the solutions they developed when trying to place children of color. Gaskins explained that there were few African American or mixed-race couples to adopt children of color in his area. This shortage caused officials on the Hennepin County Welfare Board to inquire about placing children of color in other states. Gaskins disclosed that he was only able to place the mixed-race children who appeared to be white. Consequently, he concluded that the adoption prospects for African American and Native American children in Hennepin County were not good. Similarly, Rose Graul, the consultant for Ohio's Adoption Clearance Service, contacted the Urban League to solicit tips on how best to publicize her agency's need for African American adoptive families. Graul acknowledged that agencies all over the country were facing the same placement challenge, but she still wanted help to access African American families in other states. In his reply to her request, Jackson did not commit League resources to help the Clearance Service but instead encouraged Graul to advertise her agency's needs in the African American press.[34]

Once a local agency made a commitment to the League to serve families of color, members of the League's staff would develop community-organizing strategies to publicize that agency's needs. The League used the radio, television, newspapers, brochures, and pamphlets to announce adoption options. But the thrust of each program involved the recruitment of the "volunteer corps" to bridge agency and community misunderstandings. League staff felt that community involvement was a necessary component for any successful placement program, and they relied on volunteers to provide on-the-ground assistance. Employing a variety of committee arrangements, the League fostered the idea that communities had to demonstrate an investment in the programs for them to succeed. Volunteers were always needed to conduct the surveys that were the backbone of the League's social science research into the lives and working conditions of African Americans. In Pittsburgh, Pennsylvania, the Citizen's Committee on Adoption and Foster Care of Negro Children drew on the skills of volunteers to answer prospective adoptive parents' questions at informational meetings. Milwaukee Urban League staff established a steering committee for their Family and Child Welfare Division that was made up of African American and white volunteers. This committee set the goals of the Negro Foster Home-Finding Project, which included the implementation of research to determine why there were so few foster and adoptive homes for minority children in that city.[35]

The League's coordination with national and local agencies revealed the intersection of economic and cultural issues that limited placement opportunities for children of color. In the League's early years, the agency's administration observed that white social workers judged African American families by the standards of white adoptive families. This trend continued in the decades after World War II, when League staff saw how the low economic status of African Americans increased this population's need for foster care and adoption services. Ironically, these characteristics also contributed to social workers' negative assessments of African American prospective adoptive families. But, not only did child welfare agencies resist providing services for children of color; they also failed to acknowledge the existence of African American "community resources and leadership personalities," like day nurseries and nonprofessional volunteers that provided child care in black communities. League staff concluded that these circumstances increased African Americans' distrust of social welfare agencies and their avoidance of foster and adoption services.[36]

Although Nelson C. Jackson complained in June 1954 that "we have not gotten very far," a number of League branch offices could report some progress.[37] In that same month the League's executive director, Lester B. Granger, described promising developments in thirty League branch offices. The six most successful programs had combined several protocols central to League operations. They established committees, initiated publicity campaigns, and coordinated staff and research with local agencies. The remaining twenty-four branch offices reported progress in one or more of the above areas. Based on the data branch offices gathered, Granger formulated steps to improve the services of all League affiliates. First, he hoped to generate a network to share information about the "methods, resources, successes and failures . . . where the interests of Negro children are concerned." Next, he suggested a greater investment in research to identify exactly why certain activities were more successful than others. Finally, Granger proposed the creation of a manual for national and local agencies that outlined the relationship between family resources, community needs, and the services agencies provided.[38]

In 1954, League administrators had good reason to be cautiously optimistic about the nationwide implementation of their adoption initiatives. Even though the success of these programs depended on the willingness of the mostly white adoption agencies to accept the guidance of African American colleagues and respond to the needs of African American clients, these goals seemed possible. Officials with the League thought that both components were necessary to reverse the nationwide trend that left African American clients without adequate adoption services. Significantly, the programs that exceeded League expectations made outreach and the incorporation of African Americans in advisory roles central to their reforms. However, the most notable example of the effective implementation of all of the League's strategies was the multiagency collaboration called Adopt-A-Child.

Adopt-A-Child and African Americans' Adoption Outcomes

Adopt-A-Child began in January 1955 with the goal of increasing the number of adoptive and foster homes for African American and Puerto Rican children in New York City, and Suffolk, Nassau, and Westchester counties in New York State. This interracial, interfaith venture pulled together the services of fifteen adoption agencies and combined the skills of volunteers and professionals to carry out publicity and community organizing. In its first year, this program generated 240 inquiries from interested families across the nation. A referral agency, Adopt-A-Child made sure people of color staffed its home office. These individuals explained adoption procedures and prepared African American families for their meetings with adoption caseworkers.[39]

The organizers of Adopt-A-Child used these strategies to attract families that avoided agencies because they believed or knew that they could not meet the criteria that social workers associated with traditionally successful adoption seekers. Adoption agencies customarily looked at four criteria to determine if a family could pursue an adoption. Social workers evaluated the occupation of the male head-of-household, the family's income, the age of perspective parents, and the level of education of prospective adoptive parents. Many social workers believed that couples that had a history of divorce and couples with biological children should not be eligible to adopt. Additionally, social workers could reject a family for circumstantial and psychosocial reasons, or because there was no medical proof of infertility. According to social worker and prominent child welfare researcher David Fanshel, these were the most common issues that kept many African Americans away from adoption agencies. His study of African Americans who completed domestic adoptions between 1951 and 1955 showed that this group included couples who were usually more educated than their counterparts in the general population. But they were also older, and even though some were economically stable, these couples usually had biological children and wives who worked outside of the home.[40]

To determine how agencies could improve their contacts with such families, Adopt-A-Child began its three-year intensive project with a community conference. This event brought together adoption agency representatives and leaders of the area's religious, social, and civic groups. During the conference, these agency officials and community representatives "were extremely critical of each other," as they discussed the reasons for low community involvement in local adoptions.[41] Adopt-A-Child executive director, William S. Jackson, considered this an important and healthy dialogue that forced agency representatives to see that they were not effectively reaching their target audiences. Program executives thought that the success of the project lay in its ability to demonstrate that apathy in communities of color was not the reason for the low number of adoptions. William S. Jackson reported that this attempt to encourage agency accountability had immediate results. Following the contentious meeting, several adoption agencies agreed to evaluate their placement policies. Subsequently the number of inquiries about adoption from members of communities of color increased.

Following the conference, Adopt-A-Child sponsors created committees and programs to reinforce agency and community cooperation. Project executives established both the Study Committee on Technical Procedures and an "At Home" program. Then they held open houses to address issues raised at the conference. The study committee defined eight areas that limited applicants of color. Out of the eight areas, the committee recommended that agencies review and change the age, minimum income, infertility, stay-at-home mother, and housing requirements. They further encouraged changes in agency fees, in the structure of initial family contacts, and in training for social workers to accommodate economic and cultural differences that often characterized members of communities of color. The "At Home" program recruited individuals to host small-group social gatherings to publicize adoption needs in various communities. Often, speaking teams attended these gatherings to answer questions and provide practical guidance. Speaking teams included a community member, a caseworker, and an adoptive family, all of whom possessed engaging speaking skills and extensive knowledge of local adoption agencies. The monthly open house was a recruitment event that targeted new applicants and families that had withdrawn an application after at least one agency contact. Project sponsors also advertised these meetings in the local press to promote greater community involvement.[42]

Project executives' investment in community contacts and volunteer involvement in program development was at the root of Adopt-A-Child's early success. The project's cooperating agencies relied on the services of liaisons that gave presentations about the project's goals to individuals and groups throughout Adopt-A-Child's service area. The ingenuity and persistence of these "community-rooted persons" led to many of the agency's workshops and speaking engagements. At the 1958 Adopt-A-

Child Volunteers' Workshop, project executives recognized the role this arm of the project had in promoting a "feeling of togetherness" that was markedly different from the "hostility which had been evidenced at the 1955 conference." The contacts not only reinforced agency-community cooperation, they also validated the wisdom of local community leaders whom agencies had kept out of adoption policy creation in the years prior to the project. These expanded networks lay the groundwork for a Clearance Service Committee that formalized and centralized information about available adoptive families and adoptable children. With the help of one paid social worker, the clearance service gathered all inquiries and made referrals to appropriate agencies.[43]

In his November 1955 report for the Adopt-A-Child conference, League community services director, Nelson C. Jackson, identified economic, housing, and cultural factors as the main issues the program successfully interpreted. Adopt-A-Child provided local agencies with information to demonstrate the financial disparities between African American and white households. The report noted that in 1949, the median income for white families was $3,695 annually. For this same year, the African American annual income was $1,689. Adopt-A-Child executive director, William S. Jackson, reported that in 1954 the average income of African Americans living in the North Central Region (an area that included Minneapolis and St. Paul, Minnesota) was $1,776.00 less than that of their white counterparts.[44] Economic disparities increased the housing crisis many African Americans faced. Nelson C. Jackson noted that, of the nonwhite residents in areas Adopt-A-Child served, 29 percent lived in "dilapidated dwelling units." The problem of suitable housing for nonwhite residents in this area was compounded by the fact that they had limited access to new housing developments. According to Nelson C. Jackson, a negligible percentage of new housing was open to people of color living in New York City. He concluded that, for African Americans, low incomes and poor housing made it possible for social workers to reject promising African American clients.[45]

This pattern of housing discrimination was a problem in many cities throughout the nation where legal and cultural racial barriers dictated the geography of residential spaces. The practice of demarcating and grading the boundaries of residential communities based on the economic and racial markup of neighborhoods (commonly referred to as redlining) kept many African Americans in communities on the decline. Redlined neighborhoods served the purposes of real estate agents and mortgage lenders intent on keeping nonwhite residents out of the most desirable neighborhoods. But the practice also drew attention to class differences through the grading system it established for all neighborhoods. As Robert O. Self notes in his study of 1950s and 1960s redlining in Oakland, California, what had been a redline "between black and white [became] a class boundary." African American families that had the resources to live in more desirable neighborhoods were often trapped by this dilemma. League officials hoped these barriers would become more apparent to white social workers who had the important job of screening potential adoptive parents.[46]

In addition to economic and housing problems, Nelson C. Jackson identified a number of cultural factors that Adopt-A-Child translated for local agencies. The cultural factors of interest to the League included African Americans' general distrust of white authority and an issue of color consciousness that was unique to African American clients. Regarding the first issue, Nelson C. Jackson explained that the distrust of white authority grew out of a long history of inequality. He emphasized that many African Americans experienced agency intervention with suspicion, and some terminated inquiries if their initial contacts were unsatisfying. The issue of color consciousness had more ambiguous origins and significance, which caused leading social workers to worry when African Americans made specific requests for children of a particular shade of brown. For some agencies, this pattern was frustrating because it complicated adoption placements. But some white social workers' apprehensions also stemmed from a concern about the psychological implications of this type of behavior for prospective adoptive parents and African American adoptees. These child welfare professionals believed that parents interested in children with light complexions were exhibiting a form of self-hatred that would negatively influence their ability to parent. This issue generated a noteworthy discussion among social workers attempting to determine whether this was a healthy precedent or a manifestation of applicants' internalized self-hatred.[47]

Members of the social work field articulated numerous theories about African Americans' color preferences that reveal a fascinating inconsistency regarding their matching policies and their assessments of African American communities. When a YWCA board member claimed that "many agencies" described having trouble placing "children who are dark skinned and do not have straight hair," Annie Lee Davis Sandusky of the Children's Bureau disagreed. Because she was an African American, Sandusky understood that many African Americans desired children who matched their families. Before joining the Children's Bureau, Sandusky had worked as a teacher in Louisville, Kentucky. She completed a Bachelor of Philosophy in Child Welfare in 1933 and a Masters in Social Work in 1938, both at the University of Chicago. Sandusky also taught at the Atlanta University School of Social Work after World War II. After joining the staff of the Children's Bureau in the late 1940s, Sandusky worked as Consultant on Minority Groups before she became the agency's Consultant on Social Services to Children in Their Own Homes. When she corrected the misconceptions of a YWCA Board member who was seeking information about adoptions of African American children, she acknowledged that finding homes for African American children was hard. But based on her years of experience working with African American families, Sandusky could say with authority that "Negro adoptive parents want children who look like them just as all parents do."[48]

Unlike Sandusky, a number of social workers disregarded the basic reason for matching when they assumed that African Americans preferred children with light complexions because of internalized self-hatred. African Americans were not, however, always reflecting the nation's racial hierarchy when they made their requests. But social workers who were particularly attentive to the principle of matching when placing white children in homes where their appearance did not show marked differences from their adopted families, did not seem to value this same approach for African American families. This type of matching allowed white families to keep their adoptions secret and thereby protect adoptees from unnecessary scrutiny or ostracism. White social workers seemed to miss that African Americans might desire these same protections. Some also struggled to understand the significance of gradations of skin complexion in African American communities.[49] Consequently, when members of the social work community attempted to clarify the issue of African Americans' color preferences, they often emphasized the critical role color played in defining a rigid race hierarchy in the United States. For example, David Fanshel explained that visual appearance is "tied up with economic opportunities and a social status system." Based on this premise, if African American clients were asking for children of lighter complexions than both prospective parents, it was likely they wanted to secure more opportunities for their children than they had experienced. While this pattern and explanation are troubling, they do not address the more practical reasons African American adoption seekers expressed concerns about the complexion of a potential adoptee.[50]

Some families attempted to explain why they cared about race or color differences. William S. Jackson, executive director of Adopt-A-Child, quoted a number of such families in his report that compiled the statements of couples interested in adoptions. In several instances, however, couples that reported unsatisfying experiences with social workers complained that agencies disregarded their desire for children who looked like them. Explaining to League officials why they did not complete an adoption, one family recounted that the adoption agency asked them to take a light-skinned child even though they were a brown-skinned couple. The second child the agency offered this couple had a disability and they "refused to accept the children." Another family was shocked that the agency wanted them to take a "half-white" child. This couple tried to explain to their social worker why this was a problem for them. They were darker than the child and felt this would create a problem of adjustment. One couple that did ask for a child with a light complexion did so because they were light, and they wanted a child who would "blend" with their family. In yet another case, an agency offered a couple a mixed-race child who had blue eyes and blond hair. This family wanted "a child who looks like us," and they walked away from the agency without pursuing the adoption any further.[51]

African American applicants gave similar explanations in their interactions with child welfare professionals affiliated with the US Children's Bureau. Families who contacted the Children's Bureau to get information about adopting a child of color often gave reasons for their desire for a child with a particular complexion in their initial contact. One woman explained that she and her husband were "fair complected [*sic*]" and wanted a child "whose heredity could be traced to" them. Her husband had red hair, blue eyes, and freckles and she had brown hair and brown eyes. Both were interested in a secret adoption. Another woman who asked officials with the Children's Bureau for information about adopting a child also requested one "to match our coloring if possible." She described herself as brown and her husband as olive.[52]

Some social workers seemed preoccupied by the issue of color and not necessarily their African American clients' color preferences, which is a theme that chapter 4 will revisit to discuss how this pattern affected Korean black children. In domestic adoption cases, social workers' ideas about color created uncomfortable encounters for some African American prospective adoptive parents. In a very telling example, a light-complexioned couple left an agency because the social worker asked, "Do you consider yourself colored? You don't look like an American Negro." This couple assumed that the social worker believed this was a compliment, but they were insulted. In some cases, it seems that social workers wanted so desperately to get children of color placed that they did not consider how matching or blending could matter to African Americans. Social workers in this category seemed to believe African Americans could take any child that white communities deemed "Negro." Without an understanding of the great range of complexions in African American communities, white social workers routinely misunderstood African Americans' desires. In response to this type of treatment, one African American applicant noted, "you can't raise a negro child in a white world by" the "theory and books" social workers promoted. League programs like Adopt-A-Child had to coax families who faced this kind of bias back to the adoption process with the promise that the League would interpret these issues to white adoption agency officials.[53]

Color preference was not the only issue important to African Americans, and Adopt-A-Child provided an outlet for these families to express adoption desires, fears, and concerns that white social workers often did not understand. African Americans wanted to select the child they adopted and not just take one the agency offered. A number of couples wanted to see the child the agency matched them with before they made a decision. Some wanted to know about the mental and physical health of a child and its birth parents. A number of couples wanted children of a specific sex or age. Several also expressed fear of the adoption procedures and confusion related to the adoption process. One applicant explained, "you hear so many stories, you have to have money, own your own home, I've been afraid." As African Americans conveyed these concerns to Adopt-A-Child, they revealed misunderstandings between adoption agencies and African Americans that became barriers to adoption.[54]

Several applicants worried that agencies would reject them because of their low economic standing or mixed religious affiliations. When couples interested in adopting expressed anxiety over their economic status, they often mentioned the costs associated with adoptions. One couple complained that the $300.00 fee was outside of their budget. This fee was outside of many applicants' budgets. Another couple explained that an agency rejected them in 1952 because their annual income of $3,200.00 was below the minimum qualifying income. One couple criticized the consumer nature of adoption, noting, "we don't want to buy a child. We only want to give a child a home and love, and the things a child really needs." Additionally, adoption agencies counted religious affiliations among their list of activities applicants needed to give children. This caused some applicants to wonder if agencies would harshly judge the interfaith nature of their households or their affiliations with groups like Christian Scientists. In some instances, these characteristics did prohibit couples' adoption goals. One family reported that they were "disappointed with [the] treatment" they received from a social worker who stopped helping their family when she learned that the couple included a Protestant husband and a Catholic wife. In another case, a social worker rejected the application of a Protestant husband and a Catholic wife, calling them a "split family."[55]

In 1958, Adopt-A-Child executives broached these and other placement challenges when they formulated a new approach to adoptions involving African American families and children of color. Executive director William S. Jackson suggested that "the 'right' family for a child should be chosen—not so much on similarity of racial or ethnic background, but on the ability of the child and family to complement each other in physical appearance and personality."[56] This statement signaled that William S. Jackson was encouraging more innovations in child placement that challenged ideas about race and adoption. Even as Jackson complimented the remarkable transitions some agencies made from very rigid interpretations of racial and religious matching to more practical standards, he observed that these changes would not lead to the recruitment of enough families of color to meet the growing demand agencies faced. Indeed, in its three years of operation, Adopt-A-Child experienced significant increases in the number of inquiries submitted to affiliated agencies. It referred 851 families to agencies and reported consistent improvements in adoption completions. William S. Jackson also reported that the number of minority children placed in permanent homes increased slightly, from 115 to 135 to 165 to 186 for the four-year period between 1954 and 1957, respectively. But these efforts did not keep pace with the growing caseloads of many child welfare and adoption agencies that began to include more African American and mixed-race children throughout the 1950s and 1960s. Jackson also reported that one institution in New York City with a capacity of 200 was full, and he estimated 40,000 to 60,000 children in the area were in need of foster care or adoption services.[57]

Consequently, William S. Jackson suggested that agencies should continue to utilize the skills of "indigenous leader[s]" to access suitable families, but they should also pursue new applicant pools and broader legislative and cultural approaches to address the changing needs of communities of color. He proposed a reevaluation of policies and encouraged adoption agencies to expand the field of possible applicants to include "unmarried women and widows." In a decisive break with League procedures that advocated the avoidance of legislative entanglements, Jackson called for new laws that would make childcare agencies that received public funds serve communities of color. A 1952 New York City ordinance that prohibited the use of city funds for private childcare agencies that discriminated against minority children inspired this new approach. Jackson considered this law to be an example of effective local legal intervention that could work on the national level. In a compelling plea, Jackson proposed changes in an equally important but underexplored direction. He suggested that a critical solution to the growing problem of displaced children of color began with efforts to reduce the circumstances that led to family breakdown.[58]

With his call to "strengthen families and reduce the breakdown of family life," William S. Jackson articulated a sophisticated critique of the adoption policies that linked democracy, citizenship, and community well-being with the support of adoptive and birth families of color.

From the League's earliest reports detailing the need for greater involvement in minority adoptions, the agency connected the attainment of a stable home life with a child's ability to develop the skills it would need to become a good citizen in a democracy. But these interventions always focused on the child as a separate entity from the family. Jackson was revising an older version of community responsibility that viewed reform of the family as critical to community and national strength. Early twentieth-century child welfare architects had designed programs to help unwed mothers keep their children and not become burdens on charity and social welfare organizations. These child welfare reformers approached their clients, many of whom were immigrant women, as problem women who could be reformed and made into suitable mothers and citizens. Jackson revised this model to suggest that racial inequality and not inherent dysfunction created situations that made children of color vulnerable, harmed families of color leading to family breakdowns, and disrupted communities.[59]

William S. Jackson also moved beyond the Adopt-A-Child goal to hold agencies responsible for the adoption of children of color in order to encourage people to see family-centric adoption reform as a democratic venture. He implored individuals who cared about the nation's future to work against issues that caused family breakdown. Jackson argued that the care of minority children was the best protection against the social ills that people associated with dysfunctional families and communities. He insisted that, in many instances, family dysfunction stemmed from poverty and racial inequality.[60] Jackson further outlined six areas that required community action, and he developed a critique of social practices and legal precedents that ensured African Americans' inferior economic and political status. His list explained that agencies needed to propose strategies to improve deficiencies in housing, hiring, and educational facilities to meet new standards of equal access. The similarity between these initiatives and the goals of the era's multiple civil rights efforts was not lost on Jackson. In one instance, he even referenced the May 17, 1954 US Supreme Court, *Brown v. Board of Education* decision as one example of a critical success in African Americans' fight to secure "the goals of a democratic life." Jackson demonstrated that the fight to protect families of color was in line with civil rights goals and would benefit all citizens, not just people of color.[61]

William S. Jackson labeled the problems that hindered communities of color the nation's problems, and he encouraged child welfare professionals to work to assist all children who needed adoption services. Ultimately, Jackson wanted child welfare officials to recognize the ways they perpetuated racism and segregation in child welfare organizations. However, he attempted to deemphasize the divisive potential of issues like race, class, and religion in matters of child welfare when he stated, "a child is a member of the total community—not just a member of a particular race, religion, or class."[62] Officials with Adopt-A-Child affiliated agencies and League representatives agreed that the project to secure stable homes for children of color was important. However, most white affiliated agencies were more nearsighted in their assessments of which communities benefited the most from improvements to the status of African American children and communities. Several executives with affiliated agencies conceded that a healthy family life played a role in every child's personality development, but few moved in the direction of a larger critique of racial inequality in adoption as a measure of the nation's democratic potential.

The overtly political nature of William S. Jackson's ideas and the NUL's goals in child placement drew fire from whites who found his message of inclusion and equality threatening. Beginning in 1954, White Citizens' Councils throughout the country responded to such League activities by initiating a campaign to eliminate any funding League branches received from local community chests. The community chests had been a major source of funding for NUL branches since the early twentieth century, but membership in the community chests limited branches to activities that emphasized the League's "social work orientation."[63] In spite of the economic vulnerability that their association with the community chests created, a number of NUL officials and staff demonstrated their support for the desegregation activities of organizations like the Congress of Racial Equality (CORE) and the NAACP. NUL historian Jesse Thomas Moore notes that the "Community Chest crisis" began after League executive director Lester B. Granger publicly supported the 1954 *Brown v. Board of Education* Supreme Court decision that initiated the desegregation of the nation's public schools. The crisis led a number of League branches to either end or lose their affiliation with the community chests, which allowed some to engage in forms of more direct political activism that further antagonized segregationists.[64]

In 1956, members of the States' Rights Council of Georgia used the radio to stoke resistance to League programs because they believed the NUL "arranged for Negroes to live along side white people." A representative of the Council claimed that he opposed the community chest's funding of the League because it supported "boycotts, litigations, and other activities to force race mixing at all levels of society." He made these claims knowing that if he could prove that the League was not just a charitable organization, he could argue that it should not receive funds from the community chest. This line of attack was an obvious pretense for organizations intent on derailing school desegregation and other political and social changes that challenged white supremacy. The State's Rights Councilmembers included the text of an inflammatory speech written in 1887 by former managing editor of the *Atlanta Constitution*, Henry W. Grady, in its radio attack against the League. The piece made clear the political intent of the coordinated backlash against civil rights activism that was sweeping the nation. Grady's speech was a kind of call to arms that identified any attempt on the part of African Americans to achieve equality as a violation of divine order. He asserted that "the supremacy of the white race of the South must be maintained forever, and the domination of the negro race resisted at all points and at all hazards."[65]

The backlash against the NUL and civil rights activism was not isolated to the South, and League executives had to develop a defense against attacks from White Citizens' Councils in non-Southern cities too. For example, the California League of Christian Parents in San Bernardino, California circulated an open letter that called League programs "anti-white, race mixing activities."[66] The letter referred to Lester Granger as the "Mulatto Executive Director" of the League and accused him of being a communist. It then encouraged people to contact their local community chest and threaten to end their support of that agency if it did not end its support of the Urban League. In response, League branches shared information about their efforts to correct these slanderous assaults. League officials and staff gave presentations about the League's history and evolving mission, they circulated flyers that made the activities and organizational structure of the League transparent, and they created television public service announcements that defined the League's goals. Some local organizations also came to the defense of the League and Lester Granger. One official with the United Community Funds and Councils of America asserted that Granger had received a commendation from every US president from Hoover to Eisenhower, proving that he was not an "outright subversive."[67]

None of these efforts were sufficient to stop most community chests from ending their relationships with the League. This response was especially detrimental to League branches in the South.[68] The damage done to the reputations of Southern Leagues led one official to admit that the Citizens' Councils had successfully cut off much of the League funding in local communities. By 1958, officials with the Children's Bureau noted that even Adopt-A-Child in New York was unable to recruit as many African American families as it had in earlier years. It is certain that the successful campaign of the White Citizens' Councils against the League played a role in the decline of the NUL's adoption reform project.[69]

The resistance of White Citizen's Councils and the reluctance of some agencies to implement the changes recommended by the League hindered the NUL's recruitment efforts. By the late 1950s, a few officials began actively promoting transracial adoptions that would place African American and mixed-race children with white adoptive families as one solution to the problem the League faced because of the low numbers of African American adoptive families. According to Matine T. Spence, the NUL was "among the first to endorse color-blind interracial adoption for African American children," but Adopt-A-Child's early experiments in transracial adoption in 1955 and 1956 were not "cross-color" adoptions.[70] Instead, these placements matched children who could pass as white with the white and Jewish families that applied to adopt with that agency. The practice caused NUL officials to debate the merits of transracial adoptions and ultimately conclude that they did and would benefit some African American and mixed-race children. Subsequently, in 1959, Nelson Jackson publicly acknowledged his belief that transracial adoptions were necessary.[71]

However, the NUL remained committed to a family-centric reform agenda even as it promoted transracial adoptions. At the NUL annual conference in August 1963, League members proposed resolutions that emphasized their continued support for programs that would prevent family breakdown in addition to their support for efforts to increase transracial adoptions. Officials requested that "leadership of the country undertake a massive 'Marshal Plan' approach and intensified efforts to close the wide economic, social, and educational gap which separates the large majority of Negro citizens from other Americans." Then they called for an end to "state laws restricting adoptions based on race."[72] Two months later, League officials Nelson Jackson and Jeweldean Jones met with representatives of the Child Welfare League of America to encourage that agency to revise its adoption standards to deemphasize race in adoption placements. Jackson's and Jones's insistence on both types of programs made clear that some officials believed the organization should not distance itself from either the controversial or the political nature of these issues.[73]

The Limits of Adoption Reform and Foster Care for African Americans

Many League-affiliated agencies did not pursue an overt political agenda when they promoted the role of adoption placements in stabilizing children's lives and in their local communities. Playing down the larger political implications of racial inequality in adoption services, some NUL officials characterized children of color as unfortunate victims of inequality who missed the opportunity to have "a normal, integrated personality" when they did not receive adoption services.[74] Thus, a number of adoption agencies measured their progress and the effectiveness of their programs using very concrete criteria that identified successful child placement as an end unto itself. League branches across the nation could boast a range of successful outcomes in the early years of the Foster Care and Adoption Project when these criteria were the only consideration. Often not as comprehensive as the Adopt-A-Child project, these branches initiated community-based outreach programs that did transform some local adoption agencies' activities on behalf of children of color.

League officials observed increased interest in adoption among families of color in all cities where League branches partnered with local adoption agencies. In Dayton, Ohio and Pittsburgh, Pennsylvania, League staff reported steady increases in inquiries from African Americans. Agencies that did not report measurable increases in interest did mention their continued efforts to promote good public relations and community organizing. Several League branches reported the creation of committees to coordinate services between local agencies and incorporate volunteer assistants. Other agencies identified their continued efforts to use the media to take the story of the project to targeted communities. In two cases, League members confessed that they could not report increased placements, but this did not mean that children were going without care. Officials with these agencies surmised that their low numbers were, in part, because family members were informally adopting displaced children. This pattern of informal adoption confounded a number of League staff and prompted investigations into the effectiveness of some branches. The Washington, DC League is a case in point.[75]

The Washington, DC League began its foster care and adoption project in 1957, and it experienced mixed results from its efforts to expand adoption services for children of color. The DC League incorporated and refined all aspects of the organization's community approach, making impressive use of volunteers and the media to get the story of DC's adoption needs out to the public. Branch administrators invigorated community involvement and education using a multimedia approach. Branch staff used the local press, radio, and television outlets to publicize agencies that needed adoptive parents. Members of the agency's public relations committee revised the media approach by encouraging very specific spot announcements that limited the waste they experienced from sending bulk mailings. Project director Anita Bellamy noticed that spot announcements produced the greatest responses. The branch's staff also observed that they received the largest number of inquiries because of radio and television advertising. However, printed media produced the most adoptions and foster care placements.[76]

The DC League's volunteer corps blanketed the city's business establishments with numerous flyers, posters, and brochures that attracted a more committed group of adoption applicants. In a 1960 report, Bellamy boasted that volunteers had distributed brochures "in three hundred fifty-seven beauty and barber shops," and the League received permission to advertise on buses and streetcars. The Church and Neighborhood committee used targeted literature drops to distribute 14,950 flyers to Protestant churches for their Mother's Day services. Branch staff members also used the services of the area's Medical Wives Club to place materials in dentists' and doctors' offices. Branch administrators observed greater delays in people's responses to printed material, but the families who approached the agency because of a brochure or flyer seemed to be better informed and this strategy produced lasting results.[77]

The DC League utilized face-to-face meetings and speaking engagements to recruit couples who expressed a real interest in adoption. Bellamy believed that face-to-face contacts were an essential element of the community model. Therefore, she called perspective parents to make the adoption process as personal as possible. Staff members also encouraged applicants to contact members of the Adoptive Parents Group to get answers to specific questions about the adoption process. The staff developed a personal approach to the community by hosting neighborhood exhibits and public meetings. Although they targeted professional organizations, civic groups, and fraternal orders, these contacts produced mixed results. This strategy did reach large numbers of people, but it also led many participants to share both the positive aspects of adoption and negative experiences couples remembered. Testimonials and the unexpectedly low adoption rates (given the extent of the League's promotional efforts) prompted a study to determine African Americans' attitudes toward adoption.[78]

In 1961, sociologists Leila Calhoun Deasy and Olive Westbrooke Quinn conducted a survey to identify reasons for the relatively low adoption participation of Baltimore and Washington, DC's African American communities. Deasy and Quinn led a team of research assistants affiliated with the Catholic University of America and Goucher College that contacted 484 African Americans to answer one key question, namely, "why don't Negroes adopt children."[79] The researchers designed the study to ascertain whether a lack of information or general misgivings about the adoption process influenced African Americans' ideas about adoption. The study revealed that while the majority of respondents had favorable opinions of adoption, they continued to believe that informal arrangements would provide enough homes for displaced children. Some respondents indicated that they agreed with the statement, "dependent Negro children . . . will be cared for through the device of informal arrangements by persons other than their parents, if the need arises."[80] When researchers pressed to see if respondents had problems with adoption agencies, a number of them said that their ideas about agencies were not negative. However, respondents did believe that social workers were "too inquisitive" and their standards "too stringent."[81] These respondents thought the most significant agency requirement for adoption was that families demonstrate financial responsibility. These responses caused the researchers to encourage agencies to develop strategies to gain the confidence of African American clients. The researchers echoed League officials' conclusion that adoption would improve only when child welfare officials and social workers gained the trust of African American communities.

While the subjects of the Deasy and Quinn study reported that they did not think a wife's paid labor affected a couple's adoption process, officials with other League projects found that some families did. A report that William S. Jackson shared with NUL officials suggested that League staff needed to work to interpret African American women's paid labor patterns to white social workers. One applicant reported that a social worker told her she had to quit her job as a domestic to qualify for adoption. Another applicant described that her family's application was proceeding nicely until she told social workers that she could not quit her job. Many social workers did not say that a woman's paid labor prohibited an adoption, but some female applicants believed this issue caused a breakdown in their adoption process. In one case, an applicant explained that, in her opinion, her job outside of the home caused social workers to block her adoption. A couple of women who reported negative interactions with social workers either withdrew their applications or social workers rejected them with a note explaining that the wife was "aggressive."[82] As we will see in chapter 3, conflicts between social workers and African American families over these kinds of economic issues led some couples to pursue transnational adoption and forced others to become foster parents.[83]

Foster Care versus Adoption Reform for African Americans

From the beginning of the Project in Foster Care and Adoption, officials working to place minority children saw foster care and boarding home programs as "an essential corollary to the placement of children for adoption."[84] But League staff prioritized adoption because they believed that foster care increased a child's vulnerability by limiting the chance that he or she would become permanent member of a family. This idea had its roots in the late nineteenth and early twentieth centuries, when child welfare professionals and nonprofessionals used the term "foster care" to describe a number of strategies people implemented to provide homes for displaced children. Foster placements could involve families receiving small payments to care for foster children. However, in some cases, children had to work as a condition of their care. The distinctions between boarding homes, free homes, and work homes were often not as important as the legal distinction between foster care and adoption. Although formal adoptions were uncommon in the early twentieth century, they involved the legal transfer of a child from its birth parents to its adoptive parents. Foster care placements were different. Parents could place a child in foster care without terminating their legal parental rights. Indeed, some biological parents made arrangements for short-term foster care as a part of a long-term strategy to keep their children. This type of foster care could be formal or informal and, as was the case in much of the child welfare landscape in the early twentieth century, the funding for such arrangements came from a mix of private and public sources.[85]

By the 1930s, child welfare professionals and state actors were playing larger roles in the organization and regulation of foster care. However, many child welfare professionals believed foster care would become "a last resort" strategy after the passage of the Social Security Act of 1935.[86] This seminal piece of New Deal legislation created state and federal social welfare programs to address the causes of poverty and family breakdown. Even after the law went into effect, however, foster care remained essential to the many groups that were not eligible to receive social security benefits or benefits through programs like Aid to Dependent Children (ADC), and later Aid to Families with Dependent Children (AFDC).[87] Many African Americans did not qualify for these programs because the framers of social security designed both the maternal and the entitlements programs to largely benefit white clients.[88] But in the 1930s and 1940s, boarding and foster homes began to rely more on public funds, and social workers decreased their reliance on orphanages and other residential institutions, which led to an expansion in foster care systems in the post–World War II decades. These shifts caused some child welfare officials to begin to identify and work with African Americans who could serve as foster families.[89]

While this change suggests that child welfare officials were attempting to reduce racial barriers to some child welfare services, critics of the persistence of racial inequality in US child welfare remained unconvinced. Some argued that increasing African Americans' access to foster care eliminated the pressure to improve adoption services for African American children.[90] A number of League officials held this opinion. As early as 1955, League officials attempted to combat what they believed to be the child welfare establishment's tendency to resist changes that would promote adoption over foster care.[91] Nelson C. Jackson recognized that recruitment and placement challenges were largely the result of "an acute problem in [the] field of social work."[92] He noticed that social workers in a number of agencies actively worked against League recommendations to include African American professionals and volunteers in adoption procedures. In one instance, Jackson hoped meetings with executives of affiliated agencies would "break the bottleneck which seems to be harming Adopt-A-Child," but this did not happen.[93] Some social workers continued to rely on standards that accommodated white, middle-class clients while encouraging African American adoption seekers to pursue foster care. Some agencies even seemed more willing to make accommodations for African American families to increase their participation in foster care. As Catherine E. Rymph explains, a number of agencies endeavored to change "rigid standards of placement agencies," including bans on a foster mother's paid labor, to make it easier for black couples to become foster parents.[94]

Some African American couples complained when they realized that social workers were more intent on helping them become foster parents and not adoptive parents. One couple charged, "agencies want Negroes to board children, but they only let them be adopted by wealthy people who have big homes and lots of money."[95] Another couple explained that the social worker handling their case tried "to force foster care on us."[96] This couple further reported that their social worker said that they needed foster parents more than they needed adopting parents because "only once and a while [did] they [have] children for adoption."[97] League officials noted that this pattern indicated a bigger problem with the social work profession. It seems that some white social workers claimed that there was no need for African American adopting couples and denied that there was a need to improve services to this population. Commenting on the situation in New York City, William S. Jackson placed the blame for delayed adoption placements on local agencies by insisting that agencies could get children out of foster care and institutions if they made the effort.[98]

Urban League officials were not alone in their concerns about the efficacy of foster care. Throughout 1956 and 1957, officials associated with the Child Welfare League of America worked to develop standards for foster family care. They endeavored to clarify questions about the goals and requirements of child welfare agencies and to assure quality services for all families involved in the nation's foster care systems. Members of the Working Committee on Foster Family Care began meeting in November 1956, and they worked for the next two years to draft and revise standards that would represent the agreed upon best practices for children in foster care. Published in 1959, the Standards for Foster Family Care Services outlined procedures for determining what situations warranted foster care placement, the kinds of services available to children in the foster care system, and the criteria for selecting and assessing foster families. By the late 1950s, the families most in need of foster care services were experiencing what social workers called "social disorganization," and child welfare officials stressed the importance of agency supervision for each child in need of foster care. Some Urban League officials optimistically interpreted changes in foster care standards to mean that child welfare communities were intent on equalizing services between the nation's white and minority children.[99]

Urban League officials considered foster care an interim step in the adoption process that would give social workers time to locate suitable African American adoptive families.[100] They also worried that without a substantial number of foster homes, minority children would remain in less desirable institutions, including hospitals and overcrowded orphanages. However, a 1963 study conducted by Helen Jeter and reprinted in the book *Children of the Storm* by Andrew Billingsley and Jeanne M. Giovannoni found that foster care was "more heavily relied upon for Black than white children."[101] In some cases, children of color remained in foster care for years because a parent or both parents refused to relinquish their parental rights. But NUL officials noticed that many children who could be adopted remained in foster care for many of the reasons League staff had identified when they began the Project in Foster Care and Adoption.[102] Annie Lee Davis Sandusky of the Children's Bureau made a similar observation when she insisted that minority children in foster care could become adopted children "if staff in social agencies have conviction, determination, and imagination—and at the same time enlist the interest, conviction and support of the total community."[103]

Although some agencies complained that working to formalize African American adoptions was too costly, evidence suggests that foster care created a greater fiscal burden on agency budgets and state welfare funds. Before initiating the Seybert program mentioned earlier, Walter P. Townsend had noted that the cost of foster care was outpacing the needs of Pennsylvania's Children's Aid Society. He promoted adoptions, in part, because of how expensive foster care was for that agency.[104] The first major study of the costs of foster care corroborated this assessment. David Fanshel and Eugene B. Shinn conducted their research on the costs of foster care in New York City under the auspices of the Child Welfare Research Program of Columbia University School of Social Work in 1972. The study investigated the costs of boarding children in "institutional care, foster family care, group residence, and agency-operated boarding homes." Reviewing the outcomes of services provided to 624 children over a period of five years beginning in 1966, the researchers concluded that keeping one child in foster care for four years cost more than $68,000. Fanshel and Shinn further surmised that foster care cost about five times what a low-income family would spend to raise their own child. These findings encouraged the researchers to promote "prevention and family rehabilitation" or adoption over foster care. The assessment also reinforced the argument League executives had made years earlier when they noted that reasons other than cost influenced agency resistance to adoption placements involving African American.[105]

The League initiative to transform child placement practices for children of color revealed that a constellation of political, social, economic, and cultural issues caused the increase in foster care placements among African Americans. The Foster Care and Adoption Project allowed League staff to coordinate a national initiative that encouraged adoption agencies to work with local African American community leaders and institutions. They also promoted adjustments to requirements that created unnecessary economic hardships for African American clients. Consequently, agencies that partnered with the League did not ignore families of color or dismiss them outright as dysfunctional and pathological. League officials considered this change to be a promising reversal that could correct the tendency of many white child welfare professionals to classify African Americans' family patterns as inconsistent with their definitions of stable adoptive families. They hoped these changes would alter the tendency of some white social workers to encourage African Americans to foster instead of pursuing a formal adoption. To officials and social workers associated with the NUL, this tendency reinforced African Americans' perceptions that some child welfare professionals believed that African American couples were good enough to act as temporary parents but not good enough to become permanent, legal parents.

The NUL's adoption and foster care initiatives evolved as Americans faced the challenges of resolving a history of segregation that made children of color vulnerable in the United States and abroad. Unsurprisingly, the issues that League officials worked to change because they limited African Americans' adoptions in the United States also proved limiting when some African Americans attempted to complete a transnational adoption. The recognition of this relationship was sobering for a few child welfare professionals who had been cautiously optimistic about the prospect of placing Korean black children with African American families during the same years that League officials worked to increase African Americans' domestic adoptions.

Specifically, ISS's William T. Kirk and Susan T. Pettiss conceded that recruiting African American adoptive families was harder than they had imagined in 1955 when they corresponded with the editor of *Ebony* about the magazine's article, "How to Adopt Korean Babies." As the introduction of this book demonstrated, these professionals believed that the African American couples who would adopt Korean black children would not be the same families that attempted to complete a domestic adoption. But, by December 1957, Kirk, Pettiss, and other officials on the Intercountry Adoption Committee of ISS recognized that this distinction was not automatically true. Consequently, members of the Intercountry Adoption Committee were also wondering whether their agency should attempt to find homes for "hard-to-place children in general and for Negro children in particular" in the United States. ISS was having difficulties recruiting African American families that could meet the standards of agencies in the United States that coordinated both domestic and transnational placements. These difficulties revealed that whether African Americans pursued a domestic or transnational adoption, many still had to face the barriers that officials with the NUL attempted to address.

Thus, Kirk observed that locating African American families was a "time-consuming process." Susan Pettiss wondered how many hours ISS staff could devote to this new project if the board decided to initiate a domestic adoption program for minority children. Board member Mrs. Eric H. Haight warned that US adoption agencies had trouble placing African American children, "particularly those who were rather dark, since in general Negro adoptive parents want a child lighter than they are." By the end of the December 1957 Intercountry Adoption Committee meeting, committee members decided not to pursue a separate project for hard-to-place children in the United States. Instead, ISS officials agreed that the problem was too big for their agency. They decided that they would contact officials with the Child Welfare League of America and "various national Negro groups" and ask them to "take some interest in this total problem for Negro children."[106]

However, in an article for the journal *Child Welfare*, Pettiss indicated that, in some cases, agencies had responded to her request that they adjust standards to work with African American couples interested in adopting transnationally. These attempts to increase African Americans' adoptions of Korean black children drew attention to "the scarcity of Negro adoptive homes in the United States" that had inspired NUL officials to establish its Foster Care and Adoption Project. Indeed, Pettiss acknowledged that encouraging African American couples to adopt transnationally reduced the pool of parents for children in the United States. But she concluded that the strategy was necessary when one considered "the meager alternatives for those [children] in foreign countries."[107] Yet, the failure of comprehensive adoption reform in the United States assured that African Americans would continue to struggle to adopt children of color in the States and abroad.

The National Urban League's Project in Foster Care and Adoption Services sparked debates among child welfare professionals concerning the roles African Americans would play in various adoption and foster care schemes. The goals of the project were controversial because the League wanted agencies to transform their administrative, advisory, and social work staff to include African Americans. This meant much more work for adoption agencies than simply reforming their policies to better serve African American clients. League officials and social workers also attempted to interpret African American family patterns and preferences to white social workers when these patterns and preferences seemed at odds with the characteristics of many white adoptive families. The League hoped measures like these would increase adoptions that reflected what families were like in African American communities and not the idealized version of adoptive families that agencies attempted to replicate. When League officials proposed that agencies should consider single mothers and reconsider their adherence to strict matching when placing African American and mixed-race children, they were affirming a belief that a loving, permanent family was best for children. Although they advocated for reforms that would increase adoptions, they also supported African Americans' participation in the foster care system. Yet League officials were sensitive to African American clients' complaints that some white agencies encouraged foster care when they were interested in adoption.[108]

The resistance of some social workers to extend services to African American clients, the changing status of children receiving child welfare services, and organized efforts of White Citizens' Councils limited the success of the project. When the national initiative ended in 1958, project designers could point to slight increases in the numbers of completed adoptions as proof that African Americans were invested in the welfare of displaced children. A number of League branches even continued their programs in adoption and foster care well into the 1960s and 1970s. Many of these local efforts effectively implemented a community organizational model that encouraged cooperation between African American volunteers, African American child welfare professionals, and white child welfare professionals. In their most ambitious moments, national and local League officials called the reforms that assisted adoptive families of color an integral feature of a democratic society. More often,

League personnel viewed their work as a necessary and overdue inter-vention that fit into the most basic goals of child and community wel-fare. Although the NUL encountered resistance to its efforts at national adoption reform, chapter 3 demonstrates that the confluence of Cold War anxieties and international critiques of US race relations caused some agencies to devise NUL-like strategies to help African American couples adopt Korean black children.

3

African American Families, Korean Black Children, and the Evolution of Transnational Race Rescue

When Helen Wilson learned of a proposal to implement transnational adoptions of displaced Korean children in January 1953, she considered the plan to be unwise. Wilson was the liaison for the United Nations Korean Reconstruction Agency (UNKRA) office in New York, and she insisted that the adoption of Korean children by Westerners would create problems for Korean adoptees and their new families. She cited immigration restrictions and the cultural, social, and racial differences that existed between people in the United States and Korea as factors that agencies should not ignore. Suspicious of Americans who might pursue transnational adoption for selfish or unscrupulous motives, Wilson hoped UNKRA would support US-Korean adoptions only as a last resort. Instead, she encouraged agencies to devote their resources and time to creating plans that would place children with families in South Korea. Wilson made this recommendation because she was confident that, with support from Western organizations, Korean communities could care for the nation's displaced children and war orphans.[1]

Wilson's concerns were valid. As described in chapter 1, during the war soldiers and volunteers with sectarian and nonsectarian agencies in Korea were working around US immigration restrictions to bring Korean children to the United States. When the Korean War ended, more Americans attempted to bring Korean children to the States in response to the growing humanitarian crisis in Korea that disrupted the lives of millions of families and left hundreds of thousands of children without one or both of their parents.[2] Although Wilson imagined that Koreans would be able to absorb these children, in the immediate aftermath of the war, the majority of Korea's citizens could not do so because the South Korean government and civilians were largely dependent on aid from numerous international sources. Consequently, Augusta Mayerson, the Voluntary Agencies Liaison Chief with UNKRA in Korea, reported that officials with the Republic of Korea were interested in having its "beggar and unwanted children adopted . . . that these might have a better chance in another country."[3] Many of the people involved in the first adoptions of Korean War orphans and displaced Korean children agreed with this sentiment. As the number of mixed-race Korean children grew, supporters of Korean transnational adoption also promoted transnational placements as a form of humanitarian rescue for these children, whom many called GI babies.

A number of factors caused people in Korea and the United States to advocate transnational adoption for mixed-race Korean children. First, in Korea, the patriarchal family traditions that organized social, cultural, and political definitions of Korean identity based a child's citizenship on its father's status. Thus, mixed-race Korean children were not legally citizens of South Korea, and they were not listed in the family registries that defined belonging in that nation.[4] Further, because people associated the Korean mothers of GI babies with military prostitution, these mothers and their children experienced abuse and ostracism. Finally, Koreans' emphasis on racial purity as an essential aspect of their national identity also made mixed-race Korean children vulnerable. According to Arissa Oh, Koreans applied their own interpretation of the one-drop rule when they concluded that "whiteness or blackness rendered a half-Korean child wholly American."[5] Korean black children faced additional hardships because Koreans' acceptance of elements of US racism informed their treatment of children fathered by African American soldiers.[6] However, the ideas about race that caused many Koreans to reject Korean black children motivated African Americans' participation in Korean transnational adoption. Whether or not they were biologically related to a Korean black child, many black prospective adoptive parents believed their adoptions were necessary because the racism taking root in Korea bore an unfortunate resemblance to the racial discrimination that locked African Americans into a punishing second-class citizenship in the United States.

The child welfare professionals and nonprofessionals who began arranging adoptions for Korean black children acknowledged that anti-black racism shaped many Koreans' responses to these children. But they also knew that racial inequality in the United States would constrain African Americans' ability to complete a transnational adoption. As discussed in chapter 2, African Americans frequently failed to meet many of the standards social workers used to evaluate prospective adoptive couples attempting a do-mestic adoption. Nonetheless, many social workers endeavored to identify families that conformed to the nuclear family model, as closely as possible, to place Korean black children. Conversely, nonprofessionals were much less concerned with applying what many considered to be unreasonable standards when they recruited African American adoptive couples. They believed the emergency nature of Korean transnational adoption required the implementation of the kinds of reforms the NUL was advocating for in domestic adoption. Consequently, African Americans' transnational adoptions intensified debates between nonprofessionals who established adoption programs to place mixed-race Korean children and the profes-sionals working to regulate Korean transnational adoption.

This chapter evaluates how these contests, and the need to increase adoptions of Korean black children, caused some child welfare profes-sionals and nonprofessionals to devise competing plans to recruit African American adoptive families. I argue that African American soldiers' fami-lies that conformed to the gender conventions of the nuclear family model caused child welfare professionals to redefine some of their ideas about what constituted a stable adoptive family. As a result, African American couples associated with the military became the families many child wel-fare professionals identified as best able to provide Korean black children a secure future in the immediate aftermath of the Korean War. This shift took place as nonprofessionals' strategies to recruit African American adoptive families proved to be more successful but potentially more dan-gerous because of their use of the proxy adoption method. Scholars have largely explored how and why politics, race, religion, and secular religion, to varying degrees, shaped the policies of Korean transnational adoption and white Americans' participation in the practice. This chapter considers how African Americans, and especially African American soldiers and their families, influenced and responded to these policies during the first two decades of Korean transnational adoption.[7]

Humanitarian, Military, and Political Solutions to Korea's GI Baby Crisis

Before the Korean War ended, charitable organizations, the US govern-ment and military, and officials with the ROK were already grappling with America's responsibility to Korea's displaced children. Early in 1953, officials with the newly established American-Korean Foundation (AKF) identified Korean child welfare as an integral element of that organization's mission to "bring American and Korean peoples closer together on cultural, social, and economic affairs."[8] However, co-chairman of the AKF, Dr. Milton S. Eisenhower, brother of then President Dwight D. Eisenhower, promoted the construction of orphanages as the most effective way of sustaining poor and parentless Korean children. Similarly, officials with UNKRA, such as Helen Wilson and Augusta Mayerson, mentioned above, believed that the development of coordinated child welfare programs in Korea would best serve Korean orphans. They encouraged Americans interested in adopting Korean children to send food and needed supplies instead of removing children from Korea.[9]

Even organizations interested in expanding Americans' roles in transnational adoption were unsure of the practicality of US-Korean placements. Actress Jane Russell Waterfield, president of the International Adoption Association (IAA), did not think many Americans would want to adopt a Korean child. Waterfield and her husband, ex-football player Robert Waterfield, were adoptive parents who had completed adoptions in the United States and England. The legal battle they faced to complete their transnational adoption inspired Waterfield to work to make the process easier for other families. In correspondences with US Children's Bureau officials after the Korean War, Waterfield posed and responded to questions about the feasibility of US-Korean adoptions. The information she obtained led her to propose that agencies push for the creation of a foster care program that would place Korean orphans in the homes of families in the States, much like the one that had placed English children in US homes during World War II. Waterfield felt that some of the families that participated in a program of this kind might consider adopting the Korean child they fostered. Skepticism from organizations like IAA confirmed the short-lived suspicions shared by many in US child welfare communities that Korean transnational adoptions were not feasible because (white) Americans would not adopt Korean children.[10]

The US Children's Bureau (USCB) began fielding questions from state departments of welfare regarding US-Korean adoptions early in 1953 that suggested that families in the United States would adopt Korean children. In February of that year, the child welfare supervisor of the Arizona Department of Public Welfare contacted officials with the USCB to find out if they knew of any plans to coordinate adoptions of Korean War orphans because of the many requests that agency was receiving about the children.[11] I. Evelyn Smith, consultant on foster care for the Children's Bureau, confirmed that she did not know of any such efforts.[12] Yet, by June, Smith was consulting with officials at the Child Welfare League of America (CWLA) about the need for procedures to assist American families stationed overseas who were attempting to adopt Korean children. Describing the Bureau's new focus on US-Korean adoptions, Smith explained that the agency was receiving numerous requests from families interested in transnational adoptions and state child welfare agencies willing to work with them. She also expressed concerns about the complaints from soldiers and other US personnel stationed overseas, who claimed that child welfare agencies in the United States discriminated against them. Although Smith acknowledged that adoption agencies considered the frequent relocations of military families to be potentially detrimental to the adjustment of an adopted child, she conceded that, in light of the orphan situation in a number of countries, agencies throughout America needed to consider coordinating adoption services for military families stationed overseas.[13]

As child welfare agencies began developing US-Korean adoption networks, military and government officials continued to celebrate soldiers' child-centric humanitarianism in Korea that began during the Korean War. Eighth Army Civil Affairs Officer, Colonel Vachel D. Whatley, was among the many officials who applauded soldiers' performance of charitable acts on behalf of displaced children. He saw great benefit coming from soldiers' activities that demonstrated the ways "a combat army can also perform humanitarian deeds."[14] One group of soldiers collected thousands of dollars and hundreds of pounds of packages for the 1953 Christmas program, prompting Colonel Whatley to suggest that such efforts would improve relations between soldiers and the Korean people. In 1954, Assistant Secretary of State Thurston B. Morton recognized the work soldiers were doing to construct or reconstruct several essential facilities in Korea, including orphanages. Morton reported that in one month alone, soldiers constructed thirteen new orphanages and were working on twenty-one additional institutions. Soldiers completed these structures while working for the Supplemental Armed Forces Assistance Program. The military established this program in response to suggestions made by President Eisenhower, who wanted to demonstrate that the US Armed Forces were "instruments of construction as well as war." These networks augmented the efforts of humanitarian agencies to support displaced children and orphans in Korea.[15]

The construction of orphanages and the collections of Christmas gifts for Korea's children became features of US-Korean relations that exposed a sobering aspect of the two nations' reciprocally dependent relationship. The war had crippled the South Korean economy, and that nation faced the real threat of communist aggression after the war. Consequently, the South Korean government needed the security that came from an alliance with the United States. The Korean War was largely a US-led intervention carried out under the auspices of the UN to ostensibly protect democracy south of Korea's 38th parallel. This history gave officials in the United States an incentive to act as unofficial custodians of South Korea's economic and political recovery. As such, the US government needed South Korea to succeed in order to justify the nation's tremendous financial and military investment in Korea, and to substantiate the premise that capitalism and democracy were superior to communism.[16]

As early as 1950, the UN had expressed concern over the implications of America's unilateral support of South Korea. The UN warned that certain types of American intervention would exacerbate tensions between nations in the West and communist leaders in China and the Soviet Union. Although on October 7, 1950, the UN acknowledged its responsibility for South Korea's reconstruction, the United States held the largest stake in the process. Officials in the United States agreed to assume 70 percent of the cost of Korean reconstruction. By 1954, the UN reported that the United States had contributed $84,302,614 of the $162,500,000 officials had pledged to aid Korea. In some ways, the future of this alliance depended on how these nations supported displaced children, and officials in the US government cautiously approached the creation of an adoption plan for Korean children.[17]

In 1953, permanent Korean Observer at the United Nations, Ambassador Ben C. Limb, stressed the importance of US-Korean adoptions as a means of reinforcing America's ties to South Korea. He suggested that transnational adoptions "would constitute a fine humanitarian gesture by the American people towards Korea" that would demonstrate the nation's commitment to Korea's reconstruction. He was convinced that US citizens were eager to open their homes to Korean children in spite of the legal and social difficulties they were certain to encounter. Limb explained that he had received approximately one hundred inquiries from Americans interested in adopting Korean orphans after they learned of the children's dire circumstances. In response to complaints that families were unable to obtain the legal documents they needed to bring Korean children to the United States, he urged the Department of State to support legislation to make these adoptions possible.[18]

Limb and other advocates of early US-Korean adoption recognized that immigration restrictions would make it difficult for American families to bring Korean children into the United States. Before 1953, families used the strategy mentioned in chapter 1 that involved prospective adoptive parents getting a private act of Congress to change the child's immigration status from "inadmissible alien" to "natural-born alien child." However, people complained because the process could take a long time and it involved a number of bureaucratic hurdles. The State Department's advisor on refugees and displaced persons, George L. Warren, felt confident that Congress would back immigration legislation to help families avoid such challenges. But he was skeptical that US adoption and child welfare agencies could easily develop strategies that complied with national and international adoption regulations. He was right on both counts. Later that month, Congress passed the Refugee Relief Act (RRA) of 1953, which made temporary provisions for orphans to enter the United States from any country that had exhausted its visa quota set by the McCarren Walter Act of 1952.[19]

Although Congress designed the RRA to facilitate the migrations of refugees from Europe, adopting families also benefited from section five of the act, which made four thousand visas available to orphans adopted by or to be adopted by an American family. The RRA specified that the adopted child had to be younger than ten and a true orphan or a social orphan. Officials considered a child to be a social orphan when the child had a living parent who could not care for him or her and therefore agreed to relinquish the child for adoption.[20] However, families using this provision still needed to finalize a legal adoption in the United States. And, much like the private acts that families obtained from Congress to bring Korean children to the United States prior to the passage of the RRA, the orphan provision did not automatically make the child a citizen of the United States.

The RRA did make it possible for families to use the controversial method known as proxy adoption. The proxy adoption method allowed couples to choose a proxy—a person to represent them legally in a foreign court—to complete the requirements of the child's birth country. This provision meant that parents were adopting children they had never seen, which was only one of the reasons child welfare professionals opposed the method. Proxy adoptions also allowed adopting families to avoid the evaluations child welfare professionals used to assess adoptive families in the States because the State Department, and not child welfare agencies, had jurisdiction over the program.[21] When the RRA expired in December 1956, Congress passed short-term renewals of orphan visa provisions that classified the orphans as refugees from 1957 to 1960 but assured that US-Korean adoptions could proceed, even if there were some interruptions in the process. The orphan provisions of the Immigration and Nationality Act of 1961 settled the immigration issue by eliminating the quota restrictions on foreign-born adopted children, which made this aspect of transnational adoption easier for families in the States.[22]

As Warren feared, coordinating the services of the many sectarian communities caring for Korean children with South Korean and US agencies was no easy task. Sectarian organizations in South Korea were among the first to address the daunting task of caring for Korean orphans and developing procedures to facilitate US-Korean adoptions. The Quakers, Seventh-Day Adventist (SDA), Methodist, and Presbyterian churches sponsored facilities to assist Korean children, and officials in the Korean government gave them considerable control over the disposition of the children in their care. The lack of an established legal or institutional framework for Korean transnational adoptions made it possible for nonprofessionals associated with these sectarian communities to take leading roles in the first efforts to help Americans adopt Korean children. These agencies sponsored many of the orphanages that housed Korea's orphaned and displaced children. Indeed, numerous adoption scholars have demonstrated that South Korean officials' reliance on the Western aid that was tied to these facilities, and their adoption of Western child welfare models, hindered that nation's development of in-country strategies to care for orphaned and displaced children.[23] However, the South Korean government did create state-sponsored social welfare institutions in 1952 and a foster care program to support in-country adoptions.[24] In 1954, South Korean officials established the Child Placement Service (CPS) to coordinate transnational adoptions for the mixed-race children of GIs and Korean women. By 1955, the South Korean government was attempting to draft laws that would regulate Korean transnational adoption, but these attempts failed until 1961.

Thus, sectarian communities played a significant role in the creation of networks of private agencies in South Korea that worked with "companion agencies" in the United States to place Korean children.[25] In 1953, skeletal Korean procedures for adoption conferred guardianship of any child in a public orphanage to the superintendent of that facility. But local authorities had to appoint a guardian for children in private institutions. In addition to obtaining a certificate of guardianship, agencies facilitating adoptions had to obtain several documents to initiate a transnational adoption. These documents included a statement of authority to consent, certification of guardian's consent by the US Consulate in Korea, the child's family registration certificate, and a certificate of orphanhood. Officials in Seoul and other cities and districts throughout South Korea regularly authorized the volunteers and missionaries working in sectarian orphanages that had these credentials.[26] This provision allowed guardians to help arrange adoptions and transfer custody of children to adoptive parents. As the number of children fathered by UN soldiers grew, representatives of the Korean Ministry of Social Affairs, the government agency responsible for crafting Korean adoption procedures, did not scrutinize too closely the methods these facilities employed as long as they worked to get GI children out of South Korea.[27] However, most of the people affiliated with sectarian organizations had no social work training or familiarity with US adoption standards. Not surprisingly, officials, staff, and volunteers associated with these sectarian communities encountered institutional barriers when they attempted to coordinate with agencies in the United States.

Child welfare officials' responses to the adoption work of the Adventists demonstrate how relations between professionals and nonprofessionals could become contentious as these groups attempted to devise strategies to facilitate US-Korean adoptions. Officials with the USCB and the CWLA expressed concern over the methods the Adventists used to place mixed-race Korean children early in 1954.[28] The SDA sponsored the Seoul Sanitarium and Hospital Orphanage, which would become the only hospital approved by the American Embassy and US Public Health Service to perform medical examinations for immigrating Korean adoptees. The hospital was one of the facilities that cared for mixed-race children, and Dr. George H. Rue, the facility's director, and his wife Grace were instrumental in arranging many transnational adoptions involving civilians and individuals affiliated with the military.

The Rues came to the attention of officials with the USCB and the CWLA because of newspaper coverage of the adoption of a mixed-race Korean baby girl by Irene Robson, the Director of Nurses at the Seoul Sanitarium and Hospital Orphanage. In January 1954, Richard Steinman, a representative of Welcome House, was among the officials who contacted the CWLA in response to the media's coverage of Robson's adoption. Steinman explained that the story "concerns me."[29] As chapter 5 will explain in more detail, Welcome House was an adoption agency in the United States that specialized in the transracial adoption of American-born mixed-race children of Asian descent. Steinman wondered how the Rues were arranging adoptions for the "fifty other beautiful children . . . mostly under two years—waiting at the hospital to be adopted."[30] Although Steinman seemed opposed to the methods the Rues employed, Welcome House and that agency's co-founder, novelist Pearl S. Buck, would soon become the subject of scrutiny by officials for similar reasons. By the mid-1950s, the USCB, CWLA, and other child welfare agencies would distance themselves from Buck because she endorsed proxy adoption and used methods to facilitate transnational placements of Korean children that resembled the work the Rues were doing in the early 1950s.

Robson's adoption, and Grace Rue's correspondence with Bessie C. Irvine of the California State Department of Social Welfare, also raised red flags for officials with International Social Service (ISS). Following Grace Rue's letter explaining her need for assistance to place children living in the SDA orphanage and other South Korean facilities, these officials began to question how the Rues screened and selected prospective adoptive parents. Although the Rues tried to match children based on the race of their birth fathers, professional social workers believed they were not equipped to sufficiently screen prospective adoptive parents. The Rues did attempt to conduct investigations of applicants that involved checking with the banks and employees of interested couples. But the agency's limited resources, staff, and child welfare training hampered these efforts.[31]

The Rues did not want to become an adoption agency, but the needs they observed compelled them to assist the civilians and soldiers who wanted to adopt Korean children. They also tried to help officials of other orphanages in facilitating such placements. In this capacity, the Rues saw patterns that caused them to worry about adoptions involving soldiers and Korean children. Much like the child welfare officials who were concerned that the Rues' tactics were questionable, Grace Rue worried that soldiers were taking custody of children using incorrect documents. She had learned that soldiers were obtaining statements from various Korean district offices that certified a child's status as an orphan but did not represent an official adoption decree. Soldiers then used these papers as proof of an adoption in order to gain guardianship over a child they hoped to transport to the United States. These forms were registrations, not legal adoptions, and Grace Rue feared that officials at the US Embassy in Seoul would accept them as verifications of adoptions.[32] She had good reasons to worry. Most soldiers were unaware of the many steps involved in a obtaining a visa under the RRA, which led to problems when they struggled to navigate the complicated regulations governing US-Korean adoption. But these complications did not dissuade soldiers or their families. Indeed, Ellen Visser of the Korea Civil Assistance Command (KCAC) noted that soldiers' families were responsible for the growth in US-Korean placements that began in the mid-1950s.[33]

Military officials were aware of the uptick in soldiers' efforts to adopt as well as the challenges soldiers faced when they misunderstood or disregarded important aspects of the nascent transnational adoption policies. Some officials did not support these attempts because they felt the men were too young to comprehend the seriousness of such a decision. Others worried that the development of familial bonds between soldiers and Korean children "crossed the Army's fine line between being a good soldier . . . to being an emotionally attached surrogate father to the children, a kind of sentiment and liability that the military feared would weaken its fighting force and complicate the relationship of the military to South Korea."[34] But soldiers' persistence informed a narrative of rescue that officials could not ignore. The *Pacific Stars and Stripes* included many stories describing the ways soldiers were "fighting the red tape wrapped around child-adoption laws."[35] Adoption stories had appeared in this paper as early as 1950, and by 1955, the paper was describing the efforts of military and non-military families who were trying to adopt mixed-race children as part of its coverage of Korea's evolving orphan crisis.[36]

To assist such families, the Eighth Army Public Information Officer began outlining the requirements of the RRA to clarify adoption procedures in 1955. He further lobbied for the creation of instructional movies and pamphlets to walk servicemen through each part of the transnational adoption process.[37] When he became commander of US Army Forces in Korea that same year, General Lyman Lemnitzer also began investigating what it would take to establish measures to help soldiers adopt. The growth in the number of mixed-race Korean children who were vulnerable because they were outcasts worried General Lemnitzer. To avoid what he feared the children would become if they did not have a secure family life, Lemnitzer encouraged policies to increase military families' adoptions of Korean GI children.[38]

Initially, General Lemnitzer coordinated with other military officials, representatives of the US Embassy, and ROK officials to make accommodations that would simplify immigration requirements for military families. One component of this effort involved streamlining the paperwork required of couples when a wife was in the States and her husband was serving in Korea. The RRA required couples to jointly complete paperwork, including a DSR-5 form that served as the assurance of a couple's plan to legally adopt and take care of the immigrating child. Representatives with an official public or private child welfare agency in the United States then had to complete and endorse these forms. Next, couples completing the forms in Korea had to take them to the appropriate visa or consular officer. If the parents were in the United States, they had to send the forms to the offices of the Refugee Relief Program. Soldiers were able to sidestep this requirement by getting wives in the United States to provide written evidence of their consent to adopt.

Wives who gave this assurance did not have to travel to South Korea to sign any other forms.[39]

The military also made transportation on military aircraft and ships available to some adopting families. This provision was very useful for soldiers stationed in Japan with their wives when they adopted a Korean child. The military often transported these couples to Korea to complete adoption proceedings and then brought the family back to Japan. It is possible that African American men like Major Robert L. Sweeney benefited from this kind of assistance when he adopted his four-year-old Korean black daughter, Elizabeth Ann. The *Pacific Stars and Stripes* covered this adoption, noting that Sweeney and his wife Hazel had adopted their six-year-old German black son Robert Jr. in 1952. Their first transnational adoption likely helped them navigate the bureaucracy associated with US-Korean adoption. But they also benefited from the army's effort to help adopting families. By 1956, this strategy was generating significant interest among other couples like the Sweeneys who were stationed in Japan.[40]

In some ways, these plans ran counter to the military's practice, if not its policies, regarding soldiers' paternity responsibilities. Before the Korean War, officials had resisted forcing servicemen to take care of their illegitimate children, much less children not biologically related to them. During the war the army endeavored to create policies addressing soldiers' legal and moral obligations to financially support their legal dependents. In April 1950, the Secretary of the Army informed commanders of the Far East and European Commands that they needed to ensure the servicemen were aware of the ways their poor performance in this area—paying support—violated the army's code of conduct and reflected badly on the military as a whole. The army recognized that men were often able to escape the legal judgments of civil courts in the United States because they were serving and living abroad. This behavior went against official military policies that directed soldiers to "make reasonable provision" to support children so that they did not become wards of the state or dependent on private or government assistance.[41]

The births of soldiers' children in Japan, Korea, and countries throughout Europe where the United States had troops complicated the implementation of the army's policies concerning soldiers' responsibilities for their dependents. The military had little authority to command soldiers to support a child who was not a legal dependent, which was the case for children of unmarried mothers. Too often, when a woman sought the assistance of international agencies to obtain support for a child fathered by a soldier, the alleged biological father could simply deny paternity and avoid any penalty. This pattern caused members of the UN Economic and Social Council to coordinate the international enforcement of child support for women who could prove paternity. Council members believed this type of program was necessary for the children because their mothers often struggled to support them, and this circumstance was evident in Korea. However, by the fall of 1956, military officials were still working to determine what were soldiers' legal obligations in cases where they were responsible for a "proven . . . extramarital pregnancy in Korea." The uncertain status of Korea's mixed-race children led some in the military to believe that there was an urgent need to expedite adoptions for this population. Indeed, an article titled "A Better Life" mentioned that even the wife of General Lemnitzer was "anxious to form a committee of ladies in both Japan and Korea to aid Korean orphans," as it described some of the steps officials at the American Embassy in Seoul were taking to speed up the adoption application process.[42]

The accommodations the military negotiated for soldiers' families did not lessen the challenges they faced when social workers attempted to conduct home studies, which prompted military and child welfare officials to work for an expansion in programs that provided adoption services to soldiers in Korea. General Lemnitzer approached representatives of ISS to obtain the agency's assistance with the adoptions of GI's children in Korea. General Lemnitzer was familiar with the organization's track record, which demonstrated that its officials and employees were interested in facilitating transnational adoptions by coordinating contacts between prospective adoptive families and US child welfare and adoption agencies. When transnational adoptions increased following World War II, officials with ISS had preferred to coordinate solutions for children in the countries of their births. But the situation in Korea caused them to concede that transnational adoptions were necessary for Korean GI babies.[43]

From the organization's beginnings, ISS branches routinely assisted individuals and families who had to deal with problems that arose when they migrated from one nation to another. Officials with ISS were aware of the ways the movement of people across national borders could create difficulties for families and communities in the countries of origin and destination. With branches in the United States, Japan, England, and other countries throughout Europe, ISS had already been instrumental in coordinating the foster program that brought children from England to the States during World War II, as well as adoptions involving orphans of the Greek Civil War, and the children of soldiers who fought in Germany and Japan during World War II.[44] From its inception, ISS managed cases that ranged from missing persons investigations to straightforward requests for spousal support. However, by 1953, 60 percent of the agency's caseload involved children's issues. That same year, ISS assisted with 331 transnational adoptions. In 1954, ISS officials proposed an elaborate procedural flowchart that outlined the responsibilities of US child welfare agencies, ISS America Branch, and ISS foreign branches at each step in a transnational adoption. By the end of 1957, the number of transnational adoption cases the agency handled had increased to 3,092.[45]

Even before the Korean orphan crisis expanded, ISS was considering many strategies to raise money to support transnational adoptions that fell under the jurisdiction of the organization's Intercountry Adoption Committee. One popular effort involving celebrity fund-raising developed after the Intercountry Adoption Committee partnered with the World Adoption International Fund (WAIF) to head up projects on behalf of international orphans. ISS officials identified WAIF as a resource that "transforms two tragic situations into one healthy and happy situation" by placing homeless children from around the world with infertile couples in the United States.[46] The committee appointed actress Jane Russell Waterfield to act as president. Waterfield's interest in such matters was clear from her involvement with the IAA, and that organization began coordinating with ISS in the fall of 1953. Waterfield's international adoption activism and Hollywood connections were instrumental in generating support for many projects sponsored by WAIF-ISS.[47]

Waterfield organized balls and benefits that featured celebrities like Bob Hope and Jerry Lewis, and in 1954 her Hollywood group, International Adoption Association, pledged a first and then a second $25,000 gift to WAIF-ISS. ISS used this money to establish the Korea branch, which opened its doors on May 13, 1957. ISS located the Korea branch office in the former headquarters of the American-Korean Foundation (AKF), and AKF donated a vehicle to the new branch. ISS officials could not identify any Korean social workers they trusted to run the Korea branch, so they tapped Marcia J. Speers from the ISS Australia branch to oversee the Korean programs. To assist Spears, agency officials located one Korean caseworker who had completed her master's degree in social work in the United States. Together they made the transnational adoption of mixed-race children the first priority of ISS-Korea.[48]

When ISS assistant director Susan T. Pettiss noted that the children fathered by GIs disproportionately occupied "sub-standard, under-staffed orphanages," she identified one reason child welfare communities pursued strategies to expedite their adoptions.[49] Pettiss and other observers of the child welfare situation in Korea came to believe that the racial heritage of GI babies made it unlikely that Korean families would adopt them even if they could. All GI babies occupied a precarious status because adoption was rare among Koreans, and those who did adopt traditionally did so when a couple needed a male heir. Because they did not see adoption as a child welfare issue in the same way that people in the States viewed the practice, Pettiss believed mixed-race children would remain outside of Korean family systems. She also worried because many GI babies died and would continue to die in South Korean communities and the nation's child welfare institutions. She was particularly concerned for Korean black children because their complexions made them targets. In a correspondence with officials of a South Carolina public welfare agency, Pettiss explained that "the small group of Korean-Negro children are [sic] the most needy [because] the dark skin is completely unknown in this country and carries with it a tremendous stigma."[50] These circumstances convinced officials with ISS and other agencies involved in Korean child welfare that mixed-race children's survival depended on their removal from Korea.[51]

GI babies also experienced extreme privations because many South Korean civilians and officials of the ROK associated them with their foreign fathers and therefore believed the United States should take responsibility for the soldiers' children. In some cases, these beliefs left mixed-race children open to abuse from full-Korean children and adults alike. Discrimination against mixed-race children was so strong that the few Korean civilians who took the children into their homes had to endure the scrutiny and, in some cases, rejection by their neighbors. In 1955, Ellen Visser of the Korean Civil Assistance Command reported that Korean officials supported plans that would allow mixed-race Korean children to leave the country. She also claimed that President Rhee's office was pressuring her organization to explain why the children were not leaving in larger numbers.[52] By 1956, representatives of ISS were agonizing over rumors that President Rhee "did not care what happened so long as the children were got out of the country—and quickly."[53]

Korean officials' emphasis on the quick removal of mixed-race Korean children corresponded with the goals of many soldiers and a number of nonprofessionals who founded programs to facilitate Korean transnational adoptions. The nonprofessional most associated with the expansion of Korean transnational adoption is the Oregon farmer turned Korean adoption advocate, Harry Holt. One scholar's assessment that the story of the events that led Holt to become involved in Korean transnational adoption has "acquired a mythic flavor reminiscent of [the Biblical story of] Paul's experience on the road to Damascus" is a fitting characterization.[54] Holt and his wife Bertha learned of the circumstances of Korea's orphans at a meeting of the evangelical Christian organization World Vision, in 1954. The couple's adoption journey began as they watched documentaries about the Korean orphan crisis and listened to World Vision's founder, Bob Pierce, describe ways people in the audience could help a Korean child. Convinced that he had a divinely inspired mission to help these children, Holt took the first of what would be many trips to retrieve Korean children to bring back to awaiting adoptive parents in the United States in October 1955. Holt brought twelve Korean children back on that trip. Eight were his own adopted children. He delivered the other children to families that had expressed a desire to participate in his religiously motivated mission to rescue Korean children.[55]

In 1956, Holt started his own adoption agency, Holt Adoption Program (HAP), that modeled a response to the Korean GI baby crisis that inspired many in the United States to see the adoption of Korean children as morally and politically imperative.[56] According to Oh, Holt represents an ideology of "Christian Americanism" that equated Americans' adoptions of Korean children with religious, patriotic, and antiracist motives.[57] Scholars have speculated that Korean transnational adoption might not have expanded in the manner that it did if Harry Holt, whom some people call the "father of Korean adoption," had not employed very visible and radical methods to "rescue" Korean children. Specifically, Holt's use of proxy adoption appealed to many adoptive families, including African American couples, because it allowed them to adopt a child without traveling to Korea and, if they worked with a private agency like HAP, without extensive investigation from a child welfare professional.[58] Holt's methods worried child welfare officials with ISS, but his plans, and the proxy adoption method, were in line with the objectives of officials with the Korean government.

The ROK expressed concerns that the presence of mixed-race children in South Korea compromised the nation's image by making it look weak to its North Korean adversaries. ISS officials believed the ROK's push to have mixed-race children removed from the country was one manifestation of its response to North Korean propaganda that publicized the circumstances of mixed-race children to shame South Koreans. In one case, officials worried because of the rumor that an agent from the North had arranged to have a mixed-race child kidnapped and then put on display to prove that America was colonizing South Korea.[59] Stories like this one reinforced ROK officials' plan to aggressively promote transnational adoptions of GI children. The ROK's emphasis on getting mixed-race children out of Korea also motivated Oregon Senator Richard Neuberger. In 1956, he asked Under Secretary of State Herbert C. Hoover, son of former president Herbert Hoover, for federal money to aid mixed-race children in Korea. Senator Neuberger was a leading advocate of congressional efforts to support Korean transnational adoption. He had helped pass the legislation that allowed Harry Holt to bring twelve Korean children to the United States in 1955, since the orphans provisions of the RRA stipulated that a family was only allowed to bring two children to the States for adoption.[60] In 1956, Senator Neuberger was still working to change immigration laws to make US-Korean adoptions more feasible, and he wanted the Department of State to allocate funds to feed and maintain the children while they remained in Korea awaiting adoption. Senator Neuberger encouraged Under Secretary Hoover to consider his request because the "half-castes," as he called them, were "definitely our responsibility, legally and certainly morally."[61]

Mixed-race children constituted a relatively small part of the total number of displaced or orphaned children in Korea, but they occupied a significant place in the nation's nascent transnational adoption plans. In theory, the earliest adoption programs made provisions for any eligible Korean orphan. In practice, the removal of mixed-race children was the impetus for the first wave of large-scale US-Korean adoptions. While there is no way to know the exact number of mixed-race children born in Korea in the first decades after the Korean War, estimates put that figure at a little over 12,000 for the period between 1950 and 1965.[62] This number pales in comparison to the hundreds of thousands of displaced children that lived in institutions throughout South Korea during those same years.[63] Between 1953 and 1961, when the orphan provisions of a number of US refugee acts made it possible for families in the United States to adopt a Korean child using a proxy, Korea's Ministry of Health and Welfare recorded 4,197 out-of-country adoptions.[64] American families adopted the majority of these children, and most of these adoptions involved mixed-race children.[65] However, these figures obscure how considerable were the numbers of people who tried to adopt the children of GIs during the same span of years. Although charitable organizations, the US government and military, and the ROK attempted to define the nature of American citizens' responsibility for mixed-race Korean children, the individuals who wanted to rescue GI babies had already decided that they belonged with families in the United States. But these families often had very different reasons for believing that Americans could provide the most secure future possible for mixed-race Korean children. For African American soldiers, an awareness of the ways racial inequality shaped their lives and the lives of Korean black children became a distinct feature of their involvement in US-Korean adoption schemes.[66]

African American Military Families and US-Korean Adoption

As mentioned in chapter 1, many South Koreans developed a particularly negative response to Korean black children based on their understanding of US racial hierarchies that emphasized white supremacy and black inferiority. South Koreans who engaged in commerce near the military camps, and later in the camp towns around military bases, learned and refashioned the racism of the US military. As scholar Katharine H. S. Moon describes, owners of private clubs and dance halls in the camp town entertainment districts kept these social spaces segregated until the 1970s. The women who associated with African American soldiers occupied the lowest ranks in the clubs and bars where servicemen spent their off-duty hours, and these circumstances caused many Koreans to view Korean black children with particular disdain.[67] In a report of her 1956 trip to Korea, ISS's senior case consultant Margaret A. Valk described learning that many mothers of mixed-race children lived in the woods around the military camps with their children. She also noted that the missionaries she spoke to worried about the prevalence of suicide among the mothers of the mixed-race children. Yet untold numbers of Korean mothers wanted to keep their mixed-race children, and by the 1960s, ISS officials were commenting on the remarkable efforts these women made to do so.[68]

ISS director Paul R. Cherney's notes from his field visit in July 1962 include descriptions of the ways Korean mothers of mixed-race children endeavored to maintain their families. Mothers who lived in what Cherney called a typical "prostitute pavillon [sic]" shared childcare responsibilities and the "problems and plans of one are shared and discussed with the group." In these pavilions, women and their children lived in rooms surrounding a courtyard that functioned as a multipurpose living space. The families used a common stove and washed their clothes in the courtyard where children played and received affection and correction from all of the mothers. The courtyards were more than living areas though. They also functioned as places where mothers could hide their children and insulate them from racially motivated assaults. Cherney described the children living in one such pavilion as "relaxed and contented, emotionally secure." The limited security of these spaces only protected young children, and mothers living in these circumstances often considered transnational adoption once they could no longer prevent their children from having interactions with Koreans outside of the pavilions.[69]

Some mothers who negotiated other living arrangements for a mixed-race child also agonized over the decision to consent to a transnational adoption. ISS records describe caseworkers' interactions with mothers who sent their children to orphanages hoping that they would marry and then be able to reunite their families. When these plans fell through, some mothers turned to adoption. One mother who had arranged for another woman to take care of her two-year-old mixed-race child faced this decision when she could not afford to keep making the payments the caregiver required. This woman was a part of "a tightly governmental prostitute group," and her earnings went to a madam who charged the workers high fees that kept the women in debt. Her inability to pay for her child's board meant that she had to consider other options, including adoption. Another mother sent her son to live at what Cherney referred to as "the mixed blood school at Ascom" only after she met with and refused ISS case workers three times. In spite of her meager resources, this mother remained unwilling to sign the release for adoption until she believed she had no other option. Cherney seemed convinced that this mother knew that adoption by a family in the United States would be better for the child, but she could not let him go. Instead, she wept and agreed to continue meeting to discuss her options. On one occasion, she explained that the only reason she considered transnational adoption was because the income she received from prostitution was not enough to support herself and her son.[70]

By the mid-1960s, Cherney was still reporting that a majority of mixed-race Korean children continued to live with their mothers around the camp towns. As in other field visit notes, Cherney displayed sympathy for these mothers because he knew that most had set up housekeeping with the fathers of their children, believing they would one day marry. He also repeated an earlier observation that the connections between many of the women and their children were strong.[71] Although the affection he observed caused him to question whether transnational adoption was in the best interest of children living with loving mothers, case workers affiliated with ISS continued to travel into the areas around military bases to try to convince mothers to relinquish their mixed-race children. This process could involve lengthy conversations, sometimes over a period of days or weeks, precisely because of the relationships Cherney described. However, as scholar Hosu Kim explains, other family members often made this choice in spite of a birth mother's desires because of the shame they felt regarding the child's mixed-race status.[72] ISS officials were aware of the punishing nature of the exclusions these mothers faced that constrained all of their choices and made transnational adoption seem necessary. It is revealing that even after they agreed to relinquish a child for adoption, some Korean birth mothers requested pictures of their children to prove that they were in good homes. This practice caused one ISS official to comment that one such group of mothers "have been quite insistent, needing the reassurance that such a picture would give them."[73]

Too often, Korean mothers' attempts to protect and keep their mixed-race children proved insufficient to stave off the privations that made them vulnerable. In the first few years of the Korean orphan crisis, officials with ISS were aware that the suffering these mothers and their children endured led some to commit heinous acts of desperation. In her report on her visit with Harry Holt, Susan Pettiss recounted one disturbing scene that Holt said motivated him to establish an adoption agency to facilitate US-Korean adoptions. He explained that he saw "the bodies of the little Negro [Korean] children washed up on the shore of the river where their mothers had thrown them away."[74] Observations like this one caused many international aid workers to conclude that Korean black children were in grave danger. In spite of many Korean mothers' efforts to protect and care for their mixed-race children, ISS officials continued to comment on the poor treatment and status of Korean black children throughout the 1950s and 1960s.

African American soldiers were also aware of the conditions that shaped Korean black children's lives, and some sought the assistance of ISS and child welfare agencies in the United States to learn more about US-Korean adoption. Officials with ISS were usually eager to help black soldiers get in touch with the appropriate agencies in their home states to begin the application process and schedule a home study. But a family's ability to navigate the requirements of agencies stateside varied widely. As discussed in chapter 2, many US child welfare and adoption agencies had routinely discriminated against African American clients, often choosing not to provide adoption assistance to black women wishing to relinquish a child or to black families interested in adoption. Consequently, some African Americans completed formal adoptions, but many participated in informal care networks that originated in their private or professional relationships and religious and service associations. Through informal arrangements, displaced and parentless children became the wards of grandparents, aunts, and uncles, whether or not they were biologically related. Many of these families took on the care of displaced children as a function of their understandings of extended kinship networks and obligations.[75]

Some African American soldiers activated similar networks when they attempted to adopt a Korean black child. In a number of cases, soldiers sent word back to the States to encourage family and friends to adopt members of this vulnerable population, and they alerted ISS to the presence of prospective adoptive parents in their communities. For example, when one African American sergeant realized that he could not adopt a particular Korean black child, he asked officials with ISS in the United States to contact friends of his who might be eligible. However, he did not stop there. The sergeant and his wife mentioned their concerns to people in their church and inspired another couple to eventually adopt the child.[76] Another African American master sergeant asked his niece and her husband to adopt the boy he was supporting in Korea. The sergeant knew he could not adopt the child because he was unmarried, but his inability to adopt did not stop him from paying the $24 monthly fee to house the child in an orphanage in Seoul while his relatives began the adoption process. He supported the child until ISS officials could coordinate his transportation to the United States and subsequent adoption.[77] After one veteran completed his tour in Korea and returned home, his interest in adopting a Korean black girl produced two adoptions. He and his wife adopted a child, and a short time later, his sister-in-law and her husband did the same.[78]

ISS and a number of child welfare agencies in the United States responded favorably to African American soldiers who were married and had commendable service records. But the standards agencies followed when evaluating prospective adoptive parents also disqualified some soldiers, even if they were the biological fathers of the child they wanted to adopt. The *Pacific Stars and Stripes* published numerous articles about young soldiers who attempted to adopt their Korean child but could not because they were unmarried.[79] In several cases, these men convinced their parents to pursue the adoption. The records of ISS include many such requests, and some resulted in a completed adoption.[80] Yet this was not the case for many African American soldiers. One African American serviceman asked his mother to adopt his two-year-old Korean black daughter. Although he planned to support the child financially, he felt his mother would be a better parent. ISS did not endorse this adoption because the prospective adoptive mother—the child's grandmother—was unmarried.[81] Although adoption laws and standards varied from state to state and agency to agency, by the 1950s, social workers opposed the practice of placing children with single parents even though single women had functioned as celebrated adoptive mothers in the early twentieth century.[82]

Social workers made a similar determination in the case of another African American soldier who wanted to adopt his Korean black son in 1957. The case notes on his application describe that the soldier met the Korean mother of his child during the war. When the child's Korean mother married a Korean man who did not want a mixed-race child, the soldier applied to adopt the boy. Although the boy's Korean mother agreed to relinquish him to his birth father and took him to an orphanage to prepare for the adoption, she later took the boy back. The ISS worker assigned to the case noted that the mother cared deeply for her son and she did not want to let him go to the United States. When the mother in this case finally relinquished her son for adoption, ISS workers rejected the soldier's application to adopt his son. The soldier's mother, who had sent clothes and money to her grandson since 1953, then submitted an application to adopt. The grandmother had a successful history as a single mother of three children who had maintained her employment with a phone company and only had one debt for furniture. ISS officials did not support her application and neither did the social workers assigned to the case in the soldier's home state. They questioned whether the father and grandmother would be suitable guardians for the child. Their main complaint was that both parties were unmarried. Instead of placing this child with his birth father and grandmother, they recommend a non-relative adoption.[83]

Unlike ISS and agencies in the United States, the South Korean government was willing to allow single applicants to adopt. In 1954, Carl W. Strom of the American Embassy in Seoul explained to officials at the State Department that Korean law did not require adoptive parents to be married. However, Korean laws and customs placed restrictions on adoption and guardianship to secure patrilineal lines and male authority. Korean customary laws traditionally prohibited the adoption of a child who would be the head of household or the oldest son of a head of household. But these same statutes stipulated that prospective adoptive fathers should be deemed fit by adoption agencies in their own country. Similarly, the main requirements for guardianship made no mention of marital status but rather prioritized other aspects of parental fitness. Article 908 of the Korean Civil Code Relative to Guardianship placed restrictions on minors, incompetent individuals, individuals who were bankrupt, or any person deemed unfit by the South Korean Supreme Court.[84]

Whether married or single, the costs associated with US-Korean adoptions were prohibitive for many African Americans. This caused some officials with ISS and US child welfare organizations to identify African American soldiers and their families as ideal adopting families for Korean black children. They believed the expenses and logistics of transnational adoptions would likely deter many African Americans in the States from applying to adopt a Korean child. Even though soldiers did not earn a lot, they did receive a consistent salary, and they had other benefits that made it possible for some to manage the expenses and bureaucratic demands of a US-Korean adoption. A typical adoption application involved payments at several points in the process and included many of the following steps. First, a soldier had to obtain the assistance of a child welfare agency in the state where he lived or planned to return to once his tour ended. Because soldiers were often transient, many gave their parents' address as their permanent address. Public adoption agencies charged a fee that could be $100 or more. Once the family made this payment, the child welfare agency submitted an I-600, or Immigration and Naturalization Service Petition, to the district director of the Immigration and Naturalization Service (INS). Families were also required to submit either the DSR-5 or DSR-6 assurance of care form that obligated them to guarantee that the child would not need private or public assistance. After a family completed these preliminary steps, a social worker conducted a home study, during which she assessed the family's living situation and ability to provide for a child's all-around security. Some agencies also required proof that the husband had life insurance, some savings, and little or no debt. Ideally, prospective adoptive mothers did not work for wages outside of the home, and the family owned a home that included a separate bedroom for the child. Once the social worker signed off on the home study and INS approved the I-600, the adopting family had to provide several hundred dollars to cover a child's transportation from South Korea.[85]

In many ways, the benefits African American soldiers received because they were affiliated with the military offset some of the costs of transnational adoption, and social workers were well aware of these advantages. A career in the military could make it possible for African American couples to achieve a domestic ideal that many social workers looked for in adopting families. Child welfare communities emphasized the benefits of the male breadwinner and female caregiver family for adopted children, and the chances of a soldier's family being approved for transnational adoption improved when it appeared to conform to this model. The following examples from case notes of three adopting families depict the kind of favorable responses social workers had toward the African American career servicemen they considered able to provide a good home for a Korean black child.

The social worker assigned to review the application of one serviceman of mixed African American and Mexican heritage found him to be "a superior person in every way." This man and his wife enjoyed a reasonably comfortable life because of his service in the military. He earned $425 a month, which was more than enough to cover the $90 rent they paid for base housing. He also had a $20,000 life insurance policy that would provide for his family in the event of his death. This soldier's thoughtful approach to adoption impressed the social worker investigating his home.[86]

A master sergeant in the army earned considerably more than the average enlisted man, and the social worker reviewing his case was excited about the family's prospects. His income of $508 a month made it possible for him to only owe $1,000 on the mortgage for his home worth $18,500. He also had two insurance policies totaling $8,000. The social worker noted that he had a BA and MA in education. She also mentioned that this master sergeant's wife was an attractive and kind woman who had completed college and attended business school. The fact that the family did not need the wife's income also impressed the social worker and this couple completed the adoption of their five-year-old Korean black daughter in 1959.[87]

A career in the military guaranteed a salary that social workers saw as evidence of a man's ability to care for his family whether the salary was substantial or modest. The case of one career navy man who applied to adopt a Korean black child in 1960 demonstrates this tendency. The social worker reviewing his family was impressed that the couple had lived in Japan and was familiar with Asian culture. She approved the family's adoption even though this sailor only earned $315 a month. At the time of the adoption, the sailor's wife worked in a factory, but the husband's belief that he could support the family without her income of $216 a month satisfied the social worker evaluating this case.[88]

Many of the first successful adopting families were military couples with stay-at-home wives. These couples met social workers' expectations, in part, because they aligned themselves with the military and the home, spaces that neatly represented the divide between postwar definitions of masculine and feminine. The Seavers were one such family. In 1955, they petitioned to adopt a child Mr. Seaver had grown fond of during his tour in South Korea. The social worker assigned to conduct the home study for this couple reported that the stay-at-home wife was extremely competent and qualified to parent the child in question. She also noted that the wife, who was a graduate of one of the premiere institutions of higher education for African Americans, had worked as a high school home economics teacher until she quit to take care of her family. The social worker found Mrs. Seaver to be an "intelligent woman, cultured, well educated, with sensitivity to the needs of children," and went on to compliment her housekeeping.[89]

Mrs. Seaver was not shy about her skills and she bragged about her ability to sew, cook, and budget, which was important considering how little her husband earned. She had to make her husband's salary of $350.00 a month stretch to cover all of the household expenses, which included two mortgages and life insurance policies. In the case notes describing this family, one social worker was glad to report that the wife had no inclination to seek paid work outside of the home. The agency approved this couple's adoption, and the social worker glowingly reported that, on subsequent visits, the family was adjusting exceptionally well. Although the Seavers' economic status was meager, the social worker was not concerned about the possibility that economic problems would negatively affect the placement because of Mr. Seaver's military career and Mrs. Seaver's domestic prowess.[90]

ISS records also indicate that African American soldiers and their wives stationed in Japan became highly sought-after candidates for Korean adoption because of the economic and domestic security this assignment afforded families. According to historian Michael C. Green, there were 10,000 US families in Japan by 1948, and he quotes the records of the Supreme Command for Allied Powers that described soldiers' communities as having Western style "shopping centers, recreation halls, barber shops and playgrounds."[91] By the 1950s, US military families had access to "their own bakeries, dry cleaners, bus systems, newspapers, gas stations and radio networks."[92] The observations of Ralph Matthews, the war correspondent for the newspaper the *Afro-American* mentioned in chapter 1, tell us a little more about why social workers became interested in recruiting adoptive families from the pool of African Americans living in Japan. In September 1951, he reported on the status of soldiers' families in Japan who explained that they had opportunities they could not access in the States, in part because of the absence of overt discrimination targeting African Americans in Japan. A number of respondents were happy about the modern base housing, and the fact that they could purchase food and clothing at affordable prices at the PX.[93]

Based on interviews he conducted with the wives and daughters of African American men serving in Japan, Matthews identified other reasons that these families were pleased with their lives in that country. To explain how different life was for some families, Matthews described the circumstances of African American women who had worked as maids in the United States. However, in Japan, they were able to employ Japanese women to work as their maids. Matthews noted that the inequalities that made such arrangements possible in Japan led some Americans to reorder aspects of the gender/race hierarchies that organized social relations in ways that oppressed Japanese men and women. While he condemned the rude behavior that some Americans—white and black—exhibited toward Japanese people because of the advantages they enjoyed as members of an occupying army, he could not deny the many social and economic benefits African Americans gained by living in Japan. In a second article about African American women's experiences in Japan, Matthews interviewed numerous women who worked for, served in, or had some other affiliation with the occupation forces in Japan. They all said they were happy with the opportunities they had. One teenage daughter of an African American soldier explained that she was learning Japanese, and that she enjoyed attending school in Japan because it was better than the segregated school she had attended in Texas. These were the issues military officials and ISS officials had in mind when they encouraged the development of programs to expedite US-Korean adoptions involving African American soldiers' families in Japan. These families had access to the trappings of postwar domesticity that lined up nicely with the characteristics child welfare officials wanted adoptive families to possess.[94]

Throughout the 1950s and early 1960s, African American soldiers and their wives continued to be an important pool of adoptive families for Korean black children. However, the idea that military couples could provide the most secure future possible for children needing adoption was relatively new. As mentioned above, social workers generally identified military service with a level of instability that was not desirable for adopted children. Assessments like these caused many white wives of servicemen to complain that adoption agencies discriminated against them in both US and transnational adoption schemes. One soldier's wife wrote to President Truman in 1951 asking for his help to adopt a child because social workers always put them on a waiting list upon learning that her husband was in the service. When white soldiers' wives asked for assistance from child welfare or adoption agencies, the responses they received frequently explained that there were always more suitable white families available to adopt children than there were children for them to adopt. This pattern—more white families available to adopt than white children needing adoption—was apparent even in cases of US-Korean adoptions involving children fathered by white servicemen. But social workers never complained about an overabundance of African American adoptive families. This circumstance helps explain why they disregarded the potential for family relocations—an issue that suggested instability for social workers—to negatively affect a Korean black child adopted by soldiers' families in Japan.[95]

Social workers were also willing to reevaluate their positions on African American military families because experience had shown that placements with servicemen already living in Japan were easier to coordinate than placements in the United States. As late as 1964, ISS was sponsoring a program to place Korean black children with African American families stationed in Japan. Officials with ISS were excited to report that they could count on African American families in Japan to adopt the twenty-five Korean black children who were ready to leave Korea, and representatives of ISS-Japan applied to the America Branch for a $1,000 grant to process these and other cases. ISS also planned to initiate a campaign to increase the number of adoptive families by encouraging African American army and air force couples who had already adopted to encourage their friends to do the same. ISS officials believed placements with African American military families represented a viable and desirable option for Korean black children. However, efforts to increase adoptions of Korean black children by African Americans not affiliated with the military drew professionals and nonprofessionals into contentious debates over the role nonprofessionals should play in efforts to get vulnerable Korean black children to families in the United States.[96]

African American Civilians and US-Korean Adoption

Often African American families that were not affiliated with the military learned of Korea's GI baby crisis through articles in black newspapers and magazines that made the process of transnational adoption seem relatively easy. But families frequently encountered obstacles when they attempted to adopt a Korean black child. As was the case in the context of US domestic adoptions described in chapter 2, child welfare communities evaluated African Americans' ability to parent using standards they developed based on casework with white clients. These standards often did not account for the ways that racial discrimination and segregation produced socioeconomic and cultural differences that made many African American adoptive couples appear less qualified than their white counterparts. However, officials with a number of public child welfare agencies, the US Children's Bureau, and ISS did consider a number of strategies to help African American couples living in the States adopt Korean black children. The focus of many proposals involved economic accommodations. Some agencies experimented with plans that waived fees or provided resources to help families pay for transportation and any costs associated with maintaining an adopted child in an institution in South Korea while they waited for approval to bring their child to America. A few agencies also attempted to address the institutional and cultural obstacles that limited African Americans' participation in US-Korean adoption.[97]

Recognizing the importance of increasing the public's awareness of Korean black children, officials with these agencies promoted the use of radio and other types of media to publicize the need for African American adoptive parents. The most progressive plans to increase African Americans' adoptions involved the creation of advisory committees with members from both African American and white civic organizations. In addition to the development of interracial committees, officials hoped that adoption agencies would coordinate with social welfare organizations that worked more consistently with African American populations. One official with ISS's Intercountry Adoption Committee stressed the need for adoption agencies to reduce the use of social work jargon in media and educational programming because it intimidated some clients. All of these recommendations grew out of problems social workers had observed in agencies' recruitment efforts to increase adoptive homes for children in the United States, and they were reminiscent of the proposals NUL officials made to increase African Americans' domestic adoptions. While these programs met with varying degrees of success, many public child welfare agencies still had a hard time competing with private agencies like Harry Holt's HAP because private agencies and nonprofessionals could establish their own standards. Some of these agencies were even willing to eliminate the most intrusive aspects of the application process, including home studies, to recruit African American couples.[98]

Professional social workers with many public agencies were wary of schemes like one promoted by a nonprofessional named Glenn Skogman who promised to circumvent certain adoption standards to accommodate African American couples' US-Korean adoptions. In February 1955, George K. Wyman, director of the California Department of Social Welfare, contacted Dr. Martha Eliot, the head of the Children's Bureau, to alert her to Skogman's activities because he believed Skogman was promoting a potentially dangerous plan to recruit African American families. Wyman explained that Skogman and a couple, the Reverend Hwang and his wife, had given a presentation to members of a black Baptist church to get attendees to contribute to their work and to consider adopting a child in their orphanage. The Hwangs had founded the Isabella Orphanage in Pusan, and Wyman was alarmed that Skogman and the Hwangs endorsed the use of proxy adoption. Many families took advantage of this legal provision because it usually saved them time and money. According to Wyman, Skogman had explained these aspects of proxy adoption to the crowd, and he outlined the expenses adopting parents could expect to incur if they used a proxy to complete the adoption in South Korea. Skogman then encouraged the crowd to act quickly and mentioned that he had recently given a presentation to a group of Latter-Day Saints and thirty-two couples had indicated their interest in adopting a Korean child. It is possible that Wyman's intervention worked because Skogman's plans to return to Korea to locate children to bring back to the United States stalled in April 1955. The US State Department revoked his passport after representatives of child welfare agencies complained that his methods were questionable and the adoptions he arranged likely were not legal.[99]

Although child welfare officials were disturbed by these activities, the Hwangs' desire to place mixed-race Korean children with families in the United States was genuine, and they wanted to retain some control over the selection of adoptive families. In their presentation, the Hwangs explained that they believed the children should be with Christian families.[100] In June 1955, Ellen Visser of KCAC reported to ISS assistant director Susan Pettiss that the Hwangs were getting children out of Korea, but she did not know how. Visser had learned that the Hwangs spent a lot of time in Los Angeles raising money for their orphanage, but she wondered if they were actually using the money to support the children. Visser was sure the Hwangs did not follow the standards of professional social work when they investigated families or placed children. US child welfare officials were also suspicious of the couple because the Hwangs supported proxy adoptions. While Visser and other officials with ISS and USCB worried that proxy adoptions put children at risk, they also believed proxy adoptions were dangerous for adoptive parents. Visser and officials with ISS were certain that bypassing US adoption standards allowed the Hwangs to fleece the families they selected to adopt Korean black children.[101]

While most of the private programs that facilitated proxy adoptions were run by people like Holt, Skogman, and the Hwangs, I found one example of an independent adoption program run by an African American woman I call Alice Warren that also promoted the proxy method to help African Americans adopt Korean black children. Warren's activities demonstrate both the reasons that proxy adoption appealed to African Americans, and why child welfare professionals worried when African Americans worked with nonprofessionals to complete a transnational adoption. Warren's efforts to bring Korean black children to the United States came to the attention of officials with the Children's Bureau and ISS in 1957. Officials with the State Department of Social Welfare of Kansas had begun investigating Mrs. Warren in January of that year when they learned that she was attempting to place Korean black children with families in her community. These officials believed that Warren's efforts to help children were actually putting the children in danger. They had observed Warren's questionable behavior years before when the State Department of Social Welfare had licensed her to provide transitional care or foster care for children in Kansas. At the time of the new investigation relative to the Korean black children, Warren was not boarding any children in Kansas City because of an incident involving a child she tried to keep after child welfare officials had instructed her to return the child to the Division of Child Welfare.[102]

The first time the public health nurse named Mrs. Brady tried to investigate Warren to determine the status of her Korean children, Warren would not allow Brady to enter her home. When Brady and the nurse for the Division of Maternal and Child Health, Ruth Graves, finally gained access to the home, they learned how she first became involved with US-Korean adoption. Warren explained that she had responded to an appeal in a magazine. The article instructed families interested in helping Korean black children to contact the US State Department. Warren said that representatives at the State Department referred her to Harry Holt. Warren then claimed that Holt contacted her to see if she would help him place children in the Kansas City area. Warren agreed but insisted that there be no publicity of her participation in the adoption program. According to Warren, Holt paid for her to travel to South Korea, where she collected eight Korean black children whom she planned to place with families in and around Kansas City, Kansas. On a second trip to South Korea, Warren collected five more children that she placed in Kansas City and across state lines in Missouri. Warren further explained that she had taken clothes to the children, and that a number of families were still giving her food and clothing, which she sent to Korea. Others gave her money to bring more Korean black children back to the States.[103]

At one point, Warren had contacted officials with the State Department of Social Welfare of Kansas requesting their help. These officials were concerned that Warren was attempting to establish a transnational adoption program. Nonetheless, Warren met with several staff members of the Division of Child Welfare who were willing to conduct home studies of the families Warren recommended. But the social welfare officials also warned that they could not help unless ISS had approved Warren's adoption plan. This stipulation meant that they would not allow her to place a child adopted by proxy. Facing this roadblock, it seems, led Warren to continue to arrange her own placements. When asked, Warren confirmed that she conducted the investigations of the families who received a child from her, and she tried to confirm that each couple had some savings in a bank and owned a home. She ensured there was a breadwinner with a steady job, and she checked to be sure couples were not older than forty years of age and that they had medical proof of infertility.[104] The requirements on Warren's checklist were similar to the basic standards professionals used to screen prospective families, and they indicate her superficial familiarity with adoption policies.

In spite of her rudimentary knowledge of adoption requirements, investigators Brady and Graves recounted that Warren disclosed an additional detail that was alarming to both of them. She explained that social workers had already rejected a number of the families she approved and planned to approve when these families had originally attempted to adopt in the United States. Many of these families sought her help to adopt a Korean child after they had grown tired of waiting to find out whether they could adopt a child in the States. Neither of these circumstances was unusual for families attempting to adopt a child from Europe or Asia, but they raised the level of concern child welfare officials had regarding Warren's activities.[105]

Child welfare officials in Kansas became even more uneasy about Warren's adoption work when they learned that she was planning to get more children from CPS in South Korea. Hong Oak Soon, the director of CPS, was initially optimistic about Warren's work, and in March 1957, she contacted officials with the Kansas State Board of Health regarding Warren's plan. Hong had met Warren during her visit to Korea and the two women began to work together because they agreed that Korean black children had better prospects in the United States. Hong had been the director of CPS since the South Korean government established the agency in 1954, and many adoption agencies in the United States had worked with Hong to place mixed-race Korean children. Officials with ISS were complimentary of her devotion to the children and her commitment to getting them placed with the best possible families. However, these officials worried that she was not qualified to run an adoption program because she was a nurse, not a social worker. Hong and her small staff helped arrange an untold number of US-Korean adoptions with the very limited resources the South Korean government and other sectarian and nonsectarian agencies provided. Given Hong's lack of social work experience, and her intimate awareness of the poor treatment Korean black children experienced, her desire to work with Warren makes sense. But child welfare officials in Kansas remained convinced that Warren's methods and goals were definitely unsound, if not altogether illegal.[106]

ISS officials also believed Warren was a fraud and an unstable religious kook who had lied about her activities and credentials. A memo from ISS-Korea Branch to Susan T. Pettiss claimed that on her first trip to South Korea, Warren had paid her own way. Pettiss was certain that Warren was not working with Harry Holt, even though she had told people in the institutions that cared for Korean black children that she was with his adoption program. Pettiss also claimed that after Warren's return to the States following her first trip to South Korea, the bank returned all of her checks because of insufficient funds. According to the same memo, Warren had misled people by saying she had a letter from President Eisenhower to give legitimacy to her plan to get *all* of the Korean black children to families in the United States. Warren did not explain how her plan would work but she, like Harry Holt, believed that she had divine inspiration and assistance to rescue Korean black children.[107]

Warren put her plan into action in the summer of 1958 when she established her own child-placing agency called the International Love of Humanity Aid Society, Inc. The charter for the society stipulated that the agency would have legal guardianship over the children referred to her program, which would allow Warren to make all decisions about the children's care, education, and eventual placement with an adoptive family in the United States. Warren planned to open more branches of the society in other states and countries to make it easier to arrange adoptions across state and national borders for mixed-race children fathered by African American children abroad. She rented a house in Kansas City, Missouri to begin placing children in that state as well. But Warren did not obtain a license to operate an adoption agency in Missouri or her home state of Kansas. As president of the society, Warren received money from families who applied to adopt Korean black children. It seems that Warren used some of those funds to pay for a house in South Korea to care for the children she planned to bring to the States. It is likely that Warren also used the money to pay for at least one trip to promote her adoption plan in Oakland, California and to cover the costs of another trip to South Korea in January 1959.[108]

When they learned of her plans to bring more Korean children to the United States, officials with the Kansas Division of Child Welfare intervened. Inquiries from Word Vision's Erwin W. Raetz alerted these officials to Warren's plans and the problems she was facing in Korea. World Vision was the evangelical Christian organization that also arranged US-Korean proxy adoptions, and that Harry Holt had an affiliation with for many years. Raetz was World Vision's overseas director, and he explained that representatives with World Vision and Catholic Charities had found Warren to be difficult. Officials with both organizations also questioned Warren's credentials. Raetz wondered whether Warren had a legitimate adoption agency because she was pressuring Hong Oak Soon to get more children from CPS. Based on their investigations, reports from ISS, and information they obtained from Raetz, child welfare officials in Kansas were able to stop Warren from bringing any more children adopted by proxy from Korea. By September 1959, one of the perspective adoptive parents that Warren had recruited had gotten in touch with the Secretary of State of Kansas to complain that she could not reach Warren to find out about her adopted Korean child. The woman had paid $360, and she either wanted her money or her child. ISS records do not include any further information about Warren, but it seems that the legal action against her effectively ended Warren's Korean transnational adoption activities.[109]

Warren's story highlights several of the issues that drew African Americans into US-Korean adoptions and that made proxy adoptions so appealing. Warren's vision of an agency that could rescue *all* Korean black children suggests how unsettling were the circumstances she observed in Korea that shaped her conviction that African American families had to intervene. Even though racial inequality structured African Americans' lives in the United States, she thought Korean black children would thrive. But she did not link African Americans' adoptions with civil rights goals, which was a strategy of the African American journalist discussed in chapter 1, and the African American domestic adoption reformers associated with the NUL discussed in chapter 2. Warren also did not frame her goals in terms that evoked Cold War imperatives, nor did she connect the rescue of Korean children with an ideological stance against communism. Yet Warren saw race, and specifically anti-black racism, as the central issue necessitating African Americans' involvement in Korean-transnational adoption. Her ideas likely resonated with African Americans who agreed with her assessment that the racial discrimination Korean black children experienced in Korea was far worse than what they would experience in the United States. Her use of proxy adoption also must have appealed to many families that perceived or were exposed to discrimination when they interacted with social welfare agencies. Given these circumstances, it is understandable that many African American couples chose to work with Warren or other nonprofessionals who devised their own standards and employed the proxy adoption method to skirt other social work procedures.

Many African Americans took advantage of the proxy method despite social workers' concerns that this practice increased the possibility that an adoption would fail. Some African Americans had used this provision when they adopted the children of black soldiers from Germany and Japan following World War II. It was appealing to families because they could avoid the expense of traveling to another country. This method of adoption could also reduce the costs and time delays many associated with adoptions that were completed through licensed adoption and child welfare agencies in the United States. The proxy method did not require families to work with these agencies. Thus, families could adopt with the help of lawyers, private agencies, or other unofficial agents and circumvent the interviews and home studies social workers customarily used to evaluate prospective adoptive families. While some families believed these arrangements expedited their adoptions, many child welfare officials argued that the lack of supervision from licensed agencies left transnationally adopted children and adoptive parents without the protections that sound social work investigation provided clients in the United States.[110]

Child welfare officials with ISS, the Children's Bureau, and many state child welfare agencies who wanted to end proxy adoption shared horror stories about people like Warren, but they focused considerable attention on examples that revealed the dangerous side of Harry Holt's work and use of the proxy method. Mildred Arnold, Children's Bureau director of social services, worried that Holt's organization used force to coerce mothers to relinquish children. Arnold had heard that a boyfriend of one of Holt's daughters "beat two mothers who were reluctant to give up their children for adoption."[111] The methods he used to transport Korean children were also suspect. ISS's Susan Pettiss and Mildred Arnold, and Katherine B. Oettinger of the Children's Bureau, learned of the perilous nature of the baby lifts after meeting with Dr. Roe, the director of the Pusan Children's Charity Hospital. Dr. Roe contacted Pettiss, Arnold, and Oettinger in the summer of 1958 to tell them about the conditions she observed while serving as an escort for a group of ninety-one children making the twenty-six-hour flight from South Korea to the United States.[112]

According to Dr. Roe, many of the children on the flight were infants who traveled in makeshift bassinettes that each held up to five adoptees. Most of the babies endured the unpressurized flight, but many became ill, and one died. Dr. Roe also became ill during the flight, but she still had to assist the other escorts as they prepared the children to meet their adoptive families. The families had sent clothes for the children, and the six escorts (and possibly the five assistants who also traveled on the flight) had to hurriedly dress the children as the plane neared its destination.[113] One wonders if the escorts were able to make sure they dressed the right children in the clothes sent by their adoptive parents or if the children ended up going home with a different family following such a chaotic trip. But it is unlikely that any of the thousands of couples who adopted through HAP had any idea of these conditions, which scholar Tobias Hübinette compared to slavery's middle passage.[114] It is possible that receiving parents would have continued to support Holt even if they knew about the harrowing nature of the baby lifts. Many adoptive families shared Holt's religious conviction that the children needed rescue, no matter how it occurred.

The available statistics on Korean adoptions show that the largest number of African Americans who adopted Korean black children used Harry Holt's adoption agency, HAP. According to Arissa Oh, between 1955 and 1961, HAP completed 2,420 US-Korean adoptions. During that same time span, families adopted 704 Korean black children.[115] If we assume that HAP placed the majority of these children, it is easy to see why social workers worried, and why African Americans used his services. Like the Hwangs, Holt wanted the children to go to Christian families. In letters to prospective adoptive parents, Holt asked interested couples not to apply to adopt through HAP if they were not Christians. Although Holt did not follow social work standards when screening prospective adoptive families, he did stipulate that black families adopt Korean black children.[116] Holt eagerly recruited African American families who could testify about their personal relationship with Jesus, and this fact surely appealed to African American adoptive couples who were Christians. Ultimately, Holt's methods facilitated adoptions of hundreds of African Americans who likely would not have adopted using the services of child welfare professionals.

Reports of Holt's placements of Korean black children with African American families were widespread.[117] In a letter to ISS's Susan Pettiss, Arnold Lyslo described the scene after one of Holt's baby-lift planes had landed. He noted that the African American couples "were the most strikingly dressed and groomed" of the families waiting for their Korean children. Regarding the children, Lyslo confessed that he had heard that "the combination of Korean-Negro is an especially attractive combination, and the children proved this."[118] An article in the African American magazine *Sepia* titled "Adoption By Proxy: Red Tape Abolished in Case of Koreans" declared that "Holt is a revered citizen in a countless number of Negro homes" because his liberal policies made it possible for African Americans to qualify for adoptions. The article's author, J. Morgan, encouraged readers to apply to adopt a Korean black child and join the many African Americans whom Holt had helped. "Adoption By Proxy" ended by calling HAP "essentially a Negro program," because of the obvious success Holt had with African American families.[119] Officials with ISS also noticed this success and worried because families rejected by state child welfare agencies were aware that they could adopt through HAP. Susan Pettiss recounted that one African American couple in Seattle, Washington had informed the social worker evaluating their family that they would use HAP if the agency did not complete their home study quickly.[120]

Professional social workers' concerns about Holt and adoptions by proxy were well founded, and the failed adoption of one Korean black child, Darius Jefferson, demonstrates why these adoptions were risky. When Ed and Sarah Jefferson adopted their son in 1958, they seemed excited about the prospect of becoming adoptive parents. It took a year for the Jeffersons' adoption to become official, and when four-year-old Darius arrived in the United States, he had to spend six months at the National Jewish Hospital in Denver, Colorado because he had tuberculosis. Darius joined his new family in Milwaukee, Wisconsin in the spring of 1959, and a nurse with the Milwaukee County Health Department reported that the family planned to send him to school in the fall. By August 1959, the family was in crisis. Mrs. Jefferson was pregnant, and Darius was displaying signs that he was having trouble adjusting to his new home. On her subsequent visit to the Jefferson home, the health department nurse discovered that the couple had returned Darius to HAP in Oregon.[121]

Upon further investigation, officials with the Milwaukee County Health Department learned that the Jeffersons were claiming that Darius was still living in their home months after they had returned him to the Holts. In March 1960, Mr. Jefferson had applied for financial assistance, and he listed his biological son and Darius as dependents. However, the Jeffersons had signed a form relinquishing their custody of Darius in October 1959, and the Holts had placed him with another family the following month. When questioned about what had led them to return Darius, the couple acknowledged that their financial problems began when Mr. Jefferson quit his job. They explained that the family incurred medical bills following a surgery and hospitalization of their biological son, which made it difficult for them to attend to legal matters related to Darius's adoption. The social worker assigned to the Jeffersons' case surmised that the couple rejected Darius because they had a biological son. She further concluded that they "may be inadequate as natural or adoptive parents."[122]

Social workers were also concerned about the Coopers, Darius's new parents in California. Matthew and Mary Cooper had previously adopted another child from Korea through HAP, and Holt considered them to be suitable parents for Darius. But both Mr. and Mrs. Cooper worked, and social workers had learned that their seven-year-old biological son was sometimes home alone. Compounding the family's problems, doctors found a spot on Mrs. Cooper's lung that indicated she was very sick. Social welfare officials in California and Wisconsin believed that Darius's original adoption records and the relinquishment form were fraudulent, and they worried that both children were in jeopardy. However, Darius and his older adoptive brother remained in the Coopers' home while child welfare agencies tried to determine the best course of action for these young boys.[123]

The dangers of proxy adoptions led professional social workers and officials with national and international social welfare organizations to fight for legislation that would eliminate the practice as more and more families used the method to adopt Korean children.[124] This coalition helped convince members of Congress to outlaw proxy adoption, and the 1961 Immigration and Nationality Act (INA) did just that.[125] Ironically, the passage of this US law occurred the same year that South Korea passed its Extraordinary Law of Adoption for the Orphan Child. Following the 1961 military coup that brought General Park Chung Hee to power, his administration enacted the law, which was the first modern adoption law passed in South Korea. It provided greater legal and institutional support for out-of-country placements.[126] This adoption law created standards for private agencies facilitating transnational adoptions that required them to have professional staff and provide a range of care for children awaiting adoption.[127] It also strengthened the legal basis for proxy adoptions, which affected adopting families from countries other than the United States.[128] In spite of child welfare professionals' efforts to end proxy adoptions in the United States, however, loopholes allowed families to continue to use the proxy method if they worked with a licensed agency and agreed to legally adopt the child in accordance with the laws of their state once the child was in the country.[129]

African Americans used and defended the proxy method before and after its legal status in the United States changed. As Warren's example suggests, some black families were wary of adoption and child welfare agencies because adoption policies perpetuated racial inequality. Thus, African Americans remained loyal to programs like Holt's HAP once licensed agencies became the gatekeepers of transnational adoption because of the minimal standards Holt used to evaluate families. However, as the Jefferson adoption failure suggests, the needs of Korean black children and the acceptance of the proxy adoption method among African Americans put additional pressure on social workers with public agencies. Thus, officials of several agencies talked about making changes to accommodate eligible families who faced financial limitations because they speculated that African American applicants failed to meet agency standards for mostly economic reasons.[130]

Even when agencies attempted to address the economic considerations that limited African Americans' adoptions by providing financial assistance for an adoptee's travel expenses and waiving or reducing fees, the pool of families approved to adopt Korean black children remained stagnant. In the spring of 1957, ISS's Senior Case Consultant Margaret A. Valk seemed pleased with reports of the placements of ninety-three mixed-race Korean children by one US agency that worked with the South Korean agency CPS. Fourteen of these placements involved African American families, and Valk confirmed that African Americans all over the United States were applying to adopt Korean black children. She noted that more than half of the couples were teachers or represented other middle-class professions, but a large percentage of interested families also represented working-class occupations. Although Valk was excited about the increases in the number of African Americans who inquired about Korean black children, few qualified to complete a US-Korean adoption. In a report lamenting the small number of adoptive families for Korean black children, members of ISS's Intercountry Adoption Committee noted that the work they did to recruit a particularly promising group of one hundred African American couples produced only four completed adoptions.[131] These efforts revealed to ISS officials the need to reform adoption standards when dealing with African American families because racial inequality and not just economic considerations contributed to the low number of completed adoptions for Korean black children.[132]

In one report to the ISS board of directors, Susan T. Pettiss conceded that most adoption agencies did not attempt to recruit African American couples to adopt children in the United States or in Korea. Pettiss theorized that social workers were reluctant to devote the time and resources necessary to complete the investigations, paperwork, or follow-up that adoptions involving African American families required.[133] Some agencies were unwilling to support African Americans' adoptions of Korean black children when they had American-born children of color who needed homes. Indeed, an official with the Children's Bureau speculated that the low number of prospective adoptive parents for Korean black children was partly the result of agencies encouraging African American families to pursue adoptions in the States instead of transnational adoptions. Given the urgency that characterized child welfare officials' discussions of the needs of Korean black children, it is surprising that this official did not see a problem with agencies saying they were going to prioritize the needs of African American children in the United States. But it is also possible that some officials were coming to terms with the fact that the insufficient efforts to increase adoption services for African American families in the States were at the heart of their struggles to recruit families to adopt Korean black children.[134]

In 1953, the Korean orphan crisis drew representatives of political, military, charitable, and humanitarian organizations into negotiations to arrange for the care of orphaned and displaced children in South Korea. The transnational adoptions that became a significant feature of the US and South Korean strategy to care for mixed-race GI children caused child welfare communities to work to create legislation and policies to facilitate the removal of the children many believed would perish if they remained in Korea. While politics, humanitarianism, patriotism, and religion inspired many to support US-Korean adoption, some African Americans demonstrated that their awareness of the anti-black racism that Korean black children faced inspired their response to this population. Thus, they developed ideas about rescue based on their understandings of the ways racial discrimination in Korea threatened the lives of Korean black children. But African Americans' efforts to adopt Korean children also revealed the degree to which racial inequality in the United States and abroad created the need for African American adoptive families, and also limited their abilities to rescue Korean black children.

The African American military families that adopted Korean black children simultaneously benefited from and experienced the constraints of the segregated child welfare systems that coordinated both US and transnational adoptions. This paradox may help explain why, unlike the African American soldiers and members of the black press described in chapter 1, most of these families did not connect their efforts to the larger movement for civil rights. While they recognized the role that anti-black racism played in their lives and the lives of Korean black children, some African American military adoptive parents were experiencing the economic and social benefits derived from serving in an integrated military. African American servicemen's families in the United States and Japan became sought-after adoptive families because they often conformed to the gender conventions child welfare communities associated with stable adoptive parents.

However, families not affiliated with the military also attempted to participate in US-Korean adoptions because they judged their own circumstances—constrained though they were—to be better than what a Korean black child faced in Korea. Many of these families found that they could not meet the requirements professional social workers designed to assure the safety and security of adopted children. Consequently, some used strategies that exposed the controversial nature of nonprofessionals' adoption efforts and the proxy adoption method. While most child welfare professionals working with public agencies associated with ISS opposed these methods, chapter 4 describes the ways a few used proxy adoption and combined rigorous assessment with reasonable reforms to assist African American and interracial adoptive families. The push to increase adoptions of Korean black children also led some of these child welfare officials to make case-by-case reforms that deemphasized the need for some adoptive families to conform to post–World War II gender ideals.

4

The New Family Ideal for Korean Black Adoption

When the Drummonds applied to adopt a school-aged Japanese black child in 1955, the social worker assigned to their case expressed great reservations about their prospects. Even though Mr. Drummond, a twenty-eight-year-old "light-skinned Negro," had a relatively good job as the director of their city's Boy's Club, his previous marriage had ended in divorce. Mrs. Drummond, a thirty-three-year-old white woman, also worked with children through their school system's guidance center. However, one aspect of her life raised a red flag for the caseworker. Mrs. Drummond had been an unmarried mother. While serving in the Women's Army Corps during the Second World War, Mrs. Drummond had an affair with a married soldier, which led to a pregnancy. Instead of putting the baby up for adoption, she had worked to support the child and her parents, who cared for the baby during the day.[1]

The Drummonds' limited finances also made them less than ideal adoptive candidates, as did the fact that they were expecting their first biological child together. The social worker's concern about the couple's financial situation reflected her expectation that Mrs. Drummond, who earned $7,803 annually, would discontinue work after the birth of their child and the anticipated adoption of their Japanese black child. Mr. Drummond only earned $3,800 annually. Nevertheless, the social worker noted that their desire to adopt was sincere, and that both parties had experience with children and educational backgrounds that would be useful in parenting a mixed-race child. She cautiously recommended the approval of the Drummond adoption because she believed they would be good parents to a mixed-race child. The social worker even commented on the Drummonds' plan to have help with the children. When their Japanese black son arrived, Mrs. Drummond did stop working for a short time. But she eventually returned to work, and the couple hired a "pleasant motherly colored woman" to take care of the children during the day.[2]

In 1961, the Drummonds applied to adopt a second mixed-race child, this time a Korean black girl. Once again, Mrs. Drummond was pregnant and working outside of the home, but the couple explained that they had always been interested in adopting from Korea. For Mr. Drummond, the idea began when he was a soldier in Korea, and he considered adopting a nine-year-old boy he had befriended. The social worker assigned to this case wagered that the Drummonds "would have a great deal to offer this child with their acceptance and the wonderful family unity they achieve with any child to whom they reach out." With this ringing endorsement, the agency approved their adoption. The Drummonds gave birth to their biological daughter in March 1962 and received their adopted daughter in October of that same year. In a follow-up visit to the family's home, the social worker noted that the Drummonds' Korean daughter was learning English. Both parents were also using Korean words to communicate with her, the father having learned some Korean while in the army. In a celebratory tone that one would not expect based on the earlier assessments of this home, the caseworker told an official with ISS, "we, like you, wish we had many more families like this one."[3]

The Drummonds' experience vividly illustrates the transition that took place in some adoption communities to accommodate the placements of Korean black children. Mr. and Mrs. Drummond's move from questionable to exemplary marks a crucial shift in the way some social workers perceived the characteristics of ideal families. Before the births of mixed-race World War II and Korean GI babies, social workers would have judged the family's history of unmarried pregnancy and divorce as evidence of types of gender nonconformity that would have disqualified them from consideration for adoption. The Korean crisis, in particular, encouraged a reconsideration of this position, and families like the Drummonds became desirable adoptive families. In the context of the Korean crisis, this family had unique qualities that set it apart for transracial and transnational adoption. That the Drummonds were well educated and both had some background in social work certainly helped their case. The family's residence in an interracial neighborhood with "quite a few oriental [sic] in the vicinity" was also positive. But it was the caring relationship between the African American man and his white wife toward their white son (whom Mr. Drummond adopted), their adopted Japanese black son, and their biological mixed-race son that moved social workers to imagine this home as ideal for a Korean black child. Social workers came to this conclusion *in spite of* the ways the Drummonds challenged the postwar gender and race conventions that child welfare officials looked for in most adoptive families.

The Drummonds were among the hundreds of families who worked with child welfare agencies affiliated with ISS to complete a Korean black adoption in the 1950s and 1960s. These families underwent extensive investigations, unlike the families who adopted with private agencies discussed in chapter 3 like Harry Holt's Holt Adoption Program, Alice Warren's short-lived International Love of Humanity Aid Society, and, as we will see in chapter 5, Pearl S. Buck's Welcome House. The case records of their interactions with social welfare agencies reveal family patterns that challenged the domestic ideal social workers normally required for suitable adoptive families. First, many of these families drew attention to forms of interracial intimacy and interracial marriage most social workers had not needed to accommodate prior to the Korean orphan crisis. Second, adoptive parents of Korean black children often included women who worked outside of their homes to help support the family. However, some social workers who had considered an adoptive mother's paid labor a distraction from the work of mothering began to recognize the ways women could successfully pair their domestic and paid labor with the care of their families.

When families that included working mothers and interracial couples participated in the adoptions of Korean black children, they inspired some child welfare communities to revise their commitment to the gender and race ideals most associated with the nuclear family. Scholars including Karen A. Balcom, Ellen Herman, Barbara Melosh, and Rachel Rains Winslow have described the ways that the push for greater standardization in adoption redefined the practice in the post–World War II years.[4] The result of such efforts led to the creation of a rigorous set of criteria that professional social workers used to evaluate prospective adoptive families. As mentioned in chapter 2, agencies prioritized couples that were economically stable, younger than forty years old, and infertile. Additionally, social workers favored families that did or would adhere to the male breadwinner and female caregiver family ideal. They also attempted to match families and children based on race, religion, and, as best as could be determined, "mental likeness."[5]

Social workers would adjust a few of these requirements to facilitate adoptions of Korean children. In this chapter, I argue that reforms in social workers' ideas about the value of adoptive mothers' paid labor and the significance of interracial homes and communities for mixed-race Korean children proffered a new institutional definition of "ideal families." Namely, these social workers deemphasized gender conformity and strict race matching as crucial factors in certain transnational adoptions. This new adoptive family ideal evolved as African American adoption reformers like the officials and staff of the National Urban League called for and failed to fully advance similar changes nationally. In light of such failures, the families that adopted Korean black children are all the more compelling. Countering labels of pathology or dysfunction, these adoptive families encouraged an expanded definition of ideal adoptive parents. They also helped transform social workers' responses to African American, interracial, and white couples interested in achieving greater acceptance of their transracial and transnational adoptive families.

African Americans and the Nuclear Family Ideal

The dominant version of domesticity that emerged in the second half of the twentieth century had considerable influence over the policies that would guide adoptive family formation. As historian Julie Berebitsky demonstrates, American adoption communities fashioned and adhered to standards "to create adoptive families that not only mirrored biological ones but also reflected an idealized version of them."[6] Couples who adopted Korean black children rarely reflected this idealized version of biological families. Although some possessed a few of the preferred qualities, in many ways they were unlike the white, middle-class ideal that included working fathers and stay-at-home mothers. The weight of this incongruity fell heavily on adoptive mothers who worked outside of their homes. To most child welfare officials and social workers, these working mothers represented an unhealthy break from the domestic ideal that many believed would protect families from dysfunction and disruption.[7]

The conflicts that developed between some African American mothers and child welfare officials reveal the troubling consequences of multiple forms of inequality that informed the nation's adoption policies. Beginning with the earliest efforts to enact welfare reform to assist mothers, social welfare professionals often ignored the needs of African American women. According to historian Linda Gordon, early twentieth-century reformers "did not notice these minorities—did not imagine them as indicated objects of reform." Mothers' Pension programs of the 1910s and 1920s, which were the basis of the New Deal's Aid to Dependent Children (ADC) program, provided meager assistance to women of color. Although reformers designed these programs ostensibly to assist single mothers, they often paid benefits based on the applicant's race or their adherence to specific gender ideals. In other words, they tied a mother's benefits to her worthiness to receive aid. Given the rigid requirements of the Mothers' Pension programs, it is not surprising that African American women received the least amount of assistance if, indeed, they qualified for any aid.[8] Federal New Deal programs went even further to limit African American mothers' access to assistance. The Social Security Act of 1935 excluded agriculture and domestic work from the categories of labor eligible for social insurance. This deliberate effort to exclude black women was consequential since "nine out of ten black women workers" occupied these jobs and received no benefit from New Deal legislation.[9]

African American female reformers affiliated with organizations like the National Association of Colored Women's Clubs (NACWC) attempted to counter these exclusions by addressing the needs of working mothers. Established in 1896, the NACWC became one of the most influential secular organizations for African American women in the country. While members of NACWC frequently articulated a vision of motherhood that emphasized the importance of women's domestic responsibilities, they also acknowledged the importance of African American women's participation in paid labor. Regional branches of the NACWC sponsored mothers' clubs that offered training in a range of subjects, and they sponsored day nurseries to provide child care for working mothers. NACWC historian Deborah Gray White notes that the instruction women received in mothers' clubs focused on skills that were unquestionably domestic but also included teaching "women how to buy land and build houses."[10]

NACWC members understood that racial inequality necessitated African American women's paid labor, and they created facilities to assist this population. One such institution, the Fannie Wall Children's Home and Day Nursery, in Oakland, California, provided full-time care for eighteen children and day care for twenty-nine children. Founded in 1918, the home had a staff of nursery teachers, housemothers, and social workers. These women provided instruction, care, and guidance to children with the goal of nurturing "love, security, and acceptance" in their young charges. The women who worked in facilities like the Fanny Wall Home represented a particular class of professional, often highly educated reformers who devoted their lives to community service. These reformers developed strategies to avoid and resolve community problems, including a community approach to child care that supported working mothers.[11]

Similarly, reformers associated with Atlanta University established the Gate City Day Nursery Association in 1905 to address the issues of working parents who lived in neighborhoods near that university. In 1923, they opened a second facility with the goal of providing quality child care especially for working mothers. The demand was so great that Gate City opened a third facility in 1955, and the staff of teachers and social workers that coordinated with local doctors and dentists endeavored to meet the children's social and medical needs. These professionals understood that they were doing the nurturing work that often fell to mothers, and they taught children table manners as well as age-appropriate academic and self-care skills. They believed mothers' domestic responsibilities were important, but they knew that black women often did not get to choose whether or not they worked for wages. As these examples suggest, reformers with programs like the Fannie Wall Children's Home and the Gate City day nurseries recognized the working mother as a vital member of African American families and communities. These reformers demonstrated that it was not unusual for black women to need support to fulfill their domestic responsibilities.[12]

Social welfare agencies were less accommodating to African American mothers for much of the first half of the twentieth century. However, after mid-century, African American mothers made up a larger percentage of women receiving aid through state and federal welfare programs. This transition had more to do with the changing nature of programs for unwed mothers than with social welfare officials' changing attitudes toward African American women. White women's increased access to adoption services and the stabilizing influence of the postwar boom in marriage rates reduced this population's dependence on public assistance. Thus, social welfare professionals' assessments of African American mothers became more negative as the numbers of black women on the welfare rolls increased. The needs of single African American women dominated social workers' attention and set in motion institutional debates about the ways black women defied gender ideals and operated outside of stable family units. Opinions like these reinforced the notion that African American communities endorsed behaviors that were at odds with the gender ideals of the nuclear family model. However, many African Americans aspired to the nuclear family ideal and the class stability it suggested. They just accepted that attaining that status was out of reach for some black mothers because of the racial disparities that made social welfare assistance necessary.[13]

Most African American families relied on black women's paid labor and financial contributions to household economies. Although African American men traditionally earned more than their wives, these men made considerably less than their white counterparts. For example, in 1949, the average salary for an African American male worker was a little over $1,700, while his white counterpart earned a little over $2,900 a year. By 1959, these figures increased to a little more than $2,800 annually for African American men and $5,100 for white men. In 1969, African American men earned an average of $5,341 but white men averaged $8,442. Although both African American and white men saw increases in their annual salaries during the two decades after World War II, the income gap between these groups widened each decade. Consequently, the money African American women earned as paid laborers was often necessary to make up the difference in household incomes.[14]

African American married women worked outside of their homes at higher rates than their white counterparts. According to Deborah Gray White, 42 percent of African American women were in the labor force in the 1930s. By the 1940s, the percentage of married, African American women in the labor force had dropped to 37 percent, where it remained until the 1950s. Historian Jacqueline Jones notes that 24 percent of married, white women were in the paid labor force during that same decade. Married African American women's participation in paid labor increased during the 1960s. By the 1970s, 60 percent worked outside of their homes compared to 48 percent of married white women. The wage disparity between these women was also an issue. On average, African American women earned fifty cents for every dollar their white counterparts earned between 1949 and 1959. While these numbers capture differences between women based on race, it is important to note that these statistics do not include the percentage of women who worked irregularly or performed labor that they did not report. These statistics do show that economic disparities shaped African American women's experience of marriage and family and constrained their choices. However, they do not indicate the ways African American women attempted to prioritize their identities as wives and mothers as well as their roles as paid laborers.[15]

The case notes of several families who applied to adopt a Korean black child show that the issue of a prospective adoptive mother's paid labor was significant because some social workers rejected couples because they included women who worked for wages outside of the home. As chapter 2 described, officials with the NUL struggled to interpret this aspect of many African American families' lives for white social workers evaluating families for domestic adoptions. The following examples show how black women's paid labor could also be an issue for families attempting to complete a transnational adoption. The Winslows applied to adopt a Korean black child in 1955. Although the social worker who conducted their home study had no specific complaints about the couple, she was not supportive of Mrs. Winslow's plan to continue working as a schoolteacher following the adoption. Although she conceded that Mrs. Winslow was working to maintain and furnish a home that was suitable for adoption, the social worker seemed critical of this decision. She assumed that the wife was reluctant to give up her job because the couple wanted to maintain their status more than she wanted to be a mother. But this couple would face real economic challenges if Mrs. Winslow did not work. Mr. Winslow was a school principal and the couple's combined monthly income was a mere $410. The social worker rejected their application flatly, stating, "it was not the policy of [her] agency to place a child in a home where the mother was absent most of the time."[16]

Throughout the 1950s, child welfare officials discussed the effect requiring women to leave paid labor had on adoptions involving African

Americans. Officials with a number of agencies recognized that African Americans often delayed pursuing adoptions for economic reasons. Families were aware that adoption agencies did not look favorably on women's paid labor, even when social workers understood the reasons African American women worked outside of their homes. Many couples that were aware of this tendency either avoided public adoption agencies or pursued other paths to adopt. ISS's consultant on foster care, I. Evelyn Smith, conceded that even African American professional social workers "obtained their children for adoption independently."[17] In spite of their awareness of the reasons some African American women had to continue working, social workers routinely scrutinized this choice as potentially harmful to families and communities.

Some couples felt pressure to live up to the nuclear family ideal, and a few of the African American couples who applied to adopt Korean black children took steps to make it possible for prospective adoptive mothers to leave paid labor. A small number of ISS case records describe the circumstances of African American families who were economically stable enough to live comfortably without a wife's financial contribution. The Bakers were one of these families. Together they had worked and saved enough for Mr. Baker to believe that his wife could leave paid labor once they adopted a child. The forty-nine-year-old Mrs. Baker was a postal clerk who, with her $5,400.00 annual salary, earned more than her husband. Their combined incomes had allowed them to achieve an enviable standard of living and to purchase two apartment buildings. The income from these investments made it possible for Mrs. Baker to remain home following their adoption. The Bakers were rare among African American adopting couples. They represented a small group of older adopters who had worked many years to attain their status but could not adopt domestically because their age made them ineligible by the standards of most adoption agencies. The Bakers had faced this restriction, which was one reason they chose to pursue a Korean adoption.[18]

It was not uncommon for African American husbands pursuing a Korean adoption to express a desire for their wives to remain at home full-time. When they applied to adopt a child from Korea, Mr. Curtis explained that he wanted his wife to quit her job as a nurse's aide on the children's ward of their local hospital.[19] Mr. Cooper also wanted his wife to leave her job once they began the adoption process in 1960.

Even though Mrs. Cooper earned $216.00 a month, which was a signifi-cant portion of their household income, Mr. Cooper believed he could support his family without his wife's salary. However, Mr. Cooper only earned $315.00 monthly.[20] The Curtis and Cooper families, and others like them, struggled financially without the wife's income. In a number of cases, mothers had to return to paid labor after they adopted a child in spite of a husband's wishes or the mother's stated desires to remain at home.

For some couples, the effort to strictly follow the male breadwinner and female caregiver model played a role in the ultimate failure of an adoption placement. This seems to have been the case for the Evans fam-ily of Jefferson City, Missouri, who applied to adopt a Korean black child in 1955. The Evans's application process began with promise. The social worker reviewing their case noted that Mr. Evans worked as a porter in a garage but was also an artist and carpenter who had played professional baseball in the Negro League. Mrs. Evans had worked in a peanut but-ter factory and an egg factory before she took a position cleaning ships. At the time of their application, she was attending beauty school. Mrs. Evans hoped to open a beauty parlor in her home because her earnings were essential to the household. Mr. Evans only made $1.25 an hour, or approximately $200.00 a month. But the couple had managed to pur-chase a car and a six-room home, which was impressive even though they had two mortgages on the property.[21]

The social worker evaluating the Evans family seemed to like the couple. She included detailed notes about their appearances and racial features. She described Mr. Evans as a "light complexion[ed] . . . very nice-looking man [who was] somewhat inclined to be feminine look-ing." She also noted that Mrs. Evans's complexion was darker than her husband's, and that she was attractive. The social worker went on to comment on the couple's hygiene by mentioning that both seemed to take time for grooming. As these comments indicate, the social worker liked what she saw, and she approved their adoption despite the eco-nomic challenges they faced. They received their Korean black son in 1956.[22]

Personal and financial difficulties soon disrupted this placement. The couple separated in the spring of 1957, and when social workers asked Mrs. Evans why she left her husband, she said it was because he was moving too slowly on filing the paperwork to finalize the adoption. Mr. Evans was much more candid when he confessed that she left because he had been unfaithful. The family attempted to reconcile in the summer of 1957, and Mrs. Evans returned to work. In another meeting with their social worker, Mr. Evans admitted that he carried a tremendous amount of hostility because he could not provide for his family. By January 1958, the social worker reported that the family's situation had improved but the reunion did not last. The couple divorced and social workers placed their son in a boarding home. Although this was the only breakdown of a Korean black adoption reported in their state, it suggests the challenges many African Americans faced that economic hardships only compounded.[23]

Domesticity, Maternal Care, and US Child Welfare Standards

Social workers were concerned about African American women's performance of paid labor because of what it suggested about their femininity and their ability to provide maternal care. Social workers had the job of assessing adoptive applicants' gender conformity, and they paid particular attention to potential adoptive mothers' adherence to emerging standards of femininity. Child welfare agencies and staff expected their adopting parents to display gender normative behaviors, and social workers diligently noted their positive and negative impressions of applicants' performance of their gender roles. The notes about the families that applied to adopt a Korean black child in the 1950s and 1960s in the ISS case files demonstrate how these assessments influenced social workers' decisions. For example, the social worker assigned to the Tanner family's case observed that Mrs. Tanner seemed to dominate her husband. Even though she was concerned that Mrs. Tanner's behavior might cause problems in the future, this social worker was comforted that Mr. Tanner was a successful businessman who let his wife run the house. Likewise, in 1956, ISS officials were initially concerned about the Curtis family because of the seven-year age difference between the young husband and his older wife. The age difference made social officials wonder if Mrs. Tanner was a controlling wife. But the social worker conducting their case study assured ISS officials that Mrs. Curtis "looks upon her husband as the man of the house." Based on her observations, the social worker also concluded that Mr. Curtis was a good breadwinner. Child welfare professionals applied subjective and objective measures to assess prospective adoptive parents. Characteristics like an age difference that might give a wife authority over her husband or behaviors that suggested female dominance represented challenges to the model of domesticity that many associated with healthy adoptive families.[24]

Femininity mattered as a quality associated with successful mothering. Many social workers assumed that women who seemed aggressive in speech or mannerisms lacked the maternal skills necessary to parent a child with whom they shared no biological ties. This idea explains why ISS officials were pleased to hear about families like the Lamberts, an African American couple attempting to adopt a Korean black child in 1955. The report on this family's home study includes the notation that the husband was "thoroughly masculine in appearance while [the wife] is very feminine."[25] The social worker assessing the Lawrence family in 1957 had a similar reaction. The Lawrences made a lasting impression because of their adherence to the male breadwinner and female caregiver family model. Mr. Lawrence was a house painter and owned an apartment building. The social worker conducting their home study happily reported that he seemed in charge of his family. She also commented on the ways Mrs. Lawrence displayed a maternal and feminine nature. The note explained that Mrs. Lawrence tended to all of the domestic duties well. She had been a dressmaker and practical nurse but left paid labor after having a hysterectomy. The social worker was also impressed that Mrs. Lawrence did not plan to return to work following the adoption. In this case, as in other cases where wives planned to leave paid labor after an adoption, child welfare officials responded favorably to the couple's plan. Social workers often indicated that this pattern showed that the adoptive mother was committed to childrearing as her primary job.[26]

Although child welfare officials looked positively on couples that conformed to gender expectations, they were sometimes willing to consider families that displayed what they defined as questionable qualities. If the couple was able to make a good impression in all other ways, social workers attempted to apply their skills in intervention to remedy problems. For example, social workers were concerned for one prospective adoptive mother because they believed she had "certain difficulty in accepting her role of a woman." The notes in this case file show that social workers worried because Mrs. Thomas seemed to be more devoted to being a mother than to performing the duties of a wife. In 1957, the social worker for the Thomas family surmised that the wife's issues either stemmed from her inordinate affection for her own mother or sibling rivalry with her sister. Whatever the cause, they were otherwise impressed with her. Mrs. Thomas had worked as a foster mother and then as a legal clerk for a local department store. But she planned to leave paid labor after adopting a child. The social worker who wrote up the case notes on this family went on to compliment Mrs. Thomas's skill managing the family's budget and her matter-of-fact approach to problems. These attributes convinced the social worker that they could help Mrs. Thomas face her problem with femininity and become a good wife and mother to a Korean black daughter. It is not clear what behaviors caused social workers to believe Mrs. Thomas needed an intervention, but the notes suggest they worried that a confused gendered identity should be fixed to ensure the mother's ability to nurture the stability of this adoptive family.[27]

Child welfare professionals' concerns about adoptive mothers' gender performance reflected their belief that mothers were either the cause of, or the defense against, family breakdown. In 1951, Dr. John Bowlby, mental health consultant to the World Health Organization, articulated the position of many physicians, educators, and child welfare professionals when he theorized that maternal care was fundamental for healthy child adjustment while maternal deprivation led to mental health problems in children. Bowlby defined functional families as institutional units composed of breadwinning fathers and caregiving mothers, whose role was the most important influence in child development. The primacy of mothers had everything to do with the underlying assumption that women performed the domestic duties that kept children fed, clothed, and comforted. Fathers mattered, but their primary function was to provide economic security and emotional support for their wives. Bowlby believed so strongly in the influence of mothers that he categorized paid employment that took mothers out of the home as a sign of dysfunction.[28] The persistence of this idea in child welfare circles is evinced in the work of professionals like social worker David Fanshell, who wrote in 1972 that the mother's role in a family was "the most elemental ingredient for normal development."[29]

Professionals' investment in a certain type of maternal care as a precursor to healthy child development had particular resonance for assessments of African American motherhood. Sociologist Patricia Hill Collins's effort to unpack the multiple and dynamic meanings of African American motherhood challenges the ideas produced by child welfare professionals and nonprofessionals alike. Collins calls into question the tendency of people to either demonize or glorify African American women for their varied performances of maternal care. Identifying the tendency of professionals and nonprofessionals to define black women as either "matriarchs" or the "superstrong Black mother," Collins suggests that, historically, politicians and social welfare reformers have assessed African American women against very narrow criteria. Consequently, child welfare professionals often do not address the ways that African American mothers participated in paid labor, community programs, and political activism to enhance the care of their own and other women's children. Child welfare professionals' lack of familiarity with, or regard for, these patterns led many to undervalue the contributions and sacrifices some African American mothers made to sustain their homes. This pattern is apparent in the records of social workers that evaluated African American adoption applicants. These professionals often judged African American women without a sense of what Collins describes as African American women's "innovative and practical approaches to mothering under oppressive conditions."[30]

Although many child welfare professionals were skeptical of the stability of families with working mothers, the black popular press highlighted the strengths of African American families that included wives and husbands who shared in the financial and domestic work of maintaining their homes throughout the 1940s and 1950s. The African American magazine *Our World* published a series of articles called "How Negro America Lives," that showcased dual-income black families that did "not live any spectacular lives, but who with their problems, their little joys and sorrows, reflect life." Modeled after the long-running "How America Lives" series featured in the *Ladies Home Journal* magazine that began in 1940, "How Negro America Lives" included representations of, and for, African Americans that countered negative assessments of African American family life. Historian Stephanie Coontz has explained that African American families showed the same rates of dual parent homes as white families until the early 1960s.[31] But postwar migrations and the dramatic growth of African American urban centers revived child welfare professionals' concerns that African American families were failing to adapt to the nuclear family ideal. Therefore, a series like "How Negro America Lives" operated on two levels. In one sense, it promoted the virtues of the burgeoning nuclear family ideal that was influencing all families in the 1950s. But it also demonstrated that African Americans' negotiations of the demands of the nuclear family did not lead them to simply imitate white family patterns. Instead, African American traditions and adaptations also informed black family life.[32]

The black popular press engaged in a project to attract and inspire an African American audience that embraced the characteristics of modernity. In some cases, popular magazines used depictions of successful African American and interracial families to advance the struggle for racial equality. As historian Adam Green notes, during the 1940s and 1950s, African Americans developed a collective identity that transcended differences of region and class. Green attributes this transition to the widespread availability of print media for African Americans that drew them into a national conversation to define and refine the contours of black life. Regarding African American family life, the black press repackaged certain characteristics of the nuclear family ideal to reflect patterns that would be recognizable in African American communities. Consequently, stories about African American families did not identify domestic spaces as the exclusive domain of women or suggest that economic and political endeavors were men's work. To the contrary, while African American popular magazines made their appeal to decidedly middle-class sensibilities, they acknowledged the range of family patterns and unconventional gender roles that sustained black communities.[33]

The Jacksons, the family featured in the first installment of "How Negro America Lives," provide a useful model for examining the ways black popular magazines expanded definitions of African American family success and modernity. The article lays out the qualities that made this couple noteworthy. Stanley was "a good man; quiet, unassuming, straight-forward with a corny sense of humor." His wife, Danice, was a graduate of Spelman College and she worked as an assistant librarian at Harvard University. The couple had twin boys, attended church, and owned their own home. The only African American family in Billerica, Massachusetts, the Jacksons were active members of the PTA. They also supported many local philanthropic organizations. The article portrays Stanley and Danice as partners in their marriage, sharing both economic and domestic responsibilities. With references to Danice's age (six years older than Stanley), good judgment, and intellectual and professional achievements, the profile revealed the many ways African American women played significant roles in sustaining all aspects of family life.[34]

This demonstration of flexible domestic and labor identities was at odds with the dominant notions displayed in popular depictions of white families during the 1950s. As scholar Wendy Kozol theorizes, *Life* magazine worked "to make traditional gender roles appear natural and ahistorical."[35] Thus, depictions that emphasized the gender divisions of labor reinforced the notion of separate male and female spheres, with women performing nurturing tasks and men performing paid labor. African American popular magazines resisted proscribing rigid gender divisions of labor even though they acknowledged the existence of gender ideals. When they described the move toward nuclear family models, they did so in light of practices that traditionally sustained African American families. The Jacksons lived with Stanley's parents before moving to an apartment. It was Danice's savings that made the purchase of their home possible, and her labor outside of the home provided necessary income. Stanley counted on "his wife's judgment and knowledge," and he assumed a role in the family that combined breadwinning with housekeeping. Stanley shared in domestic duties by drying the dishes and taking an active role in parenting his sons, which went a long way toward making this home stable. Far from being deemed a negative characteristic, "How Negro America Lives" implied that this type of relationship was in line with American modernity.[36]

The photographs accompanying the profile of the Jacksons show the most mundane family scenes enlivened by the family's unique advantages. There are photographs of the family shopping for groceries, playing with an elaborate train set in the basement of their home, attending church, and eating dinner in a kitchen alcove Stanley built himself. The twin boys are all smiles as they play with their dog, Sandy, do homework, watch television, and take tap dance lessons. Danice is at ease whether washing clothes in her "Easy-Spin" washer and dryer, talking on the phone, or assisting at a PTA executive board meeting. Stanley's world in pictures also revolves around family activities with two notable exceptions. The article includes a photograph of him fishing at a stream behind the family home and performing his job at the Air Force Research Center. All of these activities take place in a world dominated by white people, and the article does not hesitate to attribute Stanley and Danice's success to their ability to live a life comparable to their white neighbors. It also suggests that white pastors, employers, shopkeepers, and teachers accepted this family, and that the boys were the true beneficiaries of this privilege. The boys seemed to be flourishing in their community even though they were the only African American children in their local school.[37]

What makes this idyllic presentation additionally striking is the link the article makes between interracial interactions, economic success, and the attainment of the American dream for African Americans. All the trappings of the modern age surround the Jackson family. The television set, washer and dryer, telephone, and six-room home all signal the family's full participation in the nation's consumer culture. The family's economic worth is spelled out throughout the article and in photograph captions that list the cost of most of their possessions and the family's earning potential. Without any direct mention of segregation, this article lays claim to integrated spaces as a critical component of African Americans' progress. Stanley's access to the entry-level job that led to his appointment as purchasing agent for the Air Force Research Center came about because of his status as a military man and a helpful letter from Eleanor Roosevelt.[38] In successive installments of "How Negro America Lives," *Our World* profiled other families whose economic success and performance of unconventional gender roles contributed to family stability.

The majority of families featured in "How Negro America Lives" were decidedly not average. These families often included husbands and wives that had obtained some position of influence in their communities. Their achievements highlighted the political dimensions of family success stories that showed African Americans breaking racial barriers as they became the first of their race to assume some position of significance. Many segments of "How Negro America Lives" paired a story of family success with the description of how the husband or wife or both became the first "Negro" to assume some political office or important position in their community. For instance, "Keeping up with the Joneses" identified the multiple successes of Toni and Paul Jones, beginning with Toni's appointment as Pittsburgh's first African American schoolteacher and Paul's election to the city council, which made him that city's first African American councilman.[39] The profile of the Garretts of Montclair, New Jersey noted that Doug Garrett was the first African American real estate appraiser in that state.[40] Beyond being the first African American to accomplish some task of importance, "How Negro America Lives" further framed "first" efforts of individual families to secure homeownership as an issue of political importance that readers could readily appreciate. After the Mischals of Cleveland, Ohio purchased their six-room, two-story home, their pastor commented that they were "good people and would be a fine asset to any community anywhere in this country."[41] This comment took on greater significance because of the many stories about white people barring African Americans from living in their neighborhoods. Like the Jacksons and the Mischals, the Rhodens of Chicago sacrificed to buy their first home, and "How Negro America Lives" celebrated the hard work that couples like the Rhodens performed to achieve material and political success to ultimately secure advantages for their children.[42]

By the late 1950s, some social workers were describing the benefits of approving couples like those featured in "How Negro America Lives" that displayed stable family lives even if the potential adoptive mother worked outside of the home. In 1959, Annie Lee Davis Sandusky, the Children's Bureau's consultant on services to children in their own homes, commented on these changing notions in a speech at the National Conference on Social Welfare. She first described the challenges social workers faced as a result of "the burden of some of the established concepts and ideals of the past era . . . [that competed with] the realities of the present time." Next, Sandusky explained how gender conventions that reinforced the male breadwinner and female caregiver family model informed social work practice. Sandusky was convinced that this model was shifting and "the old conception of the masculine and feminine roles in the family is breaking down." As proof of this shift, she pointed out the ways women were "sharing—and must share—the wage earning role." Sandusky considered this transition positive for women whose labor "earns for her a place in decision making." An African American social worker who had been the Bureau's consultant on minority groups before she worked on issues related to services to children in their homes, Sandusky likely had encountered African American families whose experiences supported her conclusions.[43]

Many of the couples that worked with agencies affiliated with ISS to complete a US-Korean adoption demonstrated the pattern Sandusky described, and they called into question the notion that domestic stability required adherence to rigid gender ideals. Overwhelmingly, the women in these families maintained some kind of paid labor outside of their homes, and a number had already paired work with the successful parenting of either biological or informally adopted children. As they gained experience working with families that fit this profile, officials with ISS, and some of the adoption agencies it worked with, began to comment on the ways these potential adopting mothers were positive models of a different kind of domestic ideal. The ISS case notes describing social workers' impressions of these families contained fewer references to concerns about these couples' conformity to postwar gender ideals. Instead, social workers praised the couples who developed childcare plans that included husbands, relatives, and neighbors as key members of the childcare team.

It was not unusual for African American adoptive fathers of Korean black children to take an active role in childrearing, and many families worked alternating schedules to accommodate childcare needs. Mr. Stewart, who worked nights as a millwright, took care of his biological daughter and adopted Korean black daughter on the days his wife worked as a housekeeper.[44] Mr. Long also provided daily care for his adopted children. When Mr. Long attempted to adopt his Korean son in 1959, social workers supported his family even though they possessed characteristics that did not line up with the nuclear family ideal. Mr. Long and his wife were interested in adopting his biological Korean son, who was born after Long completed his stint in the military in 1953. He tried to adopt the child before he returned to the United States, but that plan fell through. In 1954, he married a woman whom the social worker evaluating his case described as "a very attractive Mulatto Negro woman . . . [with] small features, curly hair, a winsome smile, and very expressive eyes." Mrs. Long had a daughter whom Mr. Long adopted after they got married. Mrs. Long was completely in favor of the adoption of her husband's Korean child and planned to take time off work once he arrived in the States. But she was going to return to her job as a typist in a medical setting after an adjustment period. The social worker evaluating their case supported the adoption and noted that the family had a childcare plan. Mr. Long would take care of the children until he went to work at the post office in the early afternoon. Mrs. Long's aunt would then care for the children until Mrs. Long got home from her job in the evenings.[45] These arrangements are compelling, in part, because they are unlike the patterns historian Sarah Potter observed among the African American working-class men in the sample of Illinois Children's Home and Aid Society adoptive fathers that "did not necessarily anticipate being deeply engaged with their children" because they worked long hours.[46] They also offer a twist on the patterns black feminists associate with the roles of "othermothers" in African American communities. While historically, African American women have created and sustained networks of "bloodmothers and othermothers" that help each other care for children, the case notes on adoptive fathers of Korean black children suggest that these men were integral to the maintenance of these care networks.[47]

When husbands were unable to take a leading role in child care, female neighbors or family members often took on the responsibility. This accommodation characterized the Hunters' childcare plan. Social workers were pleased that the Hunters' arrangements included Mrs. Hunter's aunt, who lived in the apartment above the couple. Mr. Hunter worked in a foundry and Mrs. Hunter was a practical nurse in an osteopathic hospital. The couple adopted two Korean black daughters, and the final note on their case praised the couple's parenting abilities.[48] The James family had to rely on the help of a neighbor who lived below them to augment their shared childcare duties. The social worker conducting their home visit actually thought it was a good idea for Mrs. James to return to her job in a plastic factory because it would help the family meet its financial needs. In this case, the child would spend the day with their downstairs neighbor, whose daughter was an ideal playmate for the James's daughter. Mr. James would take over childcare when he arrived home from work and then Mrs. James would join the family at the end of the day.[49]

To some in child welfare communities, this pattern of relying on extended kinship networks was suggestive of a "more primitive" but beneficial model of childrearing. Dr. John Bowlby identified this type of shared child care as one remedy to the fragmentation that occurred when families moved from rural, close-knit communities to urban centers. But it was not the parenting model social workers wanted to see among all adoptive families because many believed the nuclear family was the modern era's answer to crowded communities and social dysfunction. As many white couples responded to the postwar impulse to flee urban areas in favor of suburban communities, they assumed the childcare model Dr. Bowlby identified as the new tradition that signified a "normal family." Although social workers accepted that families of color who adopted a Korean black child might replicate the more *primitive* pattern, child welfare officials continued to support the "traditional family" in other contexts.[50]

The experiences of families adopting Korean black children underscore the subjective nature of cultural interpretations of gender in this institutional context. Linda Gordon has pointed out that African American women constructed an understanding of motherhood that merged marriage and child care with "respect for the public achievements of women, in professions or civic activism or both."[51] In the context of adoption and the relationships couples formed with social workers, characteristics that once signaled a break from acceptable gender performance morphed into a series of practices that demonstrated the capacity for men and women to operate outside of prevailing definitions of appropriate male and female behavior. Fathers could take care of their children and do housework without undermining their masculinity, and mothers could work outside of their homes without damaging their children or compromising their femininity.

Many adoptive mothers of Korean black children were unusual among adoptive mothers. These women often combined paid labor and childrearing because they were members of poor and working-class communities. The majority of adoptive mothers scholars have studied were middle-class, and this status informed their performance of what Sarah Potter calls their domestic femininity.[52] Adoptive mothers of Korean black children were also not the African American club women of the 1930s and 1940s who fashioned reform work as a part of their duty to uplift their less fortunate sisters. But the women who participated in US-Korean adoption did make their homes the center of an expression of civic responsibility to resolve problems beyond the boundaries of the nation. These women did not simply fold in domestic and civic responsibility as a measure of their gender identity; they also used their unique positions to play a role in international politics that enhanced the significance of their multifaceted experiences of motherhood.[53]

When African American women joined the ranks of transnational adoptive mothers, they were able to transform the meanings of both their gender and racial identities. This newfound status for African American women derived from the ideological power Cold War domesticity bestowed on mothers. Their ability to adopt emphasized that, even though they were counted among an oppressed class, their status as mothers gave them more power than the Korean women who had to give up their children. The elevation of African American women's status coincided with the denigration of Korean women, who were the subjects of oppressive militaristic gender regimes. In many ways, the exchange of their children to African American women, another group of women with limited power who were also seen as low-status mothers, initiated a key reversal. In spite of their compromised position as members of a group systematically denied the rights of full citizens in their own country, African American women could use what power they had to provide refuge for Korean black children.[54]

It is a challenge to ascertain how African American women felt about their roles as adoptive mothers of foreign-born children, but a couple of examples suggest that some had very definite ideas about their responsibility to address the extreme racism Korean black children experienced. The words and ideas of the following sample of adoptive mothers come from case notes prepared by white social workers. They provide an important record of this community, but it is also possible that respondents were guarded when asked direct questions about their motivations, or they gave answers they believed the social worker wanted to hear. With that caveat in mind, it is still fascinating to see how some African American adoptive mothers understood their participation in US-Korean adoption. For example, several mothers offered compelling explanations for their desire to adopt a Korean child when there were children of color in need in the States. Both Mr. and Mrs. Lawrence said they were moved to adopt a Korean black child because "American children will always have enough to eat and a roof over their heads, and so it is more important to offer a home to the Oriental child."[55] The Nelsons had traveled extensively and were shocked by what they heard about the ways foreign-born children of black men suffered.[56]

Mrs. Anderson became interested in adopting a mixed-race Korean child after meeting the Korean black children adopted by her husband's cousins. Mr. Anderson added that he wanted to adopt because he had seen the desperate poverty that shaped the children's lives while he was stationed in Korea.[57] The social worker interviewing the Davis family noted that Mrs. Davis was troubled by the stories of the ostracism the children experienced.[58] She learned of their circumstances through the black press. It seems that these mothers assessed the challenges Korean black children faced as more dire than those of American-born children. They also believed that the racial inequality that constrained their lives did not compare with the extreme examples of racism Korean black children and their mothers endured in South Korea. Though adoptive mothers did not always consider their adoptions to be political acts, some African American mothers did understand that their efforts were politically significant responses to the social and political legacies of racism in various national contexts.

Color Lines and Family Ties

The families that adopted Korean black children also prompted ISS officials to reconsider the ways they advised families to deal with racial intolerance. Until the late 1950s, some officials with ISS discouraged families that adopted mixed-race Korean children from living in interracial neighborhoods. In 1956, Susan T. Pettiss had suggested that children of Asian descent fared better in communities where there were not many Asians. She worried that children's Asianness would be a liability if they lived in areas where there was a sizable Asian community and accompanying anti-Asian sentiments.[59] Some social workers and adoptive parents considered such warnings necessary to protect children who were already potential targets of racism. The Seavers endeavored to protect their Korean black child's privacy because they were aware of the isolation he might face as a mixed-race child. When ISS officials approached the Seavers for a picture to use in *Ebony* magazine as an adoption promotional tool, Mrs. Seaver was reluctant. The social worker reported that Mrs. Seaver did not want to draw any attention to her son that might make him feel uncomfortable. This was important to Mrs. Seaver, because she believed "he has enough of a handicap being part Negro . . . without adding to it by calling attention to his Korean ancestry."[60]

The Taylor family was quick to address the issue of prejudice when their Korean black son came home from school bothered because he thought his teacher called him a gook. Mrs. Taylor contacted the school as soon as she learned about the incident and discovered that the teacher had teasingly called him "goofy." Mrs. Taylor accepted this explanation and tried to help her son understand the difference between the two words. She also took the incident as an opportunity to tell him "about his Korean background . . . [explaining] that he comes from an ancient and very honorable culture."[61] However, as families of color taught their children how to manage the challenges of racism in the United States, they affirmed the need for child welfare agencies to promote racial equality in adoption service delivery and throughout US society. Consequently, some social workers and adoptive families concluded that interracial communities were better suited for mixed-race children because these communities were already working to manage the challenges of diversity. For example, in 1958, the social worker assigned to the Douglas family noted that their neighborhood was a good place for a Korean black child to live precisely because it was an integrated neighborhood.[62]

A remarkable characteristic among many families who adopted Korean black children was their residence in integrated neighborhoods. In some cases, owning a home in an integrated community was also an indication that these families were challenging inequality on several fronts. The Seavers and the Wilsons lived in desegregated base housing.[63] The Coopers were also a military family, but they chose not to live in base housing. Instead they lived in a neighborhood that included Asian, African American, and Hispanic families.[64] The Hyatt and the James families lived in integrated communities where they did not deal with racial barriers to housing.[65] These African American and interracial adoptive parents were aware of the political and generational import of crossing the residential color lines that were in place for the benefit of white families. They made these decisions to create new opportunities for themselves and their adopted and biological children.

Some families who pioneered Korean black adoptions also became the first families of color in all-white neighborhoods. The Warrens and the Nelsons crossed the color line in their respective communities. The Warrens told their caseworker that they were comfortable in their all-white neighborhood and they reported no racial incidents. Their neighbor was a Protestant minister and Mr. Warren claimed that the minister's four children were playmates of his two children—a biological son and a Korean black daughter.[66] In another case, the Nelsons moved into an all-white neighborhood in 1964 and Mr. Nelson boasted that his sons had made friends and integrated themselves into the lives of their white neighbors. The social worker in this case seemed to attribute their success to the fact that the boys were smart, well-behaved, and well-groomed.[67] The attributes that made these families desirable candidates for Korean black adoptions also made them ideal ambassadors for the cause of integration in racially exclusive communities. Descriptions of smart, well-behaved, and well-groomed African American and Korean black children playing happily with their white neighbors were potent symbols of the ideals at stake in struggles to overcome segregation and racism in the United States. The goals of adoptive parents of Korean black children like the Warrens and the Nelsons demonstrate why issues of family life motivated people to work to overcome the legacies of racial inequality.

Although some social workers demonstrated a greater acceptance of interracial neighborhoods as ideal places for Korean black children, they struggled to resolve their own, and some parents', concerns about color matching. As we saw in chapter 2, some social workers seemed insensitive to or unresponsive to African Americans' concerns about color matching. These child welfare professionals were alternately worried that families wanted light-skinned children because of internalized self-hatred, or they were confused when families rejected a child who was lighter than either prospective adoptive parent. The social workers who attempted to match Korean black children with their adoptive parents seemed to exhibit similar responses. SooJin Pate recounts that nonprofessionals and social workers made detailed and, at times, unflattering notes about the Korean child's appearance. Although I focus on the ways officials attempted to classify color, Pate explains that officials also inspected Korean children's bodies to assess their health and their attractiveness.[68] ISS records suggest that many social workers fumbled through the tricky task of classifying Korean black children's color. Social workers took detailed notes to describe the techniques they used to classify children based on their complexions. This tendency was evident when ISS's Margaret A. Valk asked her contact in Korea to assist the Korean social workers with their descriptions of each child's physical features. The descriptions of one particular Korean black child had prompted Valk to make this request because she was struggling to determine if he would match either of the families they had in mind for him.[69]

Anne M. Davidson of ISS-Korea seemed alternately perplexed by or worried about skin complexion and hair texture when matching Korean black children with their prospective parents. Describing a young girl she wanted to place with an African American family, Davidson explained that the girl's "hair is kinky for about two inches from her head, and then for the next six inches it is absolutely straight." In her report about this child, she sent objects to attempt to label the girl's appearance. Davidson explained, "the light brown paper is matched to her face . . . the light nylon stocking is an attempt to match . . . also with her face." For the child's stomach and thighs Davidson sent a dark brown sample with the warning that the girl "is this dark but may be a bit more on the browner side, and not quite so chocolate coloured [sic]." She closed her report with a crayon sample that she thought also matched the child's stomach. Although Davidson's obsessive attention to the details of this child's complexion goes well beyond the kind of observation that would allow a social worker to successfully place a child, it does suggest a troubling manifestation of racial essentialism. In her effort to devise a strategy to make a match based on color, she seems to be projecting her anxieties about race and color onto the child's body and replicating a racial hierarchy that inscribed gradations of complexion as the marked categories that mattered in adoption.[70]

Some concern about race matching was warranted, as many couples were interested in having children who matched their families. Peter and Bonnie Tanner knew that it might be hard to match their complexions since he was Filipino and she was African American. But Mrs. Tanner had attempted to contact the Refugee Relief Program to find out about adopting two mixed-race Korean children who might look like they were the biological children of this interracial couple.[71] The James family was pleased when their daughter arrived and her complexion matched both husband and wife. Mr. and Mrs. James were dark-skinned, and they assured their social worker, who must have been concerned that they wanted a lighter child, that their daughter's color did not matter to them.[72] Some couples were not as accepting as Mr. and Mrs. James. One family rejected a child because he was too dark. The mother in this case explained that she did not think her husband would accept a dark child. The social worker's notes explained that her husband was light and she was darker, and their biological child matched her complexion more than her husband's.[73] Some women seemed to have stronger feelings about the issue of color, especially when there was a marked difference in complexion between husband and wife. Mrs. Lawrence initially worried that the child they received was too dark for their family. She changed her mind when she saw how pleased her husband was with their new daughter. The social worker evaluating their case considered this to be an important revelation for Mrs. Lawrence because it might help her feel better about herself and her complexion. Apparently, Mr. Lawrence shared the social worker's hopes because he described not caring if his daughter did have a dark complexion.[74]

Families were not only concerned if children were too dark. In some cases, like that of Mr. and Mrs. James mentioned above, the couples commented when a child was lighter than either parent. In 1960, Mrs. Woods reported that she frequently had to tell people that her Korean black daughter was in fact part African American.[75] The social worker assigned to the Brady family was glad to learn that they did not have a definite color preference. They were prepared for their daughter's very fair skin even though she was lighter than they had expected. They conveyed that she was still the complexion of one of their nieces and this was reassuring for the couple.[76]

The meanings African Americans ascribed to their adoptive children's complexions ranged widely, but these examples show that some parents were not bothered if a child was lighter or darker than other members of their families. Although social workers believed that families preferred children with lighter complexions, as chapter 2 discusses, this desire was not central to all families' decisions to adopt. Some parents like Peter and Bonnie Tanner wanted a child that matched their complexions. But many African Americans, as well as whites, did acknowledge the existence of a color hierarchy that associated beauty, intelligence, and even class status with lighter skin complexions and dictated that darker tones signified a lack of intelligence or beauty. These families could not escape the influence of color in determining the way a child would fare in societies where racial identity defined a person's access to many opportunities. In these cases, both race and complexion mattered, and some parents believed an adopted child's lighter complexion was a valuable form of social currency.

Some officials with ISS and child welfare agencies in the United States also began to recognize the unique role interracial couples could play as adoptive parents of mixed-race Korean children. A few of the adopting families of Korean black children included parents who were mixed-race themselves, and they offered their children important tools to combat the teasing and taunting they experienced at school and in other public settings. The social worker assigned to the Douglas family was optimistic about this family's future because both parents were mixed-race. She concluded that because both Mr. and Mrs. Douglas had white and African American parents, they would be equipped to help their adopted child come to terms with his identity.[77]

For the Wilsons, interracial family ties helped them resolve an unpleasant incident their Korean black daughter had in 1961. When a classmate of the Wilsons' Korean black daughter called her a nigger, they took action by explaining to her the dangers of prejudice and the history of mixed-race peoples in the United States. This explanation was likely very meaningful coming from these parents because Mrs. Wilson had an African American parent and a white parent, and Mr. Wilson identified as Mexican and African American. When the Wilsons described the situation to their social worker, they acknowledged that a part of their challenge lay in the fact that their daughter "had always considered herself as Korean and believes that now she is an American." These parents had to explain that even though she was an American, some people might only see her as a person of color. They then took their adopted Korean black daughter along with their other adopted daughters—two German-black and one African American and white—to see a production of *Uncle Tom's Cabin*. They hoped it would help her better understand a part of her history.[78]

Very little evidence exists that allows us to know how the Korean black children of the first generation of Korean transnational adoptions sorted out the challenges of identity formation. However, scholarship on the experiences of later generations of Korean adoptees suggests that families like the Wilsons were offering useful tools to their adopted children. For example, Nam Soon Huh evaluated the ethnic identity formation of Korean adoptees to assess which factors allowed them to develop a sense of belonging in their adopted culture and their natal culture. Huh notes that studies have offered mixed, and in some cases, contradictory conclusions. But a number show that some transracially and transnationally adopted children demonstrated ambivalence about issues of race and ethnicity. As Kim Park Nelson theorizes, transracial and transnational adoptees' ambivalence about issues of race and ethnicity are "related to the pressure many feel to pick a side."[79] Other studies show that these adoptees identified with the ethnic identity of their adoptive parents. Still others seemed able to incorporate aspects of both their natal and adoptive cultures into their sense of who they were.

Although the parents in the Huh studies were white, the findings are still significant for this current project because they suggest that adoptees responded well in situations where there were "ethnic discussions in the home, [and] parents have friends or work colleagues who are Asian."[80] Indeed, Huh concludes that children who demonstrated integrated identities or "biethnic" identities had participated in cultural activities that reinforced their positive associations with the cultural traditions of their birth and adoptive families. Huh also observes that this type of adjustment was related to the level of parental support for and involvement in these cultural activities.[81] Consequently, it seems possible that African American and interracial parents who attempted to use Korean words at home (like the Drummonds, discussed in this chapter's opening section) or helped their children learn about their Korean and African American heritages to buffer them against racists assaults (like the Taylors and the Wilsons discussed above) might have helped equip their children for the lifelong process of defining what it meant to be a Korean black person in a nation plagued by racial conflict and tensions. Conversely, families that attempted to avoid discussions about ethnicity, race, and nationality in an attempt to shield their children or protect themselves from the emotional discomfort that such conversations could cause (like the Seavers) may have reinforced negative ideas about their children's cultural heritages. However, it seems likely that Korean black children raised in predominantly African American communities would have identified with many aspects of black culture even as they struggled with questions about Korea and their Korean birth families.

In the 1950s and 1960s, it was politically significant when child welfare agencies supported the creation of families that normalized examples of interracial cooperation and interracial intimacy. In some cases, these efforts were responses to African American freedom struggles that drew attention to the ways segregation and racial inequality influenced adoption policies. African American families adopted the largest number of Korean black children between 1953 and 1964, the same years in which civil rights activism produced significant movement on the racial justice front and revealed the most destructive aspects of US racism to the world. Child welfare officials' support of families that in any way promoted the acceptance of integration, no matter how trivial or intimate, forced a recognition of aspects of the nation's troubled interracial past that many white political leaders would have preferred to keep hidden. For this reason, the adoptions of Korean black children by racially marked families exposed the contradictions inherent in the rhetoric of democracy and the realities of US race relations.[82]

During the Cold War era, national politics became a site of protracted struggles over the pace and nature of civil rights and integration. As the federal government attempted to stabilize mainstream anxieties over social change in the United States, it also had to defend the nation's dismal record of racial injustice abroad. Political leaders who attempted to meet the demands of African American political constituencies had to fight the Southern Democrats who resisted any support of civil rights legislation. Liberal and conservative political leaders alike took advantage of anticommunist fervor to slow the pace of social change by linking many prominent liberal African American organizations with the ominous communist threat. However, in a number of high-profile cases, international pressure helped to compel the federal government to make some adjustments to prove the nation's commitment to democratic ideals. This pressure led to greater opportunities for some African Americans because "world opinion still required some evidence that the United States could respond positively to demands for racial justice."[83] In other words, the nation needed to create opportunities to showcase examples of interracial cooperation. In some instances, US-Korean adoptions helped further this project.

White Americans Interpret the New Domestic Ideal

Although few in number, white families adopted Korean black children during the first two decades of US-Korean adoption. They also benefited from the changing institutional definitions of ideal domestic spaces that evolved because of both Cold War anxieties and civil rights activism. As social workers expanded the scope of adoption options for Korean black children to include families that defied gender and race expectations, they also experimented with transracial and transnational adoptions that paired white families with Korean black children. Acting out of a range of motivations, a few of these families endeavored to demonstrate how integration and interracial cooperation were good for the nation's white and nonwhite adoptive families. And some did not "dismiss foreign orphans' racial and national differences as unimportant" as some scholars have suggested.[84]

One of the earliest recorded cases of a white family requesting a Korean black child involved the Martins. A Quaker couple, the Martins had learned of the circumstances of Korea's displaced children from Mr. Martin's father. While working with the American Friends Service Committee's (AFSC) project "Houses for Korea," he had observed the conditions that made it difficult for Korean mothers to keep their Korean black children. The AFSC had begun its work assisting Koreans in 1953, and it coordinated a program to provide materials and to train people to rebuild homes in the areas devastated by the war. After the elder Mr. Martin told his son and daughter-in-law what he experienced, they became determined to adopt two Korean black daughters. Their state child welfare agency approved their application to the surprise of ISS officials in 1956. ISS caseworkers noted that the state child welfare representatives did not see a problem with racial differences between the children and the adoptive parents.[85] ISS officials did consider that the placement might be beneficial for the two light-complexioned Korean black girls because they thought growing up in a white family might mean that the girls would not face as much discrimination as they might with an African American family. While this idea flipped the logic of placing Korean black children with African American families, it did line up with proposals that some NUL officials were making regarding transracial adoptions for light-complexioned African American children in the States. As described in chapter 2, in 1955 and 1956 the NUL's adoption project began endorsing transracial adoptions that were not cross-color adoptions.[86]

Both Mr. and Mrs. Martin worked outside the home and, in this way, they were like many of the African American and interracial couples who adopted Korean black children. Mr. Martin was an elevator salesman and Mrs. Martin was a registered nurse. Social workers also noted that they claimed mixed-ethnic ancestry. Mr. Martin shared that his family was French, German Dutch, and Indian. Mrs. Martin was a Canadian who claimed Irish, Norwegian, and Dutch ancestry. It is unclear if the parents volunteered this information or if the social worker asked for their ethnic heritage. But the fact that the social worker included this information in the case file suggests that the parents and/or social workers were sensitive to the ways that race and ethnicity shaped their notions of identity. The social worker assisting the Martins registered no reservations about Mrs. Martin keeping her job. However, she did make her evaluation of the family's finances based solely on Mr. Martin's income. He earned $6,000 annually and had investments and insurance totaling more than $6,000. The couple owned a thirty-two-acre farm and had almost $8,000 in savings. Whatever questions ISS may have had about racial difference, they were not worried about this family's ability to provide for their Korean black daughters.[87]

While religion certainly motivated some white families to consider adopting a Korean black child, other factors also led these families and the child welfare officials evaluating their cases. With the exception of one family, the following describes the ways that ideas about race motived the small sample of white families that adopted Korean black children. These cases demonstrate that, to varying degrees, the families were aware of what the adoption of a Korean black child would suggest about race relations in the United States. Although social workers considered their desire to adopt across racial lines unusual, they also concluded that certain families possessed important attributes that would allow them to parent a child with both Korean and African American ancestry. By the early 1960s, some social workers had already observed or heard about the successful transracial placements of Korean-white and full-Korean children with white families. A number had likely heard about the domestic placements of children of African American and white or African American and Jewish parents with white families that began in the late 1940s. Some child welfare agencies were also willing to place Korean black children with white parents because of the challenges of recruiting a substantial pool of African American adoptive parents. But the case notes also show that the rhetoric and ideals of civil rights coupled with the anxieties of the Cold War influenced white adoptive parents and child welfare professionals' opinions about transracial and transnational adoptions.

When the Ellisons applied to adopt a Korean black child in 1961, there were aspects of Mrs. Ellison's personal history that would have raised red flags in the 1950s. Mrs. Ellison had a son from her first marriage that ended in divorce. After the birth of her second child, she left her job as a millinery buyer to take care of their home. The life the Ellisons were able to build together appeared ideal in many other ways. Mr. Ellison was a chemist who worked in plastics and earned $8,000 annually. They had an eleven-room home that cost $20,000, and life insurance amounting to $18,000. While she seemed concerned about the problems the family might face following the adoption of a Korean black child, the social worker evaluating the family concluded that they had given significant thought to what it would mean to raise a child that had Asian and African American ancestry. She was also impressed that they had already talked about the kinds of reactions they might get from family, friends, and neighbors. They told one social worker that they knew they would face challenges, but they had talked about their plan with an African American couple they described as close friends. While there is no note of her response to this discussion, it is possible that the social worker was reassured by the idea that the family knew at least one African American couple well enough to seek out their advice on such a personal and potentially controversial choice.[88]

The potential for racial problems worried the Gatlings when they petitioned to adopt a Korean child in 1964. Social workers originally matched this family with a child they thought was Korean white but she began to show signs of being Korean black before she arrived in the United States. When social workers informed the Gatlings of their suspicion about the child's racial heritage, the couple hesitated before agreeing to proceed with the adoption. The Gatlings explained that they did not question their ability to parent or love a Korean black child, but they worried about the kinds of challenges the child would face growing up in a white family. They were also uncertain of the girl's prospects once she became old enough to date and consider marriage. However, they were not concerned about any social pressure they might experience, and Mr. Gatling said he was prepared to lose friends over the decision. Although the Gatlings decided to adopt the girl in question, the case records include a note that they did wonder if an African American family might be a better match.[89]

The Kents were less concerned about the challenges they might face when they applied to adopt a Korean black daughter in 1963. Mr. Kent was of Hungarian Jewish descent and his wife claimed German, Scotch, and Native American ancestry. They had five children, but they wanted another child for what they admitted to be selfish reasons. The Kents believed the adoption would bring them fulfillment. They specifically wanted a daughter, and they anticipated that adopting a child would be its own reward. Mr. Kent earned $14,000 annually and he seemed guilty for his good fortune. Both Mr. and Mrs. Kent explained that it was important for them to help a child who had experienced hardships.[90]

The Gordons also had motives stemming from their hope that the child would bring something special to their family when they applied to adopt a Korean black child in 1963. They saw the need for racial equality in the United States and abroad, and they believed that adopting a Korean black child would allow them to model racial harmony for their community. Prior to their effort to adopt a Korean black child, the Gordons had attempted to adopt an African American child. But social workers who handled this family's first application did not trust their motives. As Mrs. Gordon explained, while in college years earlier, she had worked in a children's home where she became concerned about interracial problems. Mr. Gordon described that his father had worked for the African American college Hampton Institute. As a child he had black playmates and went to church with black people. Mr. Gordon became a minister and his church boasted one African American family on the membership rolls and one African American on the church's board. The Gordons also knew a family who had adopted a Korean child. Although the social worker assessing the Gordons noted that these explanations were unusual, she seemed to accept them as good indications that the Gordons had thought about how they would manage the challenges they would face when they adopted a Korean black child.[91]

While most white prospective adoptive parents did not explicitly connect their desire to adopt a Korean black child with the Civil Rights Movement, the Pritchetts did. When the Pritchetts adopted their Korean black daughter in 1963, Mrs. Pritchett explained that the couple's religious beliefs predisposed them to engage in philanthropic causes. They were Quakers and Mrs. Pritchett had volunteered in settlement houses for Hispanic people. Then she had the opportunity to care for an African American baby when she worked as a caseworker. Mrs. Pritchett also had a brother who had adopted a daughter whose birth parents were African American and white. Mrs. Pritchett was proud to report that her extended family accepted this placement without any hesitation. Mr. Pritchett was more forthcoming with his motives. He explained that he wanted to integrate his family and his community. Both thought that a Korean black child would help their birth children understand their parents' efforts to advance racial equality. Social workers approved their adoption, but the Pritchetts soon had a small glimpse of the harsh realities of race in their community when the owners of a private pool denied the family a membership because they had a Korean black child.[92]

In 1971, *New York Times* reporter Gary Brooten included many families like the Pritchetts in an article, "The Multiracial Family," that described what Brooten considered to be a revolution in adoption. One family had adopted several children of different racial backgrounds, and when asked why, they stated very simply that at the beginning of their marriage they "started worrying about the population explosion." They explained, "they wanted children, they found children of other races who needed homes—and took them in." The article went on to celebrate the conviction these families demonstrated because it inspired other white families who saw the adoption of brown children as "something you do because you think it's right." Brooten described the challenges these families faced because of what they termed reverse discrimination and inverted white racism. Most often, they encountered questions about how they would help their children navigate racism and develop strong identities. Each couple seemed fairly confident that they could raise their children to be strong individuals who were "proud of [their] racial heritage." But they were baffled by the hostility they experienced from members of communities of color who questioned not only their abilities but also their motives. To combat these questions, the families described their efforts to "give black friends, black art, black literature, and culture an honored (but not dominating) place in the home." The article closed noting that a number of child welfare officials were impressed by the efforts of these adoption pioneers who were changing how people thought about race and family in the United States. These officials congratulated the white adoptive parents of African American and mixed-race children born in the United States and abroad for their "commitment to racial harmony."[93]

African American and interracial families played important roles in the US-Korean adoptions that transformed how some child welfare professionals defined ideal families for mixed-race children. But their involvement in transnational adoptions failed to capture the attention of mainstream communities or the mainstream media in the same ways that white families' transracial and transnational adoptions did. Instead, the collective memory of this episode of transracial and transnational adoption focused on the experiences of white couples that made their families the centerpieces of a new ideal in adoption. The "exciting new laboratory of family dynamics" that Brooten described owed its novelty to the fact that white couples were entering the world of transracial and transnational adoption in unprecedented numbers. Their actions were reassuring to some who worried about the state of race relations in the United States. Stories about white families that wanted to model racial harmony, like Mr. Pritchett, suggest ways the rhetoric and ideals of civil rights shaped some white people's ideas about their adoptions of non-white children. These ideas would dominate discussions about what constituted the most secure future for Korean children, including the Korean black children whom child welfare officials had originally worked diligently to place with African American and interracial families.

The changes some adoption agencies made to accommodate African Americans' adoptions of Korean black children expose how and why institutional definitions of ideal adoptive families were flexible in the first decades of US-Korean adoption. Although child welfare professionals agreed that the work of mothering should take precedence over a woman's paid labor outside of the home, they recognized that many African American women had, of necessity, paired paid labor and successful parenting for their biological children, and for their formally and informally adopted children. These women confounded the notion that mothers working outside of their homes produced dysfunction in their families. Instead, African American and interracial adoptive families that included working mothers acquainted social workers with childcare plans that involved wives, husbands, neighbors, and the local institutions that had sustained African American families for decades. These families displayed their own version of stable family life that allowed them to meet the demands of post–World War II domesticity.

The successful adoptions of Korean black children also demonstrated the inherent value of placements that put mixed-race children in interracial homes and integrated communities. A few child welfare officials became convinced that interracial couples and families that lived in integrated neighborhoods were uniquely positioned to disarm anxieties over interracial intimacies at a time when civil rights struggles and the nation's history of troubled race relations threatened to undermine US foreign relations. Additionally, these families showed that civil rights successes held intrinsic value for the nation's white citizens. Paradoxically, while communities of color helped transform the image of the multiracial adoptive family in child welfare settings, the patterns families of color introduced as healthy accommodations to institutional inequality took on new meaning when white families attempted to adopt Korean black children.

The white couples that adopted Korean black children presented a new challenge to social workers who were attempting to define the value of multiracial families in placements involving mixed-race children. Throughout the 1950s, child welfare officials had largely agreed to match mixed-race Korean children with families that were the same race as the child's father. This practice revealed the ways the nation's history of racial inequality and segregation influenced child welfare practices and policies. But the growth in transracial adoptions of children of color in the United States and transnational adoptions of Korean children caused some white adoptive parents and child welfare officials to envision an expanded role for white families in both adoption schemes. It is revealing that the white families that made up the small sample considered in this study did not describe their transracial and transnational adoptions as demonstrations of color-blind love. Rather, these families were keenly aware of the ways that issues of race and identity informed their decisions. Some even imagined that their multiracial families would demonstrate the potential for interracial love and harmony to overcome racial intolerance in the United States.

Yet, popular ideas about white families' involvement in transracial and transnational adoptions would advance the notion of color-blind love as the most significant factor in this type of family formation. Chapter 5 explores the role Pearl S. Buck played in the construction of popular narratives of transracial and transnational adoption that emphasized color-blind love. As a novelist and nonprofessional adoption reformer, Buck attempted to transform unfavorable ideas about mixed-race children and the families that would adopt them. Buck paired the ideals and rhetoric of civil rights with Cold War rhetoric to advocate for reforms to assist African American and interracial adoptive families. But she also championed white families' adoptions of nonwhite children as one of her many strategies to assist mixed-race children of Asian descent in the United States and abroad.

5

Pearl S. Buck and the Institutional and Rhetorical Reframing of US and Korean Adoption

In a 1946 article written for *Cosmopolitan* magazine, Pulitzer and Nobel Prize–winning novelist Pearl S. Buck declared that she would not adopt a child of a different race. The complicated nature of adoptions involving families of the same race convinced Buck, an adoptive mother, that there was no easy way to manage adoption with racial differences added into the mix. She cautioned couples interested in adoption to consider not only race when choosing a child but also nationality, warning that parents of "warm Italian blood, [should] not adopt a child of cool Scandinavian ancestry." Well-known for her candor and considered an authority on matters relating to China and the so-called Far East, Buck was echoing ideas that informed the social work method of matching children and adoptive parents based on racial and religious sameness. Coming from Buck's pen, these sentiments were eerily reminiscent of eugenicists' beliefs about the influence of genetics on people's characteristics. Likely, Buck knew that these ideas informed how adoption agencies matched families and how social workers decided which families and children were suitable for adoption.[1]

By 1958, however, Buck had become a nonprofessional adoption reformer and a leading advocate for transracial and transnational adoption. Because she challenged matching in domestic adoption and supported proxy adoptions of Korean GI children, child welfare professionals monitored her activities in much the same way that they tried to keep track of Harry Holt, the so-called father of Korean adoption, and less-known people like the woman I call Alice Warren in chapter 3. Each of these individuals lacked any child welfare training. But they were motivated by their sense that professional child welfare communities were not doing enough to facilitate adoptions for mixed-race children of Asian descent. These individuals also believed that they needed to facilitate adoptions for these children because they were particularly vulnerable. But Buck's endeavors preceded those of many other non-professionals, and her efforts combined both institution-building and a narrative reconfiguration of mixed-race Asian children and interracial adoptive families. In the years between 1946 and 1958, Buck co-founded Welcome House, the first long-term foster home for mixed-race children of Asian descent in the United States. Then she transformed Welcome House into an adoption agency to serve mixed-race children of Asian descent in the United States and abroad. Buck implemented adoption strategies to place Welcome House children that were ahead of social work convention. An adoptive mother to five white children, one German black child, two Japanese black children, and foster mother to several "Amerasian" children, Buck believed that her family—as well as the families she helped create through Welcome House—affirmed the idea that color-blind love could triumph over racism.

Buck frequently characterized her transition from an opponent of transracial adoption to a leading advocate for transracial and transnational placements as simply a humane response to the circumstances that constrained mixed-race children's lives in the United States and Asian nations. However, the chronicle of her transition indicates a more agonizing struggle. Buck's early ideas about transracial adoption reflected her acceptance of child welfare policies that child welfare officials created to police the boundaries of race in adoptive family formation. Buck had to confront these ideas when she became involved in the effort to find an adoptive family for an American-born child whose "East Indian" father and white, American mother could not marry or keep him. Similarly, her first transracial and transnational adoption grew out of complicated personal and political motives. Buck adopted her German black daughter because of her sincere desire to parent the young girl. But one of her associates also explained that it was a symbolic and politically motivated gesture to demonstrate her commitment to racial equality.[2] These experiences shaped Buck's ideas about the need for institutions to assist mixed-race children. Thereafter, Buck made adoption reform a part of her effort to persuade her closest peers, her neighbors, and a national audience that inequality in adoption undermined Americans' claims to truly democratic principles.

The transformations in Buck's personal and professional involvement in adoption illustrate some of the ways that nonprofessional adoption reformers attempted to provide the most secure future possible for mixed-race children of Asian descent. Buck's strategy took shape and evolved in the context of post–World War II renegotiations of family and race that linked America's return to so-called normalcy to a number of fictions about the home. One fiction identified the healthy, nuclear family as a symbol of a healthy secure nation. Buck attempted to facilitate the adoptions of mixed-race children of Asian descent in the United States and Korea by literally and figuratively inserting them in the story of US family and national stability. After Buck established Welcome House, she crafted a rescue narrative that made the transracial adoptive family a symbol of the nation's benevolence and leadership in campaigns to protect civil rights and contain communism. But she did not depend on appeals to benevolence alone. In this chapter, I argue that Buck's adoption narrative encouraged families, including African American families, to adopt mixed-race children of Asian descent because of what she identified as the children's hybrid superiority.[3]

Scholars including Peter Conn, Christian Klein, and Emily Cheng have assessed the gender and racial implications of Buck's cultural discourses on adoption. Buck biographers like Conn often point to the progressive quality of her position on a number of issues, including transracial and transnational adoption, to describe and explain the liberal, antiracist, anticolonial, and anticommunist nature of her activism during the Cold War era.[4] But a number of scholars have interpreted Buck's activities and motivations differently. For example, Cheng questions the extent to which Buck's work produced a counternarrative to Cold War ideals in her cultural productions and activism. She notes that Buck's post–World War II activism retained elements of her commitment to the ideals of secular liberalism even though her "approach to race and family were congruent with the dominant logics of US Cold War imperial expansion coupled with domestic containment, in particular the political investment in the family."[5]

Similarly, scholars that explore the development of US transracial and transnational adoption in the post–World War II era have mixed assessments of her adoption activism and work as an institution-builder. For example, Laura Briggs identifies Welcome House, the adoption agency Buck founded, as "one of the most important midcentury liberal adoption efforts,"[6] and Ellen Herman explains that Buck was one of the three "most important early critics of matching."[7] However, while many agree that Buck was instrumental in the creation of transracial and transnational adoption, Christina Klein characterizes aspects of Buck's post–World War II adoption work as a departure from her more progressive prewar anticolonial and antiracist activism. Klein identifies Buck as a leading liberal activist whose critiques of racism in US domestic and foreign policy through her popular writings positioned her solidly in the public and political spheres. However, she suggests that Buck responded to pressure from the right to soften her position on political issues, which led her to pursue family- and child-centric activism, including founding Welcome House. Klein does acknowledge that Buck's advocacy of transracial and transnational adoptive families was the result of her desire for "racial justice," but she contends that it represented a retreat "into the private, traditionally female sphere of the family" where Buck could continue to "speak out on issues of racism and US-Asian relations, although in a less direct way."[8]

I contend that Buck's motives for and methods of promoting adoptions of mixed-race children of Asian descent evolved to meet changing needs and sociopolitical contexts. As the contexts changed, so too did Buck's activism and her sense of mixed-race children's experiences and needs. Buck deliberately designed her early writings about adoption, such as her 1946 *Cosmopolitan* article mentioned earlier, to include rather mild criticisms of the cultural, social, and institutional forms of racism that affected mixed-race children. But later, her work in support of the institutions she founded contained more pointed critiques of the political systems and ideologies that sustained inequality. This chapter begins with an assessment of the ways Buck created an institutional framework and a rescue narrative that helped transform how white adoptive families responded to mixed-race children of Asian descent born in the United States. It then evaluates how Buck's efforts to define what constituted the most secure future for mixed-race Korean children helped transform the roles that white families and, to a lesser degree, African American families played in the adoptions of and long-term care strategies for mixed-race children of Asian descent in the United States and mixed-race children Korea.[9]

Welcome House and Buck's First Personal and Political Adoption Endeavors

The daughter of Presbyterian missionaries, Buck had spent most of her youth in China, where she met and married her first husband, John Lossing Buck. The couple had one biological daughter, Carol, and the circumstances of her birth would lead to Pearl's first interest in adoption.[10] Following Carol's birth, Buck underwent a hysterectomy because doctors identified medical problems that would have made a second pregnancy difficult and potentially dangerous. Unable to have another child, Buck turned to adoption to fulfill her desire to parent more children. She adopted one daughter, Janice, in 1924 while still married to John. In 1935, Buck divorced John and married Richard Walsh, president of John Day Publishing Company. Together they adopted two sons in 1936, when Buck was forty-three years old and Walsh was fifty. The couple adopted another son and daughter a year later. Walsh and Buck's struggles to adopt these children introduced them to the adoption practices and standards that she would lash out against when she established Welcome House. The couple's final adoptions brought one German black and two Japanese black daughters into the family and exposed the couple to the challenges of transracial and transnational adoption. Although they did not legally adopt more children, they fostered many and called themselves grandparents to the children that would live at the permanent foster home, Welcome House.[11]

Buck would always say that her adoption work began with two young boys that child welfare professionals labeled unadoptable because they were mixed-race children of Asian descent. She learned of the first child in December 1948. Since returning to the States in the 1930s, Buck had written extensively in popular magazines describing her support for China, weighing in on other issues related to the "Far East," and detailing her experiences with adoption agencies. These writings and her contacts with people from India living in America brought her to the attention of a very concerned representative of the Community Home for Girls in Rochester, New York. This official contacted Buck because she was worried about the fate of Robbie, a child she could not place using normal channels. The child's mother was a white American woman and his father was a young man from India. Unmarried, the couple could not keep their son. Neither of the parents' families wanted to take the child, whom the official described as "of high intelligence . . . the finest child they had ever had." The representative from the Community Home was concerned that the last option for this toddler was placement in a segregated institution that housed "Negro" children. The official with the Community Home for Girls believed it would be unjust for Robbie to end up in a facility for children of color because she considered both of his parents to be technically "Caucasian."[12] In many of her published accounts of this story, Buck denied the blatant racism in this comment and was quick to defend the representative, saying she was not prejudiced against African Americans. But Buck and the representative well knew that placement in the "Negro" orphanage would fix the child's status as a second-class citizen.[13]

After calling several of her friends to see if they had room for this *exceptional* child, and learning that no one wanted him, Buck consulted with her own family, and they decided to take him into their home. Within a week, she learned of another mixed-race child who also needed a home. Her family took him, too. Buck knew that social workers would not allow her or her husband to adopt the boys legally because of their ages. Buck was fifty-six. Walsh was sixty-three. Most adoption agencies in the United States applied restrictions that classified couples older than forty years of age as ineligible for adoption. These events motivated Buck to open Welcome House, a permanent foster home, to accommodate mixed-race children of Asian descent in the United States. She opened Welcome House after talking with her friends Kermit and Margaret Fischer, residents of her hometown of Doylestown, Pennsylvania. Working with the Fischers, Buck registered Welcome House with the Pennsylvania Department of State in December 1948.[14] They received approval to operate a single-family dwelling, and five children entered the home in 1949. Seven more children joined the Welcome House family in 1950.[15] Agencies as far from Doylestown as the Cradle Society of Evanston, Illinois sent children to Buck, and by 1951, Welcome House was at its capacity. Consequently, Buck and the agency's board decided to open Welcome House II.[16]

While Buck was a pioneer in these areas, she was not alone. A small number of child welfare professionals and non-professionals were beginning to experiment with transracial and transnational placements and adoptions in the late 1940s. Here it is worth mentioning the innovations Louise Wise Agency introduced because they were similar to Buck's and represented the "cutting edge" of the domestic adoption reforms that took place in the 1950s. Philanthropist Louise Waterman Wise started the Free Synagogue Child Adoption Committee in 1916. Originally an agency that specialized in the placement of Jewish children with Jewish adoptive parents, Wise's agency also faced the challenge of placing the mixed-race children of Jewish and African American parents, and the mixed-race children of Jewish and Puerto Rican parents. Like the many Catholic and Protestant agencies that were placing children in the early twentieth century, Jewish agencies adhered to the requirement that they place children with families that shared the religious beliefs of a child's birth parents.[17]

However, Wise's daughter, Judge Justine Wise Polier, encouraged the agency's board to abandon race and religious matching protocols after she became president of the Committee in 1946. A graduate of Yale Law School, Polier was a family court judge and the first female appointed to serve as a judge on Manhattan's Domestic Relations Court by Mayor Fiorella La Guardia in 1935. Polier's experiences serving on the court informed her ideas about adoption. By the late 1940s, Polier and officials with the newly renamed Louise Wise Services had observed the ways that matching did not serve the best interests of some children. After 1952, the agency began to abandon matching to arrange transracial adoptions. Throughout the 1950s and 1960s, several public child welfare agencies in states including Minnesota, Oregon, and California followed suit and approved transracial placements for mixed-race, African American, and Native American children.[18] The efforts of non-professionals who worked to expand adoption options for mixed-race and minority children were instrumental in pushing more child welfare professionals to devise strategies to assist children they labeled "hard to place" or "unadoptable." Buck and Welcome House modeled one version of the kind of strategy that inspired such innovations.

Although Welcome House was Buck's idea, the venture would not have been possible without the support of key members of her community. Buck first consulted with Margaret Fischer, who had been a social worker. Years later, Fischer remembered that their next move was to convince their husbands that a facility like Welcome House would work

in a small, insular community. They consulted with Judge Edward Biester and his wife Muriel, hoping that the local judge's connections on
the Orphan's Court would help them navigate that court system. Seeing
a conflict of interest, Judge Biester declined but Muriel accepted. Buck's
neighbor David Burpee and his wife Lois Torrance Burpee, a botanist,
also became board members. David was heir to and owner of the W.
Atlee Burpee Company and Burpee Seeds, the largest seed company in
the world. It is likely that the company's work in hybrid seed cultiva-
tion influenced some of Buck's ideas about the mixed-race children she
often referred to as hybrids. Buck and Fischer considered the first board
strong enough to raise money and positively influence people's ideas
about the children once the well-regarded lyricist and librettist Oscar
Hammerstein II and his wife Dorothy became board members.[19]

The funding for Welcome House came from donations and the
board's fund-raising efforts. Lois Burpee remembered that board members' first responsibility was to raise money, and they did in a number
of ways. Some gave talks for civic organizations or at local churches.
Christmas themed efforts were popular, and they sponsored a yearly
Christmas card fund drive. The Biesters hosted an annual Christmas
dance party that once collected approximately $1,000 for the house. The
Hammersteins held several fashion shows in their home that featured
professional models. Dorothy Hammerstein donated money she earned
as an interior designer, and she organized a number of theatrical shows
that raised money for the Welcome House. Other board members gave
money and resources to support the Welcome House family, and they
encouraged friends and colleagues to do the same. Oscar Hammerstein's
writing partner Richard Rogers financed the first Welcome House mortgage. Hammerstein's son-in-law Philip Mathias wrote the play "With the
Happy Children" about the Welcome House to raise funds for the peren-
nially cash-strapped venture. Doylestown residents also contributed the
proceeds of a volunteer thrift shop to show their support for the family.[20]

Buck's effort to reconfigure the mixed-race children and the interracial Welcome House family involved manipulating the family's lived
environment to create distance between them and the unfavorable circumstances of their pasts. To accomplish this shift, Buck attempted to
make the lives of the Welcome House children look like the lives of other
children in the community. Buck surrounded the children with the trap-

pings of postwar modernity. Once she gained the permission and support of Doylestown's storekeeper, local leaders, and school officials, Buck fashioned lives for the Welcome House family that could rival those of any of her well-to-do neighbors. Buck asked the Yoders, a well-known and liked Mennonite couple, to serve as Welcome House parents. She also purchased a sixteen-room farmhouse adjacent to her lavish country cottage and remodeled the home to make it suitable for the Welcome House family.[21]

It seems that Buck succeeded in actually making the children's lives quite exceptional. Viola Yoder, the first Welcome House mother, remembered that Buck supervised the meal planning, insisting that the children ate "spinach and baked potatoes . . . cereal that came from a certain mill, [a] certain bread."[22] Buck personally purchased new clothing for the children, refusing to accept donated clothes that were not good quality. Dana Akins, a schoolmate of the Welcome House children, remembered envying their clothes because they always had the latest fashions.[23] Buck worked to get the children into the local schools, and they had tutors to assist with their education. Using her own strained resources, Buck often paid for toys, repairs to the house, and family vacations. She seemed determined that the children would not simply have parents, a home, and access to food, clothes, toys, and education: they would have the best Doylestown had to offer.

Buck designed the permanent foster homes Welcome House and Welcome House II to meet the needs of American-born, mixed-race children of Asian descent that other agencies labeled unadoptable. Buck believed this population was even harder to place than African American children who were consistently overlooked by most adoption agencies.[24] As discussed in chapter 2, child welfare professionals used the terms "hard-to-place" and "unadoptable" to describe older children, children of color, or children with congenital or developmental disabilities who were often underrepresented in statistics on completed adoptions. In 1950, Buck noted that few white families were willing to adopt a mixed-race child.[25] Consequently, these children often became wards of institutions. One of Buck's associates remembered hearing that social workers placed some mixed-race children of Asian descent in institutions for children with developmental disabilities because they were not accepted in any other setting.[26] Although not an adoptive family, Buck believed that the permanent foster home setting of the Welcome Houses was significantly better than such options. She capped the number of children in each home to keep either from resembling an institution. As child welfare agencies contacted her, referring more and more mixed-race children to the Welcome Houses, Buck and the board became concerned that they could not meet the needs of this ever-increasing population. By 1958, Welcome House II had closed, but Welcome House I was receiving approximately seventy referrals from agencies in the United States, Korea, Japan, Hong Kong, and Taiwan.[27]

During the first years of Welcome House, Buck worked to counter any negative ideas her neighbors might have had about the children by drawing attention to the ways the family's interracial makeup was an asset. Buck's approach played upon popular ideas of family life in the Cold War era. While dominant popular cultural representations defined the ideal family as white, nuclear, and middle-class, Buck believed people would accept her family because it conformed to postwar family ideals in all ways except for race. Americans consumed mainstream popular images that identified the family as a significant site where children learned morality, civic duty, and social order. Buck's interracial families took this idea a step further by modeling racial cooperation and acceptance. As several historians of American families in the Cold War era note, popular representations of the home and family offered reassuring messages about the safety and security of these spaces and relationships to people who were anxious because of Cold War conflicts. Buck configured the Welcome House family such that it could also allay fears about interracial intimacy and the integration of public and private spaces.[28]

However, pulling off this cultural inversion was challenging. The Welcome House children represented racial identities that revealed a level of interracial intimacy that confounded many in her community. The ledgers of the Welcome House that include an entry for each child referred to the agency show that the first children who lived in the permanent foster home setting represented some combination of American white, East Indian, Chinese, Japanese, and Korean. Although most US adoption agencies rarely arranged adoptions for mixed-race children of Asian descent born in the States, the ledgers show that these children were becoming a growing placement challenge by the early 1950s. Successive entries record intimacies between white women and Chinese men, Italian American women and Chinese Hawaiian men, Puerto Rican women and African American men.[29] These relationships exemplified interracial intimacies that were culturally taboo, if not legally prohibited in some states.

The interracial intimacies represented in the Welcome House ledgers provide a glimpse into the hidden history of interracial sex and marriage in the United States that scholars including Martha Hodes, Mary Ting Yi Lui, and Beth Bailey and David Farber have explored. Throughout the colonial era, intimacies between European men and Native American women evinced the gendered and racial nature of colonial conquest that made women and children particularly vulnerable. Extant evidence suggests that Native American and African women had relationships with European men that were largely coerced and violent. The children born of these relationships often experienced legal and social marginalization as a result of the laws the colonies enacted to constrain or deny their citizenship and status.[30] Throughout the nineteenth century, contests to increase the legal standing of individuals who chose partners across race revealed that people of African, Asian, and European descent were crossing color lines and creating families that often lacked the legal protections that white families enjoyed.[31] Twentieth-century challenges to the laws that prohibited interracial marriages would culminate in the 1967 *Loving v. Virginia* Supreme Court ruling that struck down the country's remaining anti-miscegenation laws.[32] But negative ideas about such interracial intimacies, and the children born to interracial couples, were dominant in the decades before and after the *Loving* decision. This history suggests the daunting nature of adoptive placements that Buck hoped to facilitate for mixed-race children.

According to Buck, this situation and the arrival of Lenny, a mixed-raced baby of Japanese and white descent, motivated her to mention the status of her charges during one of her public talks. Buck wondered aloud if communities like hers could embrace children whose racial differences would make it impossible to hide the fact that they were adopted. Muriel Biester remembered that Buck posed this question to a group during a talk in the neighboring town of Langhorne, Pennsylvania in 1951. According to Biester, Buck was speaking on a topic unrelated to adoption when she unexpectedly asked if anyone would adopt the charming Japanese child in her care.[33] At the end of the talk three couples approached Buck to say that they were interested in adopting Lenny. A minister and his wife, one of the couples at the talk, ultimately would adopt the child and become one of the first Welcome House adopting families. This response suggested to Buck that the answer to her question about the ability of white families to love and adopt non-white children was "yes," and she jumped at the opportunity to expand the agency's mission. Lois Burpee recalled that the Welcome House accepted ten children and placed six in 1951. In 1952, the agency accepted twelve children and placed ten. By the end of 1952, more than eighty families had submitted applications to adopt a Welcome House child.[34] From that point on, Welcome House would also serve as an adoption agency. In her book describing people's positive responses to the Welcome House Adoption Agency, Buck happily proclaimed that her "faith in Americans [was] renewed with every adoption."[35]

Buck and the Narrative of Hybrid Superiority

When Welcome House expanded from a permanent foster home to a full-fledged adoption agency, Buck crafted an adoption narrative for the media that highlighted the successes she observed in the residential home. Whether speaking to small crowds, writing to women's organizations or for women's magazines, or soliciting money to support the Welcome House, Buck's goal was to change the opinions of people in areas where families were likely to adopt a Welcome House child. She always described the children as beautiful and intelligent, and this tendency rubbed off on some of the families who adopted from the agency. Alice Hammerstein Mathias was the daughter of Oscar Hammerstein, and one of the first to adopt a child from Welcome House with her husband Philip. She referred to the intellectual prowess of her half-white, half–Japanese American children in an interview she had with one Buck biographer. Mathias proudly proclaimed, "both of them are very bright," and she called them "cute as a button."[36] Eve Eshleman, one of Buck's associates, remembered that Buck always described the Welcome House children as smart. Buck frequently mentioned the superiority of the Welcome House children to demonstrate that, unencumbered by the burdens of de jure and de facto segregation, the children's finest qualities would flourish.[37]

Buck's narrative of hybrid superiority contained elements of the model minority stereotype that emerged in the 1960s, in part, because of Chinese and Japanese activists' decades-long efforts to counter negative characterizations of their communities. These activists' goal was to improve Asians social and political standing in the United States. As historian Ellen D. Wu describes the process, Chinese and Japanese Americans utilized cultural, social, and political institutions to facilitate their transformation from "assimilating Other" to "model minority." Buck's narrative and institutional strategies to increase adoptions for mixed-race Asian children challenged negative stereotypes about the children by making them both the "assimilating Other" and the model adoptee. However, scholars in Asian Studies, Asian American History, and Critical Adoption Studies have shown why the model minority idea that Buck promoted was and is troubling. Although Wu identifies the ways that Japanese and Chinese activists mobilized the idea to resist oppression, many scholars argue that the myth of the model minority actually obscures differences among and between Asians and Asian Americans, and it reproduces oppression and exclusion. Indeed, the idea of the model minority that gained traction in white popular culture and among white politicians in the 1960s allowed these communities to celebrate Asians' assimilation and achievements and condemn African Americans for failing to do the same. In this way, the myth became a tool that allowed white communities to deny institutional racism.[38]

Further, adoption scholars have described the ways the media, adoptive families, and child welfare officials had a hand in constructing the Korean adoptee as an ideal immigrant because of her or his youth and assimilability.[39] The idea undergirding these efforts was that the children's *Asianness* was inconsequential, even erasable. Buck's narrative also emphasized the assimilability of her mixed-race subjects, but she endeavored to reverse unfavorable assessments of the children's Asian identities. She suggested that circumstances—and in her construction the love of good families—would shape how the children's "superior" qualities developed. This strategy led some white adoptive parents, who had historically avoided transracial placements, to believe that adoptions of nonwhite children benefited them as well as the children. It also reduced the children to a set of stereotypes that Buck originally framed as positive attributes.

The language Buck used to rehabilitate the image of mixed-race adoptive children was always positive but varied based on the audience she needed to persuade. For example, she often changed the story of the first Welcome House child, Robbie, to make the circumstances of his birth more romantic. The basic story begins with the letter Buck received telling her about a child born to a white, American mother and an "East Indian" father. The only details this version includes are that Robbie's parents were unable to keep him even though the boy "was of high intelligence."[40] In another version, Buck described the relationship between the Indian father and white American mother as defined by love. Having moved to India with her missionary parents, this young woman believed the "gospel of love—the brotherhood of man" that her parents preached. But when she became pregnant, her missionary parents sent her back to the States "alone to bear her baby."[41] No matter which details were embellished or omitted, the significant message of the story was that mixed-race children were victims of racial intolerance who needed "superior families who have no fears."[42] With the help of such families, Buck believed that mixed-race children would be assets to their families and the nation.

In order to appeal to a larger audience, Buck's narrative also recast mixed-race children of Asian descent as the embodiment of the best characteristics of every part of their heritage. This shift was central to the development of her version of the model adoptee. Buck's emphasis on the beauty and intelligence of the Welcome House children resembled theories promoted by sociologists in the early twentieth century who challenged negative ideas about mixed-race Chinese children—based on the theory of hybrid degeneracy—by theorizing that mixed-race children possessed superior qualities from both sides of their ancestry. According to scholar Emma Jinhau Teng, sociologists developed the notion of hybrid vigor that characterized Asian hybrids as "intelligent, strong, fit, and beautiful."[43] Similarly, Buck's reconfiguration incorporated culturally salient signifiers to reverse the negative consequences associated with interracial intimacy. When she described the children as "superior in intelligence and certainly superior in beauty,"[44] Buck identified two major concerns that limited the adoption of mixed-race children. Opponents of interracial intimacy repeatedly charged that mixed-race children were a threat to the health and progress of the nation. These ideas flourished during the nineteenth century to ensure the legal and social inferiority of nonwhite peoples. But they took on new significance in the early twentieth century as fears of immigration and race mixing increased. Beginning with statutes prohibiting whites from marrying African Americans or Native Americans, states passed a host of laws to prohibit whites from marrying people identified by a range of racial, national, and religious labels including Chinese, Japanese, Korean, Malay, or Hindu. The proliferation of these anti-miscegenation laws allowed states to punish people who attempted to legitimate either their interracial intimacies or their interracial children.[45]

Although Pennsylvania did away with its anti-miscegenation laws in the late eighteenth century and outlawed school segregation in the late nineteenth century, resistance to racial equality persisted throughout the state. Events like the 1954 *Brown v. Board of Education* Supreme Court decision outlawing school segregation revived concerns throughout the nation that integration would lead to increased interracial intimacy. Even in communities like Doylestown that lacked any significant racial diversity, the prospect of interracial dating and marriage could create problems. Some residents of Doylestown based their disapproval of the Welcome House children on their fears of future interracial marriages. Buck claimed that one older man in her community railed, "If any of those damned half-breed children marries one of my grandchildren, I will see you goddamned to hell."[46] The first Welcome House mother, Viola Yoder, also remembered that some of her neighbors asked questions about whom the children would date when they got older.[47]

Buck did not shy away from the controversial issue of interracial dating. In 1955, she confronted the question of whom the Welcome House children would date by insisting that they were ideal dating prospects for any of the Doylestown youth. Citing the positive qualities they possessed that trumped any concerns about racial difference, Buck noted that the oldest of the Welcome House children "had more girls interested in him than the average boy has." Referring to the oldest Welcome House daughter, Buck assured that she was also a sought-after dating prospect. In both cases, she based her assessment of the young peoples' prospects on their physical appearances, winsome personalities, and gender appropriate behaviors. According to Buck, the young man was "a handsome fellow and a good athlete," and "a volunteer in the armed services." She also bragged that the young woman was "pretty and sweet."[48] Here we see how Buck's efforts to make the Welcome House children's activities and attributes fit with postwar definitions of gender effectively essentialized both the gender and racial characteristics of the children.

When Buck's neighbors voiced concerns over the dating choices of Welcome House's mixed-race children, they were articulating long-established fears of miscegenation as race suicide.[49] Buck observed these fears in one Junior League volunteer who panicked when her friends asked how she would feel if one of her children dated or married one of the Welcome House children. According to Buck, the woman told her she answered by explaining, "because I give money to help and because the children come and play with mine doesn't mean they have to marry them."[50] But she later discontinued her support of Welcome House. The prospect that a Welcome House child might date or marry with one of Doylestown's white children posed a threat to enduring beliefs that interracial intimacy led to genetically inferior offspring. Buck responded to these fears by proclaiming that "there are many Americans who would yield democracy itself rather than accept the scientifically proved fact that color does not decide the place of a human being in life."[51] Buck was referring to genetic research that, as early as the 1920s, had invalidated the scientific basis for these beliefs. But, as her neighbors' comments demonstrated, ideas about race as a marker and determining factor of a person's inferiority or superiority still held significant cultural influence throughout the twentieth century.[52]

The American eugenics movement of the early twentieth century encouraged the belief that genetically inferior people threatened society. Eugenicists believed that saving the nation from the so-called unfit required aggressive reproductive control. American eugenicists assumed that the unfit passed on their undesirable traits to their children. Thus, they promoted reproduction among white, middle-class couples—positive eugenics—and discouraged reproduction in numerous communities defined as unfit—negative eugenics. Eugenicists counted immigrants, the impoverished, the mentally and physically disabled, and people of color among the unfit. Early twentieth-century eugenicists targeted several communities for negative eugenic interventions like sterilization without a specific focus on race, but they were still concerned that race mixing led to race suicide. Many policymakers who believed in eugenics were eager to save America from the degradation of race mixing, which was at odds with Buck's belief that race mixing was an undeniable characteristic of the nation.[53] Buck wrote, "the people of the United States . . . are certainly a mixed people, which may account for their energy and achievements."[54] Buck designed these statements to reverse ideas developed during the heyday of the American eugenics movement of the early twentieth century. Following World War II, eugenicists' efforts to *save* the white race through negative eugenics lost cultural and scientific support but not social currency.

Eugenics played a significant role in the legal and social policies that stigmatized mixed-race children and informed the adoption policies Buck found objectionable. Beginning in the 1920s, child welfare professionals had worked with doctors and psychologists to develop evaluative measures that would reduce certain risks in adoption. Many of these professionals believed that a child's nature and abilities were biologically determined. As mentioned in chapter 2, child welfare professionals also thought that by increasing standards and using tools to ascertain a child's mental and developmental status, including IQ tests, they could appropriately match children with families of similar status and aptitude. Child welfare professionals also judged the fitness of prospective parents based on interviews and home studies.[55] Although these measures often said more about prospective parents' social class and access to education than their intellectual abilities, social workers and adoption agencies used these practices, believing they were beneficial for both adoptive parents and children. These practices would become less influential in the 1950s and 1960s as popular and professional ideas about "children's hereditary taint [had] faded" for white children in the child welfare system.[56] But this transition was not as quick to take hold in the cases of nonwhite or mixed-race children in need of adoption.

Thus, Buck used a narrative reconfiguration of the Welcome House children's inherited characteristics to counter charges that they were inferior. Specifically, Buck relied on the language of hybrid superiority that originated in botanical science to reverse negative assessments of mixed-race children's attributes. When she compared mixed-race children to hybrid strains of corn and roses that possessed "rare qualities, so rare that the waste [of these children] was intolerable," she echoed the ideas of geneticist George Snell.[57] Snell's survey of decades of research led him to conclude that hybridity was a vital element in the formation of civilized societies. He believed this pattern occurred because "race crossing . . . produces individuals of exceptional vitality and vigor."[58] Buck was familiar with Snell's work and in one instance she paraphrased him, saying, "a hybrid people has always a higher intelligence and a beauty greater than is possessed by the so-called 'pure' races."[59] Proponents of hybridity saw potential in selective race mixing that could lead to stronger traits among the hybrid generations. Though these scientists conducted most studies of hybridity on plants, some were willing to extrapolate their findings onto humans. Luther Burbank was one of the earliest horticulturalists to suggest that race mixing was positive for the US population. He aptly named his treatise on this subject *The Training of the Human Plant*. Anthropologist Ashley Montagu's writings on hybridity also influenced Buck's thinking. Peter Conn notes that Buck referenced Montagu's book, *Man's Most Dangerous Myth: The Fallacy of Race*, to support her claims that hybrids were superior.[60] The research and theories that challenged scientific racism became the basis of Buck's effort to undermine the suggestion that race mixing diluted positive characteristics from either side of a child's ancestry.

In addition to disputing adoption standards informed by eugenics, Buck publicized her objections to the ways adoption agencies adhered to a form of the one-drop rule that fixed mixed-race children's membership in communities of color. Based on the principle of race matching, agencies considered same-race adoptions healthiest for children, but mixed-race children confounded the logic behind this idea. As discussed in chapter 3, since these children did not fit one racial category, social workers attempted to match children with any known or visible nonwhite ancestry with families that represented that racial or ethnic identity. Buck challenged this practice of hypodescent by suggesting that love and not race should influence placement decisions. She rejected the justification for race matching by asking, "did it matter whether there was such matching? Who really matches his parents? The genes that carry the master plan of any human being may be given him by distant, even unknown, ancestors and not by his parents."[61] Buck insisted that love and compatibility mattered most in families. Describing Welcome House's successes with transracial placements she explained, "time and again we have proved that race and religion do not matter. All that matters is the ability to love."[62]

Buck challenged the lingering influences of eugenics and the one-drop rule of racial identity, which became the foundation for her sustained critique of what she considered to be racist adoption policies. She hoped that more social workers would be willing to experiment with transracial placements. To foster this idea, she recommended that agencies abandon matching and rely on "criteria . . . from the human sources of experience and common sense to which textbook knowledge is helpful but secondary."[63] In many ways, Buck was reinforcing critiques that African American child welfare professionals with the NUL were making as they developed their Foster Care and Adoption Project discussed in chapter 2. However, instead of working through existing agencies to promote reform, which was the NUL model, Buck made the Welcome House the centerpiece of her reform plan. Buck imagined that Welcome House could provide leadership in this area. Buck's approach to these early transracial adoptions represented a significant departure from the matching standard that she had supported until the late 1940s, when she first began to identify matching as an impediment that kept eligible mixed-race children trapped in institutional settings.[64]

Once Welcome House began placing children for adoption, Buck's writings celebrated the existence of transracial adoptive families as a challenge to racial inequality and communism in the United States and abroad. In a number of instances, she equated race prejudice with communism, and she called prejudiced people "un-American."[65] It was common for Buck to follow up on assertions like this with an appeal to her readers to consider adopting a Welcome House child. In a 1952 interview with Rochelle Girson of the *Saturday Review*, Buck commented that she was encouraged when she found willing parents to adopt mixed-race children, and these families proved to her that there was true democracy in the United States. These families also refuted the "communist propaganda [that] tells [Asians] that Americans hate Asians," and they made it possible for people "to see if we do treat the children with Asian blood as our own."[66] Cognizant of the international critiques of the nation's poor race relations, Buck suggested that transracial adoptions could disprove this accusation and evince Americans' commitment to democratic principles.[67]

Buck and Korea's Mixed-Race Children

By the mid-1950s, the stories detailing the suffering of Korea's war orphans and displaced children compelled Buck to revise her institution-building strategy and rescue narrative to promote transnational adoption for Korea's mixed-race children. As chapters 1 and 3 describe, the media's coverage of the orphan crisis in Korea had chronicled the ostracism and abuse mixed-race Korean children faced. South Koreans' investment in the notion of racial purity as a key element of their national identity, and their association of the children's mothers with military prostitution, led many to reject mixed-race children. Further, in South Korea, citizenship flowed from fathers to their children. Therefore, mixed-race children were stateless and many, including Buck, believed the United States was responsible for these children of US soldiers.[68]

Buck changed her adoption narrative to celebrate adopting parents by contrasting them with biological parents who relinquished children. She repeatedly claimed that the biological parents of American and Korean-born, mixed-race children were themselves the victims of prejudices that severely restricted their choices. She considered it "natural, that young men, sent abroad at a time when their instincts are strong . . . will find their own way to companionship."[69] In the case of mixed-race Korean children, Buck certainly wanted biological fathers to support their children, but she knew the US military resisted holding men accountable for children unless there was proof that a soldier was the father of an illegitimate child. And, as we saw in chapter 3, many soldiers either denied paternity or were no longer in South Korea to care for their mixed-race children born during and after the War. So, Buck encouraged Americans to be responsible for their support. With statements like "there is only the old American way of concerned individuals taking responsibility," Buck appealed to American citizens to pick up where Korean communities, American fathers, and the US government and military dropped the ball.[70]

Buck attempted to refute negative stereotypes about mixed-race Korean children using the strategies she developed in her appeals on behalf of the Welcome House in such magazines as *Good Housekeeping*, *Ladies' Home Journal*, *Women's Home Companion*, *Reader's Digest*, and *Ebony*. Imitating her earlier strategy of invoking the hybrid superiority of the Welcome House children, she described Korean mixed-race children as "beautiful, nearly always . . . more handsome and intelligent than either side of their ancestry."[71] Emphasizing the attractiveness of displaced children and orphans was not new. As Kelly McKee notes, orphanages in Korea often constructed children awaiting adoption as attractive and healthy even though "the language [case workers] utilized to express the 'uniqueness' of adoptees was not distinctive."[72] Thus, these case histories marketed children in ways designed to appeal to Western consumers. Further, Laura Briggs explains that journalists and aid organizations had used images of poor women and children that cast them as "Madonna-and-child" or "waif" to promote a number of political agendas for several decades before the 1950s.[73] In the 1950s, international aid organizations used these images to stir "pity and ideologies of rescue to position some people as legitimately within a circle of care and deserving of resources."[74] Buck's reconfiguration of mixed-race Korean children combined these methods but added the emphasis on the children's inherent superiority.

Buck designed this message about the superior qualities of mixed-race Korean children to appeal to white prospective adoptive families like the ones in her community. Because of what she knew about the low number of transnational adoptions of Korean black children, she also tried to craft an institutional strategy that would address the reasons African Americans struggled to complete Korean adoptions. Buck believed that African American families' reluctance to work with adoption agencies stemmed from their sense that social workers would not respond favorably to their applications. As chapter 4 described, even though the expansion of US-Korean adoption motivated some child welfare officials to view African Americans as the most appropriate option for Korean black children, adoption agencies continued to struggle to reach and recruit African American adoptive parents. Most agencies had only recently begun providing adoption services to African Americans, and many continued to judge these families using standards that did not account for the ways that segregation and racial inequality limited their opportunities for decent housing, good jobs, and quality educations.[75]

To counter negative stereotypes about African American families and promote standards to assist their adoption efforts, Buck rhetorically placed African American adopting families on the same level as their white counterparts. Buck cast adopting parents of mixed-race Korean children as more enlightened than people who would turn a blind eye to Korea's child welfare crisis.[76] In her fiction and nonfiction writing, she celebrated the husbands and wives who adopted these children, describing them as "loving" and "superior families." Buck never limited these attributes to white adoptive families. She further insisted that African Americans' participation in US-Korean adoption was significant because they were rescuing children and demonstrating a commitment to democracy even though they did not enjoy the full benefits of citizenship.[77]

Buck felt qualified to speak to issues facing African American communities because she had maintained personal and professional relationships with prominent African American individuals and organizations throughout her adult life. Even before Buck returned to the United States to live in 1934, she sought out affiliations that would make obvious her support of civil rights. In 1932, at the invitation of Elmer Carter, editor of the Urban League's magazine *Opportunity*, Buck attended a discussion of problems facing black people in the States. According to Peter Conn, Carter noted that African Americans had "implicit faith" in Buck. In the early 1930s, Buck worked to open labor unions to African Americans and she was active in the anti-lynching legislative campaign with Mary White Ovington, an African American women's and civil rights activist. By the 1940s, Buck was speaking out against wartime racial discrimination, and she encouraged the American Civil Liberties Union to set up the Committee Against Racial Discrimination. Further, Buck and Eleanor Roosevelt were two of a small number of prominent white American women who spoke out against racial segregation during World War II. In addition to the work that allowed her to direct national and international attention to lynching and wartime discrimination, Buck also served on Howard University's board until 1964. She was a lifetime member of the NAACP, and she agreed to publish articles in leading African American publications to show her support for civil rights. Buck equated racial discrimination in the United States with the tactics used by Hitler and the Nazi party. She also espoused a version of Afro-orientalism consistent with that of the African American intellectuals and journalists discussed in chapter 2. Accordingly, in her 1941 commencement address at Howard University, she encouraged the

African American audience to see their challenges as similar to those of other oppressed nonwhite peoples in India and other Asian nations.[78]

Buck received mixed reactions to her efforts to expand African Americans' participation in US-Korean adoption. As discussed in chapter 3, couples who encountered resistance from mainstream adoption agencies responded to the attempts of private agencies like Welcome House because they did not follow many of the most restrictive placement guidelines. But the records of the Welcome House suggest that not many African Americans adopted through that agency, even though, as we will see below, many responded to her appeals to learn more about US-Korean adoption. Conversely, agencies with longer track records in domestic and transnational child welfare were skeptical of Buck's approach and critical of her support of the proxy method of adoption.[79] Criticism from ISS and other agencies working to regulate US-Korean adoptions were valid given what happened when a transnational adoption failed. As described in chapter 3, if a family decided they did not want to or could not keep their Korean adoptee, the child entered the US child welfare system. This meant that in the event of a failed adoption, local agencies had to make provisions for the lodging and care of the mixed-race Korean child until they found a new family to adopt or they could make other arrangements. Buck was aware of the risks ISS officials identified, but she considered the dangers far worse for Korea's mixed-race children if they stayed in the nation of their births. Many of Korea's displaced children experienced neglect, starvation, and death. These circumstances were Buck's justification for her endorsement of proxy adoptions.

Before Buck became involved in Korean transnational adoption and openly supported proxy adoption, her agency attempted to work with established organizations to place children in the United States. However, Buck's methods put Children's Bureau officials on the defensive. They frequently received letters and memos from child welfare officials describing outrageous or disparaging claims Buck had made about social workers or adoption standards.[80] For example, throughout the fall of 1955, the Children's Bureau received letters from a number of angry child welfare officials because of comments Buck made in the September 1955 *Woman's Home Companion* article, "The Children Waiting." In that article, Buck claimed that 62,000 children were awaiting adoption in one

US state alone because of inefficiencies in adoption agencies. The article also inspired at least one concerned citizen to write to President Eisenhower to ask that he "please look into this matter."[81] His office forwarded this request to officials at the Children's Bureau, and they remained wary of Buck's transracial and transnational adoption activities throughout the 1950s, 1960s, and 1970s.

In 1956, when Welcome House did get involved in Korean transnational adoption, officials with Welcome House and ISS corresponded to see if the two agencies could coordinate their efforts on behalf of Korean adoptees. The plans fell through because each agency wanted to take the lead in defining protocols for US-Korean adoptions. But this disagreement did not sour ISS officials' opinions of Buck, and she joined the advisory council for ISS's America Branch the following year.[82] That same year, Agnes T. Miller, executive director of Welcome House, contacted ISS officials to find out whether there were funds available to ISS to help economically disadvantaged families like "the Negroes who are applying for Korean-Negro children."[83] However, the relationships between Welcome House and agencies including the Children's Bureau, the Child Welfare League of America, and ISS became antagonistic over time. Buck and officials with ISS began to part ways following their attempt to issue a joint appeal to increase adoptions of Korean black children. Because of Buck's reputation as an advocate for civil rights, ISS assistant director Susan T. Pettiss asked her to write an article for *Ebony* magazine.[84] ISS wanted Buck to direct all inquiries to their America Branch office, but she made no mention of ISS in the article. Instead, Buck encouraged the magazine's readers to contact her agency, Welcome House. This slight infuriated ISS director, William T. Kirk, and in the years that followed, ISS officials were reluctant to collaborate with Buck or Welcome House.

The article that Buck did write, "Should White Parents Adopt Brown Babies?," made a significant impression on the magazine's readership. Welcome House received 625 inquiries from African American families interested in adoption in the months after its publication. In the article, Buck used her standard formula of identifying the need and dramatizing the situation to evoke a response. With moving descriptions of the tragic circumstances of racial intolerance in Korea, Buck declared that unless Americans intervened, most of the children born to Korean women and African American soldiers would perish. She also optimistically reported that she had received many adoption applications from interested African American families. Even as Buck identified African Americans as her target audience, she also asked a provocative question that would become central to her efforts to rescue Korean black children in the years to come. In a moving appeal to "families like [hers] who would be happy to have a child they can naturally love, whatever the color of the child's skin," Buck again asserted that love and not race should determine placement decisions for Korea's mixed-race populations.[85]

Buck encouraged greater sensitivity to the struggles African Americans faced for humanitarian and political reasons. Although Buck would claim that her early humanitarianism was a response to the oppression she observed growing up in China, racism in the United States also informed her antiracist activism. Her support for civil rights causes made her aware of the ways that, even in the area of child welfare, racial inequality affected African Americans' opportunities. Buck would often note that African Americans and people in Asia had much in common. She believed "the [Negroes] were obsessed with the same deep injustices and cruelties that had burned in the minds and hearts of the Chinese revolutionists."[86] To Buck, efforts to assist victims of the Chinese Revolution and victims of American segregation were related. Her parents had told her stories of the greatness of the United States when she was a child growing up in China. As an adult, racial oppression and inequality challenged the ideals her parents had described. According to Peter Conn, racially motivated tragedies like the Scottsboro case of 1931 and lynchings throughout America deeply disturbed Buck. Challenged by these events and the Chinese Revolution, Buck attempted to encourage white Americans to seek justice and equality for victims of colonialism and racial inequality while she attempted to assist families adopting Korean children.[87]

For Buck, the fight against racism and communism at home and abroad was necessary to safeguard future generations against anticolonial retribution. She was aware that America's reputation throughout Asia suffered as a result of the nation's neocolonial relations with Japan and Korea. Buck saw the rescue of children ostracized because of their mixed racial heritage as more than a moral obligation—it was also a nation-saving imperative. She maintained, "prejudice invalidates our democracy to others because it makes us support old imperialisms and decayed governments which other peoples have suffered and are still suffering from the inequalities of imperialisms and tyrannies."[88] Buck posited that US-Korean adoptions helped stem the growth of communism and bridge the gap between Americans and Asians because the world was watching America.[89] Although Buck believed African Americans' adoptions of Korean black children provided compelling evidence of the link between anticommunist and antiracist humanitarianism, she worried that there would not be enough black families to adopt Korean black children.[90] However, she believed white families would adopt these children for the same anticommunist and antiracist humanitarian reasons. Returning to an idea established in her efforts to place American-born, mixed-race children of Asian descent, Buck lobbied for the placement of full Korean, Korean white, and Korean black children with white families.

Korean black children proved to be hardest to place, and Buck's doubts about the availability of enough African American adoptive families developed because of her experiences at Welcome House. Between November 1951 and November 1957, Welcome House Adoption Agency received eighteen referrals for children who had at least one African American parent. Eleven of these children were mixed-race and had one parent that was not African American. Four of these children were African American, and the notation in the ledger indicates that Welcome House staff were unsure of the racial makeup of two of the children. Welcome House had to close the November 1951 case for a child with an "American white" mother, and an "American Negro" father, likely because they could not find an African American couple to complete the adoption. By February 1956, Welcome House began using the notation "we had no Negro homes" to designate cases of children with at least one African American parent that they had to close. Welcome House did not complete its first successful placement and adoption of a child with an African American parent until December 1958.[91]

The Welcome House ledgers reveal that the agency had similar difficulties placing Korean black children. Between 1957 and 1961, Welcome House received only twelve referrals for Korean black children. This number dropped to seven in the years between 1962 and 1966. The largest number of referrals for Korean black children came in the period between 1967 and June 1971, when Welcome House received thirteen referrals for Korean black children. The numbers are quite different for children who were full Korean or Korean white. Between 1957 and 1961, Welcome House received ten referrals for full Korean children and twenty-five referrals for Korean white children. Those numbers increased to eighty-eight and three hundred respectively for the period 1962–1966, and 124 and 292 respectively for the period 1967 to June 1971.[92] In an article for *The Hartford Times*, Buck expressed concerns for the Korean black children who remained in South Korea because she believed officials in Korea were pressing agencies like hers to explain why they had more success placing Korean white children and not their Korean black wards.[93]

Pearl S. Buck's Foundation for Korea's Mixed-Race Children

Buck's limited success facilitating Korean black adoptions was one of the many reasons she began investigating ways she could provide services for the mixed-raced Korean children who would remain in South Korea. In September 1960, Buck approached South Korea's Child Welfare Committee to learn more about the lives of mixed-race children and their mothers. The Child Welfare Committee could not provide the answers Buck wanted because there was no accurate census of mixed-race children. With the assistance of a $1,000 donation from Buck's personal finances, the committee agreed to conduct a national survey. The Child Welfare Committee created a subcommittee, the Children's Survey Committee, which reported that there were 1,518 mixed-race children, and that African American men had fathered 205 of them. The report further suggested that many of the mixed-race children were homeless and resorted to crime to support themselves, which made them a growing concern to the public and the government.[94]

This information led Buck to encourage a change in Welcome House policies that would expand the agency's activities beyond adoption. According to one of the first Welcome House board members, Lois Burpee, in the early 1960s Welcome House considered the request. Buck advocated for the creation of a center in South Korea that would provide job training and services to both mixed-race children and their mothers. She imagined that the center would reduce the likelihood that this population would become a burden on the Korean government or US agencies involved in humanitarian aid. Burpee remembered that the Welcome House board members did not share Buck's convictions, and they were concerned that the agency did not have the resources to expand its operations. Oscar Hammerstein, whose presence on the board of directors drew celebrity attention and support, resisted Buck's plan to expand operations into Korea. Burpee explained that Hammerstein liked the small family structure of Welcome House and believed that the agency did not have a strong enough fund-raising operation to underwrite a Korean center.[95]

After Hammerstein's death in 1960, the board lost its main fundraiser, and they increasingly considered Buck's role in the agency more dangerous than helpful. Lois Burpee explained that several board members felt that the agency was finally becoming financially stable at the time of Hammerstein's death. Additionally, some board members worried that the agency would suffer because of Buck's outspokenness on controversial political issues, which made her an object of social and political scrutiny. They were not being paranoid. Buck had been a target of critics who believed she was a communist. National news outlets including the *New York Sun* and *Time* magazine more than once accused her of voicing dangerous leftist ideas.[96] Two other members of the Welcome House board, Muriel Biester and Margaret Fischer, remembered that the work of operating the Welcome House could be dangerous because people also called them communists.[97]

The attacks against Buck's character and allegations that she was a communist began many years before she became an advocate of US-Korean adoption. As an outspoken supporter of racial equality and a fierce critic of colonialism, Buck had attracted the attention of Federal Bureau of Investigation (FBI) director J. Edgar Hoover, who suspected that she was involved in subversive activities. Buck had been on the FBI's watch list since 1935, when the Bureau was created, because of her writings against colonial rule and the legacies of colonialism in countries such as China and India. Hoover was also uncomfortable with Buck's involvement with organizations including Buck's own East and West Association and the American Civil Liberties Union, for which she had chaired the Committee Against Racial Discrimination. In 1946, Buck attracted even more attention to herself because of her public critique of

Winston Churchill after he delivered his "Iron Curtain" speech in March 1946. According to Peter Conn, Hoover ordered further investigations of Buck's activities, writings, and speeches after she accused Churchill of encouraging a view of the world that would extend the subjugation of people living under oppressive regimes. Although the FBI concluded that Buck was not a communist, accusations against her loyalty to the United States followed her throughout her life and cast a shadow over some of her efforts to aid oppressed peoples, including her work on behalf of Korean orphans.[98]

Unwilling to give up her plan to establish a center in Korea or back down because of the attacks on her character, Buck made a public break with the Welcome House and proceeded with plans to open an opportunity center in South Korea. Although Buck remained committed to transnational adoption as one option for mixed-race Korean children, she understood that many mixed-race children would never be able to leave Korea.[99] This reality convinced Buck that the opportunity center would be the way she could devise an institutional mechanism to obtain the most secure future for mixed-race Korean children who would remain in that nation. When Buck announced her intention to proceed with the foundation on her own during a ceremony where she received the Gimbel Award for humanitarian work, she had very little money to back her new project.[100] Sara Rowe, a member of the Pearl S. Buck Foundation's staff, remembered that Buck never had enough money for all of her projects.[101] However, as was the case when she started the Welcome House, Buck committed a large amount of her personal funds to open the opportunity center. She took the $1,000 Gimbel award as well as $2,000 she received from Howard University's board of directors in honor of her twenty years of service and used this money to start the Pearl S. Buck Foundation.[102] Through the foundation, Buck planned to raise money to support a pilot opportunity center in South Korea. Her ultimate goal was to open similar centers in all of the Asian countries where American soldiers resided.

Buck's vision for the opportunity center was expansive and expensive because she hoped it would provide comprehensive assistance to mixed-race Korean children and their mothers. She hoped to cultivate a network of Korean child welfare specialists including doctors, social workers, and pharmacists who would provide for the children's and their mothers' physical, medical, and psychological needs. Buck did not want professional social workers to run the foundation or the center. Instead, she relied on a group of young nonprofessionals to carry out the work of fund-raising and the center's day-to-day management. Buck explained that she chose young people without professional training in child welfare because "the Amerasian child is a young people's problem," and she wanted "a fresh approach to Asia through young and brilliant Americans."[103] But unlike the dedicated group of nonprofessionals that helped Buck develop and expand Welcome House, the inexperience of the individuals she chose to head up the foundation threatened to compromise the undertaking. Peter Conn notes that she made poor decisions regarding the young people she hired for this task. Buck's bad judgment in this area led to controversies that damaged the center's credibility and reputation in both the United States and Korea for many years. But the foundation and the center survived the scandals, which allowed Buck to continue coordinating services to assist mixed-race Korean children and their mothers.[104]

To raise money for the foundation, Buck returned to strategies she had perfected while working on behalf of the Welcome House. She organized a board of influential people, conducted fund-raisers, and crafted a rescue narrative designed to appeal to donors and government officials alike. Buck believed that the board of governors had to include people "highly and generally respected, since the Asian-American children have no status of their own at present."[105] In 1965, the foundation's board of governors included Art Buchwald, Joan Crawford, Robert Kennedy, and R. Sargent Shriver. Influential members of the board also gave the agency some credibility and served as a draw to encourage donors. Lillian W. Wolfson, another of the Pearl S. Buck's Foundation employees, remembered that Buck only used their names, she did not ask them to do any service on behalf of the Foundation.[106]

The Pearl S. Buck Foundation's fund-raising endeavors allowed Buck to solicit support from private individuals, military personnel, and government officials. She also attempted to set up volunteer chapters in many communities all over the nation to raise money through a range of activities including banquets, fashion shows, and auctions. The Harrisburg, Pennsylvania chapter boasted a $3,000 profit from one of its programs.[107] The Miami, Florida chapter encouraged its members to attend a dinner benefit and sell tickets to their friends.[108] The Miami chapter also reported that the International Debutante Ball planned to donate all of the proceeds from its fund-raiser to the foundation. This was because a Mrs. Donald Sills sat on the board of the foundation and was chairman of the Debutante Ball committee. The same Mrs. Sills helped arrange for the foundation to receive half the proceeds from the ball that took place following the premier of the movie, *The Sand Pebbles*.[109] In letters to Secretary of Defense Robert McNamara and Vice President Hubert Humphrey's wife Muriel, Buck mentioned her idea to get a dollar from every serviceman, which would cover the Foundations costs.[110] Additionally, Buck literally danced her way around the country to raise money for the foundation, in the hopes that people would attend the benefit balls hosted in her honor.[111]

Buck continued to publish articles and write books and letters to garner assistance for mixed-race Korean children, but her rescue narrative changed when transnational adoption was no longer her primary goal. In addition to promoting the children as the best, brightest, and most beautiful, she resorted to a more urgent message that "they are a potential danger for the future."[112] Instead of being an attribute, Buck saw how these characteristics could be a liability for children who would remain in South Korea. She insisted, "I know from history and experience that lost and angry children, especially if they have brains and beauty, grow up into dangerous people."[113] Describing the children's needs to politicians and average citizens alike, Buck explained that beautiful and intelligent mixed-race children often end up supporting themselves by illegal means.[114] She imagined the opportunity centers as havens where children would be educated and receive medical care, food, and clothing as a first step to safeguarding their futures.[115]

Buck's highly dramatic appeals incensed officials with ISS that were also attempting to establish programs in South Korea to assist children that would not be adopted. ISS was among the sectarian and nonsectarian agencies that "increasingly emphasized the important role of indigenous social services [in South Korea] to alleviate the plight of mixed-race children" in the early 1960s.[116] ISS created the Han River Project to extend foster care services to mixed-race children who would remain in South Korea. Many of these children were in the process of being adopted, and ISS encouraged families in the United States to send

$15.00 a month to offset the costs of an adopted child's care. According to ISS director, Paul Cherney, $8.00 went directly to the Korean foster family and the rest was supposed to cover the child's board and the cost of food and clothes.[117] The program began as a short-term solution to help South Koreans adjust to mixed-race children being a part of Korean families. But the program offered some agency and government officials hope that mixed-race children could be integrated into Korean society. ISS officials were hopeful because Korean government officials seemed to be in favor of expanding services for mixed-race children, and they had approved plans to allow some of these children to attend integrated Korean schools. In this context, integration involved mixed-race children attending schools with full Korean children.[118]

Indeed, in 1964, Presbyterian missionary George Whitener placed the first group of mixed-race sixth graders in a school for full Korean children in Seoul, South Korea. Working through the program he founded in cooperation with ISS called Eurasian Children Living as Indigenous Residents (ECLAIR), Whitener was optimistic that this pilot program would influence positive changes for Korea's mixed-race populations. Prior to the founding of ECLAIR, there was only one school in Seoul that accepted mixed-race children. The successful launch of the school integration program suggested to officials with a number of sectarian agencies that Koreans had become more accustomed to seeing mixed-race children. They acknowledged that mixed-race children were not accepted fully into Korean society, but they were at least tolerated. As programs developed to integrate these children, one official with ISS hoped these examples would prove that keeping mixed-race children in segregated situations would only perpetuate negative stereotypes. These child welfare officials and missionaries wagered that integration would give mixed-race children a chance to prove they could compete alongside full Korean children.[119]

Buck was not as optimistic. In her appeals for support, she continued to stress the need for Americans, through her foundation, to aid mixed-race children in South Korea. Consequently, she designed the final component of a revised rescue narrative to drive home the threat the children could pose if, because of poverty and isolation, they embraced communism. Buck claimed that communists and the North Korean military targeted mixed-race children for recruitment. In a poorly veiled reference to communists' recruitment strategies, she warned, "rejected by their fathers and neglected by their mothers' peoples [sic], they are ready to join any group which says, 'Comrades, we want you.'"[120] Taking advantage of the Cold War fears of communist aggression, Buck insisted that the children could become enemies of the United States. In each of these appeals, Buck called the children "the New People—the Amerasians," a term she coined in the 1930s, which, in this case, brought attention to the children's shared American and Korean identities.[121]

Buck also wanted to inspire Americans to act through appeals to their sense of national pride and not only national responsibility. She conveyed to Dun Gifford, Senator Edward Kennedy's legal advisor, that Americans' responses to the circumstances of Korea's mixed-race children were a stain on the nation's reputation.[122] She explained to Secretary of Defense Robert McNamara that she established the foundation out of patriotic motivations. In a letter to the publisher of the Call-Chronicle newspapers, Buck expressed her desire to provide the tools to allow the Amerasian children to "become good citizens rather than as, at present, criminals and beggars."[123] However, Lillian E. Wolfson remembered Buck asserting, "I am not a humanitarian, I am a humanist. There is a problem; it has to be dealt with."[124] The foundation became Buck's solution to a problem she considered relevant for the children's futures and the success of US-Korean relations. The foundation served Amerasian children because Buck considered them to be the most needy of Korea's displaced populations. In 1966, Buck estimated that approximately five hundred mixed-race children lived in the areas around the center. By 1968, Buck claimed that the center was "caring for over fifteen hundred" Amerasian children whom she hoped would eventually find a place in South Korean society.[125]

When Pearl S. Buck began the permanent foster home, Welcome House, in 1949, she did not think white families in the United States would adopt American-born, mixed-race children of Asian descent. This fact did not stop her from making the lives of the Welcome House family appear to be as good, if not better than, those of their neighbors to combat the negative stereotypes that led child welfare communities to label these children unadoptable. With the help and support of many of her friends and neighbors in Doylestown, Pennsylvania, Buck transformed Welcome House into the first US adoption agency dedicated to finding homes for mixed-race Asian children. After the first adoption of a Welcome House child, Buck devoted her resources and energy to the work of facilitating transracial adoptions for other mixed-race Asian children in the United States, and she employed an evolving narrative of hybrid superiority to alter popular perceptions of the children she placed through Welcome House. This narrative and her day-to-day efforts to make the Welcome House children recognizably American revealed her desire to transform the assimilated "Other" into the model mixed-race adoptee.

Following the Korean War, when the desperate circumstances of that nation's orphans and mixed-race children became a social and political issue, Buck's efforts to assist them included many of the strategies she had developed to increase adoptions of mixed-race Asian children in the United States. But her narrative of hybrid superiority, which continued to describe the beauty and intelligence of mixed-race children, also emphasized their vulnerability. Buck's awareness of the ways prejudice against African Americans in both the United States and Korea made Korean black children particularly vulnerable led her to propose reforms to address the reasons African Americans often failed to complete adoptions of Korean black children. Although Buck's appeal in the black popular press did generate significant interest from African Americans, Welcome House did not experience an increase in adoptions by this group. Instead, Buck aggressively publicized the message that love and not race should inform people's adoption decisions. She also encouraged white families to see their adoptions of all mixed-race Korean children as antiracist and anticommunist acts.

By the 1960s, the successful adoptions of mixed-race Korean children led South Korean officials to promote transnational adoption for full Korean children too. This shift drew more white families to Korean transnational adoption, and these families became potent symbols of the ideal of color-blind love that some agencies referenced to justify transracial adoptions. This shift also coincided with the creation of programs in South Korea designed to assist the displaced, and often mixed-race, children who would not be adopted by families in the United States or other Western nations. The care of this group became the focus of Buck's transnational child welfare activism, and she transformed her rescue narrative once again to generate support for her ambitious plan to establish an opportunity center in South Korea to help mixed-race children and their mothers gain access to health care, education, and job training.

Buck established the Pearl S. Buck Foundation to oversee the work of the opportunity center, and by the time of her death in March 1973, there were PSB opportunity centers in "Okinawa and Taiwan (1967), the Philippines and Thailand (1968), and Vietnam (1970)."[126] But the opportunity center in South Korea became the subject of numerous controversies because of her staff's lack of professional child welfare experience or training, and accusations that they were participating in criminal activities and were abusive to the children. Buck always defended the individuals at the center of these controversies, and she defended her decision to rely on nonprofessionals to carry out the work of the opportunity center. These positions would not have surprised child welfare officials who knew about her work at Welcome House. After all, many child welfare professionals were already familiar with the ways that she had rejected the authority of social workers and challenged child welfare standards like matching to promote transracial adoptions. Many child welfare professionals remained skeptical of Buck's tactics and concerned—in some cases justifiably so—that her schemes were not in the best interest of the children she wanted to assist. But the institutions Buck built to promote her ideas about what constituted the most secure future for mixed-race children of Asian descent in the United States and mixed-race children in Korea continue to influence US and Korean child welfare strategies in the present century.

Conclusion

The traditional arc of popular stories about the origins and evolution of US-Korean adoption often begin with Harry Holt's widely publicized baby lifts of mixed-race Korean children to families in the United States. Next, they explain the reasons for the transition that led to larger numbers of families in Western nations adopting full Korean children instead of mixed-race Korean children. Finally, these stories discuss the role that international media attention played in highlighting the economic basis of South Korea's adoption industry as a result of the 1988 Seoul Olympics. Indeed, the accusations that South Korea's economic recovery since the Korean War was partly due to the nation's export of the children of the poor and single mothers were embarrassing to Korean officials.[1] This unwanted attention caused South Korean officials to recommit to increasing domestic adoption and reducing out-of-country placements. While much of the scholarship on Korean transnational adoption narrates these same transitions, the story of US-Korean adoptions for Korean black children unfolded differently because of the ideas about family, race, and nation that this book has explored.

Although the Korean government was anxious to rid the nation of its mixed-race children for the first decade after the Korean War, economic considerations encouraged the nation's leaders to aggressively promote adoptions of full Korean children by the 1960s. However, the growth in transnational placements for full Korean children began in the late 1950s. In 1959, adoptions of full Korean children surpassed those of mixed-race children for the first time.[2] This shift would reoccur for a number of years during the 1960s. According to British demographer Peter Selman, 1,190 adoptions from Korea took place in 1969, and that number would continue to grow throughout the 1970s when the number of Korean out-of-country placements would skyrocket.[3] Although the number of children adopted by families in European countries declined in the 1980s, families in the United States continued to adopt large numbers of foreign-born children. In 1985, the number of US-Korean adoptions reached its all-time annual peak of 8,837.[4] Estimates suggest that between 1953 and 2004, South Korea relinquished more than 150,000 children for adoption by families in Western nations. The majority of those children became members of white families in the United States.[5]

The trajectory of adoptions for Korean black children was quite different. Although the total number of Korean children placed transnationally increased from the single digits to the thousands between 1953 and 1974, adoptions of Korean black children were more sporadic. There was a remarkable increase in the number of adoptions involving Korean black children from 1955 to 1958, but they dwindled after this brief surge. In 1955, the South Korean government recorded nine adoptions of Korean black children.[6] Over the next three years, that number climbed into the hundreds and reached its annual peak of 227 in 1958.[7] During that period of time, adoptions of Korean black children represented 24 percent of the total out-of-country adoptions. From 1959 through 1974, the number of Korean children adopted out-of-country reached 25,044. But adoptions of all mixed-race Koreans whose fathers were not white equaled 955, or only 3.8 percent of the total.[8]

Using the theory of goal displacement, Rosemary C. Sarri, Yenoak Baik, and Marti Bombyk explain how this shift happened. These researchers define goal displacement as the process by which agencies that attempt to address one social problem actually end up perpetuating the problem because their existence and funding are based on the existence of a social problem to resolve. In the case of Korean transnational adoption, the aid orphanages and agencies received from Western sources that allowed them to care for displaced children "relieved the South Korean government of having to establish domestic programs."[9] The support of first the US military, then the US government and aid organizations led to the staggering increase in the number of orphanages that began during the Korean War and resulted in the existence of "over 600 orphanages" by 1965.[10] But, with the exception of the children housed in Harry Holt's Il San orphanage, most of the children in these institutions were not mixed-race. Consequently, mixed-race Korean children "disappeared from the [Korean] international adoption system" because orphanages coordinated these placements and most mixed-race children remained with their mothers who usually lived in camp towns around the US bases.[11]

Even though mixed-race children did not figure prominently in Korean transnational adoption by the 1970s, the US military's presence in South Korea ensured that mixed-race children would continue to be born in that nation. After representatives of the United Nations Command, the North Korean Army, and the Chinese People's Volunteer Army signed the armistice to end the fighting associated with the Korean War, the United States and the ROK entered into the 1954 Mutual Defense Treaty that sealed these nations' postwar alliance.[12] To support its commitment to defend the DMZ, the United States stationed the Seventh and Second Infantry Divisions in South Korea. Subsequently, the number of US troops in South Korea dropped from more than 300,000 to just under 60,000 between July 1953 and December 1955. Beginning with President Richard Nixon's administration, US political leaders attempted to reduce the US military presence even further. In 1969, Nixon proposed a reduction in US troops that resulted in the withdrawal of the 20,000 soldiers assigned to the Seventh Infantry Division.[13] Although President Jimmy Carter's efforts to withdraw all of the remaining ground troops from South Korea in the late 1970s failed, his administration did withdraw an additional eight hundred combatant and more than 25,000 non-combatant military personnel from South Korea.[14]

Throughout the 1980s and 1990s, Presidents Ronald Reagan and George H.W. Bush would increase both US nuclear defenses in the Asian-Pacific and US economic support for South Korea's military. But their administrations also encouraged the ROK to increase its military spending and its "defense capabilities" so that the US military could play a "supporting role" in South Korean defense.[15] President Bill Clinton's administration would work to emphasize diplomacy in its relations with North and South Korea as it relied on sanctions to advance the goal of denuclearization. To this end, Clinton's administration put in place "augmented US offensive capabilities" to support the ground and air troops in South Korea.[16] By the 2000s, during President George W. Bush's administration, US troop presence would be just above 37,000 ground forces and support personnel.[17]

The policies enacted under these presidential administrations that shored up US-Korean relations during the first five decades after the Korean War resulted in waves of soldiers in and out of South Korea. This movement of men and bases was especially disruptive for South

Koreans living near the camp towns that sprang up around US military bases. Because the military did not pay for family members to accompany soldiers assigned to complete a tour in Korea, military prostitution expanded and became a fixture of base and camp town life to accommodate the social and sexual desires of soldiers. Katherine H. S. Moon has powerfully argued that policies regulating the bodies of Korean women caught up in camp town prostitution were fundamental to the negotiations that maintained the US military presence in South Korea.[18] Thus, the agreements that US government and military officials made with Korean officials to regulate prostitution institutionalized the oppression of poor, uneducated women. Their lack of economic and social status made these women subject to "physical, sexual, and emotional abuse" from Koreans and US soldiers alike.[19]

The stigma associated with camp town prostitution also shaped the experiences of mixed-race children born in the decades after the war. Although abortion and the use of contraceptives in the postwar years kept the number of mixed-race children born in South Korea low,[20] many Koreans shunned this population because they were the evidence of "the joint legacies of colonialism and imperialism imposed on the nation."[21] Estimates indicate that at least 11,000 mixed-race Koreans were born between 1955 and 2005.[22] Their status as legal and social outsiders has made this population's struggle to integrate into Korean society invisible in many respects. But the children of single mothers, and not only women associated with US military camps, have also suffered because of gender inequality in South Korea that has constrained unmarried mothers' options.[23] Until 2008, single women could not pass citizenship on to their children because only husbands and fathers had that right under the South Korean Civil Code. Even after the South Korean government ended the family registration system in 2008, many women remained marginalized. According to Kelly McKee, this legal change did not significantly alter the ways that poor families and single mothers struggle to gain status in South Korea.[24] Consequently, the children of poor, unmarried mothers are overrepresented in out-of-country adoption statistics.

Mixed-race children's disappearance from Korean transnational adoption agendas has suggested different things to different people. In the late 1960s, officials with ISS believed that the reduced number of mixed-race children available for adoption was a result of the successes of transnational adoptions (meaning that they had solved the problem), the practice of deploying soldiers to zones where they had less access to civilian populations, and increased marriages among Korean women and US soldiers.[25] While these conditions did influence the demographic shift that led to more full Korean children being available for transnational adoption, other factors that involved changes in US adoption priorities played a role as well. Namely, white parents became more involved in transracial and transnational adoption in the 1960s and 1970s. This shift was certainly a response to the perceived needs of Korean children, but many white adoptive families were also responding to a perceived shortage of adoptable white babies. Korean transnational adoptions were also attractive to adoptive parents who worried that birth mothers in the States might change their minds or in some other way interfere in the lives of adoptive families. Additionally, Arissa Oh and SooJin Pate have shown that the US media influenced white adoptive couples' decision to adopt from Korea by suggesting that Korean adoptees were easily assimilable.[26] Therefore, some white adoptive parents assumed that they could shape their adopted children to meet their (the parents') needs. This cultural reconfiguration of the Asian adoptee aroused what Pate calls "yellow desire," which made adoptions from South Korea seem less controversial than adoptions of nonwhite children in the United States.[27]

Another factor that facilitated the disappearance of mixed-race children from the Korean transnational adoption system was the creation of programs for mixed-race children in South Korea that emerged in the mid-1960s. Many of these programs ascribed to a model of care that was eerily reminiscent of the first plans representatives of the United Nations Korean Reconstruction Agency (UNKRA) had proposed at the war's end. Officials with UNKRA had warned that there would be difficult racial and social adjustments for Korean children in Western nations, and they encouraged the creation of programs that involved the Korean people in the care of their nation's orphans and displaced children instead of transnational adoption. Officials with UNKRA predicted that transnational adoption would not provide a long-term solution to Korea's orphan crisis, and this proved to be most accurate in the cases of Korean black children. The inability of transnational adoption schemes to resolve the challenges this population faced revealed the real limitations of programs that did not address the ways that Korean/black/white racial hierarchies shaped perceptions that some children were more desirable than others and that some families were better suited to complete transnational adoptions than others.[28]

African Americans' part in this history suggests that they challenged barriers to their participation in formal adoptions and adopted or attempted to adopt US and foreign-born children throughout the 1950s and 1960s. By 1971, officials with the Child Welfare League were sharing statistics compiled by the US Children's Bureau that showed that African Americans' rates of domestic adoption were similar to, and possibly slightly higher than, the rate of white families adopting in the States.[29] However, there has been limited analysis of the prevalence or patterns of African Americans' participation in formal adoptions of US or foreign-born children. Rose M. Kreider and Elizabeth Raleigh have theorized that not enough is known about African Americans' adoptions because they are not as visible or controversial as transracial adoptions that place nonwhite children with white adoptive parents. Indeed, while most adoptions in the United States are not transracial, the laws that mandate a color-blind approach to adoptions arranged by publicly funded agencies have drawn an inordinate amount of attention to the place of transracial adoption in US child welfare schemes.[30] Specifically, the passage of the Multiethnic Placement Act (MEPA) of 1994, which Congress amended in 1996 with the Interethnic Provisions (IEP), outlawed the use of race as a criterion in adoption placements. Although the MEPA did encourage agencies to attempt to recruit families of color to adopt children of color, it also specified that agencies could not prohibit a foster or adoptive placement that involved families that did not share racial, ethnic, or national backgrounds if that placement was in the best interest of the child in question.[31] Once amended, the MEPA-IEP eliminated the requirements that agencies had to work to recruit families of color to adopt children of color. This shift was consequential because, as Laura Briggs explains, the decision "guaranteed white families' access to adoption of non-white children." Briggs further identifies the MEPA-IEP as a part of conservative politicians' comprehensive effort to eliminate government programs that helped communities of color keep their children.[32]

While critics of transracial adoption insisted that the MEPA-IEP was disruptive for communities of color, politicians framed the passage of these laws as a response to the perennial problem adoption agencies had locating families of color to foster and/or adopt children of color. Indeed, throughout the first decades of US-Korean adoption, social workers continually complained that there were never enough families to place the Korean black or African American children available for adoption. Unsurprisingly, Korean black adoptions stirred debates over the place of African American families in both US and transnational child welfare systems. Although there were many projects designed to reform the policies that made it harder for African Americans to complete formal adoptions of both populations, the short-lived and underfunded nature of most of these initiatives produced inconsistent outcomes. Regarding African Americans' Korean adoptions, the increased regulation of transnational adoption also eliminated some of the mechanisms that had facilitated African Americans' Korean adoptions, including proxy adoption. Thus, African Americans' participation in Korean black adoptions was inconsequential by the late 1960s. Up to that point, segregation had dictated that social workers place Korean children fathered by black GIs with African American families.[33]

The relatively small scale of Korean black adoptions does not mean that the practice was insignificant. Another critical feature of the accommodations some agencies made to facilitate Korean black adoptions was the space it created for African Americans to inform not only the policies affecting adoptive family formation but also the popular discourses about the political significance of African Americans in domestic and foreign adoption programs. The black and white child welfare professionals and nonprofessionals that worked to increase African Americans' domestic and Korean transnational adoptions demonstrated that such placements were a part of, and not the sum of, African Americans' work to remedy the challenges brought about by oppressive political systems in the United States and abroad. Some reformers in these communities also connected the needs of specific African American families to the sweeping goals of civil rights activism and thereby inserted their struggles to actualize family rights into larger contests for racial equality. However, as discussed in the introduction, the attempts by African American social workers associated with the National Association of

Black Social Workers to eliminate transracial adoptions in the 1970s received more attention than the successes professionals and nonprofessionals were having in the area of African Americans' domestic and transnational adoptions. Thus, the expansion of US-Korean adoption would mark the beginning of large-scale transracial and transnational placements for white families in the States, while it signaled the decline of African Americans' participation in large-scale transnational adoption efforts. However, the lack of visibility for these efforts has obscured the ways that African Americans contested their exclusion from efforts to adopt children in the United States and abroad, which has skewed both the popular and historical record of the transformations that took place in adoption policies and practices in the 1950s and 1960s.[34]

This inattention to the ways that African Americans' Korean adoptions evolved has also affected the ways political officials and officials with child welfare agencies in Korea described, or did not describe, what happened to Korean black children after the nation's transnational adoption priority shifted to full Korean children. One of the questions I had when I began this project was, "What happened to Korean black children who were not adopted transnationally?" The answer to this question suggests that all mixed-race children continued to experience punishing forms of exclusion and segregation in South Korea but Korean black children were particularly vulnerable to abuse and exploitation. SooJin Pate's work demonstrates that in the mid-1960s, demographic shifts at Harry Holt's Il San orphanage were already indicating that integration might not work for Korean black children. By the late 1960s, Holt was categorizing Korean black children as unadoptable, along with disabled children and older children. This label meant that the children would remain at the orphanage until they were eighteen years old, at which time they were often on their own.[35] Evidence suggests that the first generation of Korean mixed-race children that remained in Korea all experienced economic and social marginalization once they left orphanages. However, Korean black children also experienced forms of racism that reflected the prejudice many Koreans had against African Americans. Arissa Oh relates that, while some Koreans believed that Korean black children were biologically predisposed to become "entertainers or athletes," others treated Korean black children like spectacles. This was the case for one Korean black man who was forced to become the freak-show oddity in a Korean circus.[36]

These stories indicate that attempts to truly integrate mixed-race populations in South Korea ultimately failed. Mixed-race children remained vulnerable in spite of child welfare officials' hopes in the 1960s that the integration of these children would eventually lead to their acceptance. Mixed-race Koreans' absence from transnational adoption meant that they were also "rhetorically erased" from the story of Korean child welfare.[37] Activists and scholars have begun the work of correcting this omission. They have emphasized the need for revisions to both scholarly and popular perceptions of what happened to mixed-race Korean children following the remarkable growth of Korean transnational adoption.[38] The unequal status of Korea's mixed-race children also received sporadic international media attention in the last decades of the twentieth century, which has caused some Korean officials to consider legal ways to alter the status of mixed-race children and their mothers. The story of Hines Ward Jr. is a case in point.

In 2006, Ward Jr. became an international celebrity because of his performance in the 2006 National Football League's (NFL) Super Bowl. At that time, Ward Jr. was a wide receiver for the Pittsburgh Steelers, and he became the first Korean African American to win the League's Most Valuable Player Award. In the United States, the media played up his rags-to-riches story in the weeks and months after his win. The coverage highlighted the following details of Ward Jr.'s life. Ward Jr.'s father, Hines Ward Sr., was an African American soldier who had met Kim Young-He while stationed in Korea. The couple married after they realized that they were going to have a child. When Ward Jr. was a toddler, his father moved the family to the States. It is likely that Ward Jr.'s mother experienced social ostracism as first the girlfriend of and then the wife of an African American soldier. As Katharine H. S. Moon explains, many South Koreans discriminated against African American soldiers and the women who associated with them because of the history of Korean military prostitution that haunts such relationships.[39] Social ostracism and social isolation were also a part of Kim's life in the United States. According to Ji-Yeon Yuh, the Korean wives of US soldiers faced barriers in the states because of their race and class, which informed these women's relationships with Americans and other Korean military brides. In many cases, Korean wives of white men did not associate with the Korean wives of African American men. It seems that this pattern was consistent in Kim's life, and she had little support as she attempted to transition to life in the United States.[40]

In the States, the family's situation quickly deteriorated. Before Ward Jr. was seven years old, his parents had divorced and his father had remarried. After leaving Ward Jr. with his mother to complete a tour of duty in Europe, Ward Sr. returned and took Ward Jr. to live in Louisiana with his (paternal) grandmother.[41] Although Kim spoke little English, she fought to regain custody of her son. Once she did, she worked three jobs to support them. Ward Jr. struggled to adapt to life with his mother, and in several interviews, he described feeling embarrassed as a child because she was different. Many people considered Ward Jr. to be different too, and he endured teasing and rejection from Korean Americans because he was part African American, from African Americans because he was part Korean, and from white Americans because he was not white. Over time, Ward Jr. grew to be proud of his mother, and he credited her with teaching him the value of hard work. He also acknowledged that his mother's example helped him overcome hardships and excel in football in high school, college, and ultimately the NFL.[42]

During the interviews, Ward Jr. expressed pride in his Korean heritage, and he had an opportunity to return to South Korea in April 2006. Although most mixed-raced Koreans live as outcasts in South Korea, Ward Jr. and his mother received a celebrity's welcome. During his trip, Ward Jr. met South Korea's then president, Roh Moo-Hyun, received honorary citizenship, and dined with the nation's leaders. He also met with some of the city's mixed-race population and saw how their systematic exclusion from educational and employment opportunities affected their lives. Ward Jr. acknowledged that had he and his mother remained in Seoul, they would have suffered the ostracism he observed. Consequently, he promised to "make the struggle to end bi-racial discrimination [his] chief cause." After visiting Pearl S. Buck International, Ward Jr. made another public commitment to work to change the status of Koreans like himself. True to his word, Ward Jr. used $1 million of his own money to establish the Hines Ward Helping Hands Korea Foundation, and he has become a symbol of what journalist James J. Na called a "hybrid success story."[43]

The US media's framing of Ward Jr.'s story emphasized South Korea's history of exclusionary laws and practices, which was embarrassing to South Koreans. Ward Jr.'s return drew attention to the mistreatment of the nation's mixed-race populations. It also exposed the related story of the nation's history of transnational adoption that expanded in the years after the Korean War as one solution to the question of what the nation would do about the growing number of mixed-race GI babies. Some South Korean officials attempted to use Ward Jr.'s return to signal that the nation was committed to helping its mixed-race populations. But the legacies associated with these painful histories could not be erased by declarations like that of President Roh when he said that Ward Jr. "came back a hero." During this same period in 2006, other political leaders spoke of changing transnational adoption laws to limit out-of-country placements. They also discussed eliminating laws that limited mixed-race Korean citizenship. Some saw the need for changes in the language of the nation's educational curriculum that affirmed its commitment to the idea of one nation, one blood.[44]

Advocates of greater equality for Korea's mixed-race populations have highlighted the hypocrisy of these public gestures by pointing out that officials designed them to deflect international criticism of both the history and contemporary story of Koreans' rejection of mixed-race people. Although they were rightly skeptical of officials' pronouncements, they also used the occasion of Ward Jr.'s so-called triumphant return to draw international attention to the nation's painful history of colonial exploitation that fed a national intolerance for racial and ethnic minorities. While each nation attempted to mobilize Ward Jr.'s success to show off its turn toward more inclusive laws and customs (albeit in different historical contexts), the story ultimately exposed the difficulties both nations have had dealing with the legacies of militarization, racial inequality, and gender oppression that linked South Korea's history of transnational adoption with policies that continue to constrain the opportunities of mixed-race people in South Korea.[45]

South Korea's mixed-race populations have endured exclusion and isolation since the 1950s when the South Korean and US governments, sectarian communities, and international child welfare organizations attempted to devise strategies to resolve the problems of the first generation of children born to US soldiers and Korean women. Ward Jr.'s efforts to help the newest generation of mixed-race Koreans were in line with the attempts that soldiers, civilians, and adoption reformers had put in motion in the decades following the Korean War. He was interested in identifying ways to address their day-to-day needs, and he was willing to raise awareness and invest his own money to secure the long-term success of programs for mixed-race children. However, unlike the early generation of reformers who emphasized strategies to get GI babies out of Korea, contemporary activists are fighting for changes in South Korea's laws and customs to make the integration of mixed-race children and their mothers a reality. Activists (many of whom are adult Korean adoptees) are also working to bring an end to Korean transnational adoption by demanding social justice for single mothers and poor families.[46] Together, these groups are challenging the historical silences that have hindered efforts to expose the ways that contests over the meanings of belonging, citizenship, identity, and family remain unresolved.

ACKNOWLEDGMENTS

I could not have completed this book without the support of many people. When I began this project, I really had no idea how long it would take to complete or how much my life would change in those years. Many thanks to my colleagues in the History Department at the University at Albany. From my first presentation of my work to the final days of completing this book, they have asked questions and offered advice about research, writing, and teaching that has helped me immensely. I owe a special thanks to Richard Hamm, who has been a phenomenal mentor. He has graciously given his time and energy to help me think about what the book could be, and he has been the model of a conscientious scholar and engaged teacher. Thanks also to Irene Andrea and Jamie Winn. Although their official job title is (and in the case of Ms. Andrea, was) Assistant to the Department Chair, they have been my sounding board.

I received generous support from the NYS/UUP's Dr. Nuala McGann Drescher Leave Program that made it possible for me to focus exclusively on research and writing. The University at Albany's College of Arts and Sciences also funded my research at a number of archives and libraries as well as trips to conferences. My research began at the Social Welfare History Archives at the University of Minnesota, and archivists David Klaassen and Linnea Anderson were the best guides through the records of International Social Services (ISS). Each time I went back to sift through the records of ISS or the Child Welfare League of America, I met dedicated individuals who were always helpful. I cannot say enough about the archivists, librarians, and student workers at the Amistad Research Center; Emory University's Manuscript, Archives, and Rare Book Library; Lipscomb Library, Randolph College; the Special Collections and Archives of Fisk University; and the Robert W. Woodruff Library and Archives Research Center of the Atlanta University. I always seem to underprepare when I conduct research at the Library of Congress,

Manuscript Division and National Archives II, but the staff at each of these amazing sites were infinitely patient with me as they guided me to the right finding aids and offered thoughtful advice that helped me strategize my research. A special thanks to the librarians at the University at Albany and especially the interlibrary loan team. There have been many days when I have whispered a "thank you" to my computer when an article I requested that morning arrived in my email by that afternoon.

A number of people associated with the Alliance for the Study of Adoption and Culture (ASAC) encouraged me to get the book done at moments when I was not sure that I could. My deepest gratitude to Karen A. Balcom, Laura Briggs, Cynthia Callahan, Kelly Condit-Shrestha, Silke Hackenesch, Eleana J. Kim, Arissa H. Oh, Kim Park Nelson, and Rosemarie Peña. I consider myself exceedingly fortunate to have had so many opportunities to learn from these scholars and participate in the vibrant community of scholars, activists, adoptees, birth parents, and adoptive parents who are shaping the field of adoption studies.

I am also thankful to the organizations whose records made this book possible. In particular, I am grateful to Julie Rosicky, the executive director of the International Social Service–United States of America Branch (ISS-USA) who granted me access to the collection. Although these records have been invaluable to the project, points of view in this book are mine and do not necessarily represent the official position or policies of International Social Service, United States of America Branch, Inc. For more information about ISS-USA, see http://www.iss-usa.org. Sheila Scott with the *Afro-American* Archives helped me sort out the requirements of that organization whose online archive is a phenomenal collection. Finally, former archivist, Lyn Stallings, and staff at Pearl S. Buck International helped me conduct research in the PSB records and Buck's extensive collection. They were also supportive of this project from the first years I began researching at that site.

In graduate school, I was fortunate to have a committee that was excited about the project and confident that I could pull it off, even when I was not. Nan Enstad, Susan Lee Johnson, Brenda Gayle Plummer, Christina Greene, and Charles Kim provided invaluable guidance that helped me begin the process of putting my work together to write this book. Clara Platter, editor at NYU Press, was an unfailing advocate for me and she provided support and encouragement at key moments when I was revising the manuscript. Without her patient persistence, I do not think the process of finishing the book would have gone as smoothly as it did. It was a pleasure to work with editorial assistant, Amy Klopfenstein, and the editorial and marketing teams at NYU Press who were quick to answer questions I had about the nuts-and-bolts of publishing. The constructive critiques I received from the readers of the manuscript were thoughtful and encouraging. I will be forever grateful to them for the time they gave this book and the assistance they offered to me.

Friends and family sustained me through the years it took to complete this work. I happily owe a debt of gratitude to many of them and especially Dorothea Browder, Andrea Christofferson, Paul and Patricia Ferrell, Erica Fraser, Ellen Hickman, Michel Hogue, Susan Lee Johnson, Sarah, Kelly, and Abe King, Danielle Kinsey, Story Lee Matkin-Rawn, Holly McGee, Adrienne Middlebrooks, and Gwen Walker. My sister, Naomi O. Shingles, and my aunt, Gloria Hazard, have always been in my corner. My mother, Angelia Marie Thompson (1949–2006), was an amazing teacher. I credit her with instilling in me the desire to puzzle out problems and a willingness to look silly in the process. Her example inspires me still. It is my greatest joy to share my life with my husband, Ted Riese, and our son, Orion David Riese. They have encouraged me, traveled to archives with me, cooked for me, read with me, reminded me to have fun, and helped me stay grounded. I dedicate this book to them.

NOTES

INTRODUCTION

1 "How to Adopt Korean Babies," *Ebony*, September 1955, 31.

2 William T. Kirk to Editor, *Ebony*, August 29, 1955, Box 35, Folder: ISS Branches, Korea "RRA-5" 1954–December1955, International Social Service, American Branch records, Social Welfare History Archives, University of Minnesota (hereafter ISS records).

3 Susan T. Pettiss to Directors, Divisions of Child Welfare, State Departments of Public Welfare, August 29, 1955, Box 35, Folder: ISS Branches, Korea "RRA-5" 1954–December 1955, ISS records.

4 Kirk to Editor, *Ebony*, August 29, 1955.

5 Plummer, "Brown Babies," 67–91; and Fehrenbach, *Race after Hitler*.

6 Green, *Black Yanks in the Pacific*, 89.

7 Ibid., 104.

8 Dorow, *Transnational Adoption*, 26.

9 Balcom, *Traffic in Babies*, 197; and Dubinsky, *Babies without Borders*.

10 Briggs, *Somebody's Children*, 33–48, 77–93, 137–178, and 201–216.

11 The field of critical adoption studies developed as a result of efforts by scholars in the fields of Asian American studies and adoption cultural studies to advance literary, feminist, and cultural critiques of the historical and contemporary practices of adoption. For more on the history of and future directions in critical adoption studies, see articles in Special Issue: Critical Adoption Studies, *Adoption and Culture* 6, no. 1 (2018).

12 Choy, *Global Families*; Hübinette, *Comforting an Orphaned Nation*; Kim, "Wedding Citizenship and Culture," 49–80.

13 McKee, "Monetary Flows," 139.

14 Kim, "A Country Divided," 11.

15 Berebitsky, *Like Our Very Own*, 2–3; and Porter, "A Good Home," 27–28.

16 Melosh, *Strangers and Kin*, 12–50; and Rymph, *Raising Government Children*, 17–24.

17 The Orphan Train movement of the late nineteenth and early twentieth centuries is one of the most famous examples of boarding out that involved the movement of children on trains from urban areas to families in the countryside, often in Midwestern states. Congregational minister Charles Loring Brace began sending children, many of whom were the children of Catholic immigrants, from New

York to rural families in 1854. There was very little regulation of this practice, and many orphan train children experienced violence and exploitation because the families treated them like indentured servants (and in some cases the children were legally indentured servants). For more on Charles Loring Brace and the Orphan Train movement, see Berebitsky, *Like Our Very Own*, 41–42; and Rymph, *Raising Government Children*, 37–40. The failure of the New York Foundling Home's effort to place white, Irish Catholic children with Mexican Catholic families in the small copper-mining towns of Clifton and Morenci, Arizona in 1904 is a remarkable orphan train case that revealed how issues of religion, ethnicity, class, and race structured adoption and child-placing strategies in the nineteenth and early twentieth centuries. In this example, a group of white, Protestant families forcibly removed a number of white, Irish children from the Mexican Catholics who had agreed to adopt them. For more, see Gordon, *Great Arizona Orphan Abduction*.

18 Gordon, *Pitied but Not Entitled*.

19 Balcom, *Traffic in Babies*, 62, and 166–194; and Herman, *Kinship by Design*, 31–41.

20 Herman, *Kinship by Design*, 134–154; and Melosh, *Strangers and Kin*, 36–43.

21 Balcom, *Traffic in Babies*, 197; Briggs, *Somebody's Children*, 34–35; and Herman, *Kinship by Design*, 229–238.

22 Solinger, *Wake Up Little Susie*, 24–25 and 148–204; For more on the cultural and social factors influencing social welfare programs for single mothers in the twentieth century, see Franklin, *Ensuring Inequality*, 138; Kunzel, *Fallen Women, Problem Girls*; and Rickie Solinger, *Beggars and Choosers: How the Politics of Choice Shapes Adoption, Abortion, and Welfare in the United States* (New York: Hill and Wang, 2002). Many of the American unmarried mothers who relinquished their children for adoption in the postwar years experienced pressure from their parents, the fathers of their children, and social workers to do so. The stigma associated with unmarried pregnancy forced many women to also keep their pregnancies secret, leaving them to struggle with the pain and remorse of the loss and separation in silence. For more on first mothers' experiences, see Ann Fesseler, *The Girls Who Went Away: The Hidden History of Women Who Surrendered Children for Adoption in the Decades before* Roe v. Wade (New York: Penguin Books, 2007); Lorraine Dusky, *Birthmark* (New York: M. Evans, 1979).

23 Balcom, *Traffic in Babies*, 197.

24 Ibid., 195–231; Herman, *Kinship by Design*, 195–252; and Solinger, *Wake Up Little Susie*, 148–186.

25 White, *Too Heavy a Load*; and Wolcott, *Remaking Respectability*.

26 Rymph, *Raising Government Children*, 34–36. One of the earliest orphanages established by an African American was the Carrie Steele-Pitts Home, founded in 1888 by Carrie Steele. Steele worked as a maid for the Union Station in Atlanta, Georgia. She began the orphanage to care for the abandoned children she found at the station. For more on the Carrie Steele-Pitts Home, see Albert J. H. Sloan II, "The Carrie Steele-Pitts Home and the Church Partners in Mission" (master's

thesis, The Interdenominational Theological Center, 1969). White benevolent reformers in northern cities also opened orphanages for African American children. For more on nineteenth- and early twentieth-century orphanages for African American children, see Jessie B. Ramey, *Child Care in Black and White: Working Parents and the History of Orphanages* (Champaign: University of Illinois Press, 2012); and William Seraile, *Angels of Mercy: White Women and the History of New York's Colored Orphan Asylum* (New York: Fordham University Press, 2013).

27 For more on nineteenth- and twentieth-century initiatives to care for displaced African American children, see Jacqueline Rouse, *Lugenia Burns Hope, Black Southern Reformer* (Athens: University of Georgia Press, 2004); and Stephanie J. Shaw, *What a Woman Ought to Be and to Do: Black Professional Women Workers during the Jim Crow Era* (Chicago: University of Chicago Press, 1996).

28 Mabel Alston Grammer's Brown Baby Plan was the most successful private effort to place German black children with African American families in the United States. Grammer was an African American journalist who wrote for the black newspaper the *Afro-American*. While living in Germany with her husband, Oscar Grammer, a serviceman stationed in Mannheim, Mabel had her first encounters with German black children. Publicizing her plan in the *Afro-American*, Grammer helped coordinate hundreds of placements. For more on Grammer, see Fehrenbach, *Race after Hitler*, 147–156.

29 For a description of the child welfare services available to African American children in New York, NY; Philadelphia, PA; and Cleveland, Ohio in the 1930 and 1940s, see Billingsley and Giovannoni, *Children of the Storm*, 101–139.

30 May, *Homeward Bound*.

31 Potter, *Everybody Else*, 49. For more on the US cultural emphasis on childbearing and childrearing in the Cold War era, see May, *Barren in the Promised Land*.

32 Briggs, *Somebody's Children*, 32–34; Herman, *Kinship by Design*, 236–238; Melosh, *Strangers and Kin*, 171–174; and Spence, "Whose Stereotypes and Racial Myths?."

33 For more on the history of white families' adoptions of African American children, see Bell, *The Black Power Movement and American Social Work*; Briggs, *Somebody's Children*; Day, *Adoption of Black Children*; Fogg-Davis, *Ethics of Transracial Adoption*; Herman, *Kinship by Design*; Melosh, *Strangers and Kin*; and Reid-Merritt, *Righteous Self Determination*.

34 Kennedy, *Interracial Intimacies*, 450. Herman provides a more detailed account of the first recorded transracial adoption of a black child by a white family. For more on that placement, see Herman, *Kinship by Design*, 238–239.

35 Audrey T. Russell, "Transracial Adoption Workshop-Speech," in *Diversity: Cohesion or Chaos-Mobilization for Survival; Proceedings of the Fourth Annual Conference of the N.A.B.S.W.* (Nashville, TN: Fisk University, April 1972), 285–297; Lauretta Flynn Byars, "Transracial Adoption: A Deviant Behavior," in *Diversity: Cohesion or Chaos-Mobilization for Survival; Proceedings of the Fourth Annual Conference of the N.A.B.S.W.* (Nashville, TN: Fisk University, April 1972), 298–307.

36 Briggs, *Somebody's Children*, 27–58; and Carp, *Family Matters*, 168–170. For more on the NABSW's position on transnational adoption, see Bell, *Black Power Movement and American Social Work*, 136–148; Berebitsky, *Like Our Very Own*, 168–170; Herman, *Kinship by Design*, 248–252; Melosh, *Strangers and Kin*, 174–177; Reid-Merritt, *Righteous Self Determination*, 31–58; and Winslow, *The Best Possible Immigrants*, 151–153.

37 Herman, *Kinship by Design*, 250.

38 Hübinette, *Comforting an Orphaned Nation*, 38–44; Oh, *To Save the Children of Korea*, 57–63; and Pate, *From Orphan to Adoptee*, 30–33.

39 Oh, *To Save the Children of Korea*, 127.

40 Choy, *Global Families*, 17.

41 Dorow, *Transnational Adoption*; Kim, *Adopted Territory*; Park Nelson, *Invisible Asians*; and Winslow, *The Best Possible Immigrants*.

42 Winslow, *The Best Possible Immigrants*, 10.

43 Plummer, "Brown Babies," 78–82.

44 "Britain's Brown Babies," *Our World*, July 1949, 16–19; "'Mulatto,'" *Our World*, January 1951, 50; "War Babies of Japan: Shunned and Deserted, More than 2,000 Racially Mixed Youngsters Face Tragic Future," *Ebony*, September 1951, 15–18; "Unwanted Babies," *Our World*, April 1952, 22–26; A. Gould, "Germany's Tragic War Babies: Children of Negro GI's and Frauleins Face Nazi-like Bias," *Ebony*, December 1952, 74–78; "British Foster Mother: London Housewife Has Cared for More Negro Children than Any Other English Woman," *Ebony*, January 1954, 62–63; "The Tragedy of Brown Babies Left in Japan," *Jet*, January 14, 1960, 14–17; "Fear 6,000 Brown Children of Negro GI's and German Women May Face Color Bar in Adult Society," *Jet*, January 28, 1960, 13; "Nation Rallies to Aid Japanese Brown Babies after Their Tragic Plight in Japan's Revealed," *Jet*, February 25, 1960, 19; "Negro-German Tots Making Good Adjustment in Germany," *Jet*, April 7, 1960, 47; "Tragic Story of German Brown Baby's Home-Coming," *Jet*, May 19, 1960, 14–17; and "Japanese Race Bars Dropping for 'Brown Babies,'" *Jet*, June 2, 1960, 15.

45 Choy, *Global Families*, 40; Hübinette, *Comforting an Orphaned Nation*, 42–58; E. Kim, *Adopted Territory*, 43–77; Jae Ran Kim, "Scattered Seeds," 151–162; and Oh, *To Save the Children of Korea*, 23–38 and 79–112.

46 Herman, *Kinship by Design*, 121–154.

47 Dudziak, *Cold War Civil Rights*.

48 Borstelmann, *The Cold War and the Color Line*, 59.

49 For a discussion of US domestic and foreign policy during the Cold War, see John Lewis Gaddis, *The United States and the Origins of the Cold War, 1941–1947* (New York: Columbia University Press, 1968); Melvyn Leffler, *A Preponderance of Power: National Security, the Truman Administration, and the Cold War* (Stanford, CA: Stanford University Press, 1992); Plummer, *Rising Wind*; Von Eschen, *Race against Empire* and *Satchmo Blows Up the World*; and William Appleman Williams, *The Tragedy of American Diplomacy* (New York: Norton, 1959).

50 Plummer, *In Search of Power*, 63.

51 Herman, *Kinship by Design*, 229.

52 Winslow, *The Best Possible Immigrants*, 12.

53 Choy, *Global Families*; Hübinette, *Comforting an Orphaned Nation*; E. Kim, *Adopted Territory*; McKee, "Monetary Flows"; Oh, *To Save the Children of Korea*; Pate, *From Orphan to Adoptee*.

54 Ngai, *Impossible Subjects*; Shah, *Contagious Divides*; Takaki, *Strangers from a Different Shore*; Yung, *Unbound Feet*.

55 Pate, *From Orphans to Adoptee*, 19.

CHAPTER 1. AFRICAN AMERICAN SOLDIERS AND THE ORIGINS OF
KOREAN TRANSNATIONAL ADOPTION

1 US Congress, House, Committee on the Judiciary, *For the relief of Rhee Song Wu Act: Report* (to Accompany S. 1731), 82nd Cong., 2nd sess., 1952, H. Rep. 2237, courtesy of Karen Balcom, PhD. Booker also claimed that Rhee's mother had died by the time he was able to bring him to the States, which made Rhee a true orphan.

2 Ibid.

3 Ibid.

4 Statistics charting the number of Korean children adopted between 1953 and 1970 can be found in Dong Soo Kim, "A Country Divided," 8.

5 Bill Purdom, "Officer Wins Fight to Adopt Lad: Korean Boy Starts for U.S.," *Pacific Stars and Stripes*, August 23, 1952, 5.

6 "Korean Orphan Lad Leaves for New Home," *Deseret News*, February 4, 1953, 11A.

7 Several magazines and newspapers carried the story of Booker's adoption, including: "New Yank," *New York Daily News*, 29 August 1952, 31; "Korean War Orphan, 9, Coming 'Home' at Last," *Los Angeles Times*, 5 February 1953, 26; "Negro Officer Adopts Korean War Orphan, 9," *Idaho State Journal*, 8 February 1953, 3; "Korean, Adopted by Negro Couple, Arrives in U.S.," *Jet*, 19 February 1953, 21; "First Hand Greetings," *Edwardsville Intelligencer*, 25 February 1953, 6; "Army Captain Adopts Korea Orphan," *Ebony*, September 1953, 25–26, 28, and 31–32; and Grace P. Oursler and April O. Armstrong, "Genius for Living," *The Boston Globe Fiction Magazine*, 19 September 1954, 4.

8 Pate, *From Orphan to Adoptee*, 35.

9 Oh, *To Save the Children of Korea*, 27–28.

10 Criticism of African American soldiers' performance followed them in all of the wars in which the United States participated, and several scholars endeavor to provide context for these, including Bowers, Hammond, and MacGarrigle, *Black Soldier, White Army*; Foner, *Blacks and the Military*; Green, *Black Yanks in the Pacific*; Knauer, *Let Us Fight as Free Men*; and Phillips, *War! What Is It Good For?*.

11 Pate, *From Orphan to Adoptee*, 21–40; and Oh, *To Save the Children of Korea*, 23–31.

12 Green, *Black Yanks in the Pacific*; Knauer, *Let Us Fight as Free Men*; and Phillips, *War! What Is It Good For?*. To varying degrees, scholarship on Cold War civil

rights also situates the Korean War in the historiographies of civil rights and global anticolonial struggles, including Borstelmann, *The Cold War and the Color Line*; Dudziak, *Cold War Civil Rights*; and Plummer, *Rising Wind*.

13 Knauer, *Let Us Fight as Free Men*, 31.

14 Moon, *Sex Among Allies*, 2.

15 Julius Wesley Becton, Jr. Collection (AFC/2001/001/75519), Veterans History Project, American Folklife Center, Library of Congress; John E. Mann Collection (AFC/2001/001/19265), Veterans History Project, American Folklife Center, Library of Congress; and Bowers et al., *Black Soldier, White Army*, 81, 82–85.

16 Rishell, *With a Black Platoon in Combat*, 13, 16–17, and 26–28.

17 Julius Wesley Becton, Jr. Collection, Veterans History Project; and Rishell, *With a Black Platoon in Combat*, 38–39 and 45–46.

18 Cumings, *Korea's Place in the Sun*, 276.

19 Bowers, Hammond, and MacGarrigle note that poor troop preparedness was a problem, but of the total deaths of African American soldiers, 352 occurred in noncombat situations. For more on the UN and KPA strength and losses in the early part of the war, see Bowers et al., *Black Soldier, White Army*, 26–29, 68, and 159.

20 Charles Earnest Berry Collection (AFC/2001/001/05950), Veterans History Project, American Folklife Center. Library of Congress.

21 Charles Bernard Rangel Collection (AFC/2001/001/89089), Veterans History Project, American Folklife Center, Library of Congress.

22 Hanley, Mendoza, and Sang-Hun, *The Bridge at No Gun Ri*.

23 Cumings, *Korea's Place in the Sun*, 271–275; and Green, *Black Yanks in the Pacific*, 114–115.

24 Cumings, *The Korean War: A History*, 21.

25 Hal Boyle, "Panic-Stricken Natives Stream Out of Taegu," *Boston Globe*, August 19, 1950, 2; "Iceland Sending Enough Cod Liver Oil to Take Care of 250,000 Korean Children," *Boston Globe*, October 8, 1950, 2; "Korean Children to Get Yule Gifts," *Los Angeles Times*, October 27, 1950, 23; "Glimpses of the Korean War: Pastors Hope to Deck Their Houses of God," *Boston Globe*, December 25, 1950, 38; and "Beggar Boys, Girls Given U.N. Aid, *Los Angeles Times*, January 22, 1951, 27.

26 "U.N. Fund Sets Aside $500,000 For Feeding of Children in Korea," *New York Times (NYT)*, July 28, 1950, 4; "Child Aid Agency Proposed by U.S.," *NYT*, August 4, 1950, 6; "I.R.O. Offers to Aid Korean Fugitives," *NYT*, August 5, 1950, 2; "1,500,000 Koreans to Receive U.N. Relief," *NYT*, August 19, 1950, 3; "Youngsters in Brooklyn Vacation School Start 'Kartons-for-Korean-Kids' Drive," *NYT*, August 19, 1950, 3; Lansing Warren, "UNESCO Heads Meet on Korea Program," *NYT*, August 27, 1950; and "6,000,000 Is Asked by U.N. Child Fund," *NYT*, October 3, 1950.

27 Nora Waln, "Our Softhearted Warriors in Korea," *Saturday Evening Post*, September 23, 1950, 29. For more on military officials' resistance to soldiers' efforts to house mascots in camps and barracks, see Woo, "A New American Comes 'Home,'" 63–68.

28 Woo, "A New American Comes 'Home,'" 66.

29 Ngai, *Impossible Subjects*, 17–90; Takaki, *Strangers from a Different Shore*; 14–15; Yang, *Asian Immigration*, 44, and 76–78.

30 Hübinette, *Comforting an Orphaned Nation*, 45.

31 Charles Dumas, "Lead Scouts of God," *Pacific Stars and Stripes*, July 7, 1951, 6.

32 Waln, "Our Softhearted Warriors in Korea," 66.

33 "Rugged GIs Weep as 'Mascots' Depart," *Pacific Stars and Stripes*, May 14, 1951, 5.

34 Pate, *From Orphan to Adoptee*, 54, 55.

35 Oh, *To Save the Children of Korea*, 27–28, 31–42. *Pacific Stars and Stripes* ran many articles about mascots and houseboys, including Sheldon Shapiro, "Little Children War's Biggest Casualty," *Pacific Stars and Stripes*, June 6, 1951, 2; and "8th Cav Regiment, ROKs Help Orphans," *Pacific Stars and Stripes*, July 27, 1951.

36 A reference to the pattern of soldiers arranging for the last man in a unit to adopt a mascot is included in Paul Cherney, "Notes on Field Visit—ISS Korea Staff," July 12, 1962, 17, Box 35, Folder: Korea–General/Adoptions from 1961, Discard, ISS records.

37 Lee, *A Troubled Peace.*

38 For more on soldiers' reconfiguration of Korean orphans as militarized subjects, see Pate, *From Orphan to Adoptee.*

39 Gilbert, *Men in the Middle*; Huebner, *The Warrior Image.*

40 For more on soldiers' relationships with Korean houseboys and mascots, see Hübinette, *Comforting an Orphaned Nation*, 35; and E. Kim, *Adopted Territory*, 47–53.

41 Pate, *From Orphan to Adoptee*, 52.

42 Milton Al Smith, "VA Officer Feeds 15,000 Daily in Korea: Lt. Al Brooks Bosses Army's Big Warehouses," *Afro-American*, December 9, 1950, 13.

43 Charles Earnest Berry Collection, Veterans History Project; and William Henry Harvey Collection (AFC/2001/001/27509), Veterans History Project, American Folklife Center, Library of Congress.

44 "Parson Tends Big Parish," *Pacific Stars and Stripes*, July 10, 1953, 7; and Malcolm Nash, "Missionary to Drug Addicts," *New York Amsterdam News*, April 9, 1955, 8. Reverend Charles C. Blake would later work with drug addicts in a program at Riverside Hospital.

45 "U.N. Services Give $70,373 to Korean Children Amputees," *Pacific Stars and Stripes*, October 29, 1952, 7. In addition to its coverage of soldiers' assistance to Koreans in hospitals and orphanages, The *Pacific Stars and Stripes* made stories about soldiers' Christmas charity a regular feature during the Korean War. For examples of such articles, see "UNCACK Seeks Sponsors to Bring Yule to Orphans," *Pacific Stars and Stripes*, December 9, 1951, 13; "Christmas in the Far East Command," *Pacific Stars and Stripes*, December 25, 1951, 10; "2d Div St. Nicks Give Korean Tots Taste of Christmas, *Pacific Stars and Stripes*, October 5, 1952, 6; "49th Wing Donates $4000 for Party, *Pacific Stars and Stripes*, November 15, 1952, 5; "X Corps to Deliver Christmas Presents to Korean Children, *Pacific Stars and Stripes*,

December 14, 1952, 10; "Christmas Party Grows into 'Avalanche' of Aid," *Pacific Stars and Stripes*, December 24, 1952, 6; "57th FA Unit Runs Workshop for Toys," *Pacific Stars and Stripes*, December 8, 1952, 7; "MSTS Gives Waifs Food, Candy, Money," *Pacific Stars and Stripes*, January 2, 1953, 6; and "Blood Donating Champ Gives Tots Belated Party," *Pacific Stars and Stripes*, February 8, 1953, 7.

46 E. Kim, *Adopted Territory*, 51.

47 "U.N. Services Give $70,373 to Korean Children Amputees," *Pacific Stars and Stripes*, October 29, 1952, 7. Throughout the war, the *Pacific Stars and Stripes* ran articles that talked about race, but often in a manner that showed the military's response to racial issues in a favorable light. Some examples of this type of reporting can be found in articles including "Equality Forecast In Armed Forces," *Pacific Stars and Stripes*, May 23, 1950, 4; "Last Negro Regt to Be Disbanded," *Pacific Stars and Stripes*, July 27, 1951, 1; "Billy Graham Praises Non-Segregation in FE Forces," *Pacific Stars and Stripes*, December 19, 1952, 16; "Bibles, Not Pinups, Seen By Billy Graham in Korea," *Pacific Stars and Stripes*, January 11, 1953, 7; and John J. Casserly, "American Returnees Score Red Captors' Prison Color Line," *Pacific Stars and Stripes*, August 11, 1953, 2.

48 "Inside Korean War Info," *New York Amsterdam News*, July 29, 1950, 6; Knauer describes that President Truman and several white newspapers also celebrated the 24th's victory at Yecheon. Knauer, *Let Us Fight as Free Men*, 179–181.

49 Knauer, *Let Us Fight as Free Men*, 179–181.

50 Jimmy Hicks, "24th Infantry Takes Yechon [*sic*] in 16 Hours," *Afro-American*, July 29, 1950, 1–2.

51 "Tan GIs See Action on Korea Front," *Chicago Defender*, July 1, 1950, 1 and 6; "Mass Troops for Push: Men Toiling Day, Night for Big Move," *Chicago Defender*, July 22, 1950, 1–2.

52 "Negro GI's Hit Korean Beaches," *New York Amsterdam News*, July 8, 1950, 1.

53 For more on the military's assessments of and responses to the 8th Army's performance in the war, see Bowers et al., *Black Soldier, White Army*, 121–123, 128–129; and Knauer, *Let Us Fight as Free Men*, 96–98, 195–202.

54 For more on African American civil rights leaders' conflicting positions regarding the Korean War, see Green, *Black Yanks in the Pacific*, 119–129; and Phillips, *War! What Is It Good For?*, 156–160.

55 Knauer, *Let Us Fight as Free Men*, 125–162.

56 Hicks's status as a correspondent reporting on the all-black 24th Infantry became even more significant following the tragic death of Albert L. Hinton, associate editor of the *Norfolk Journal and Guide*. Hinton and Hicks traveled to Japan together but were not on the same transport from Japan to Korea. Hinton died in a plane crash en route from Japan to Korea. He would have covered the war for his paper and five other African American newspapers, including the *Kansas City Call, Cleveland Call and Post, Houston Informer, Chicago Defender*, and the *Atlanta World*. "Hinton's Plane Explodes in Air," *Afro-American*, August 5, 1950, 1–2.

57 Farrar, *Baltimore Afro-American*, 1–22.

58 Ibid., xvi.

59 Ibid.

60 "Jimmy Hicks Off to Korea as Afro Correspondent, *Afro-American*, July 22, 1950, 1–2; "Afro Cover War in Korea," July 29, 1950, *Afro-American*, 4; and James L. Hicks, "159th Gets Smallpox Shots in Battle," *Afro-American*, September 23, 1950, 13. For more on the black press's coverage of the Korean War, see Broussard, *African American Foreign Correspondents*, 142–155; Farrar, *Baltimore Afro-American*, 172–173; Knauer, *Let Us Fight as Free Men*, 144–162; and Phillips, *War! What Is It Good For?*, 131–133.

61 "Korean Boy Gets English Lesson from Sergeant," *Afro American*, December 30, 1950, 7.

62 James L. Hicks, "GI's Attack Savage as News Comes In," *Afro-American*, September 23, 1950, 1–2; and James L. Hicks, "24th Hit Hard," *Afro-American*, August 19, 1950, 1 and 19.

63 A few examples of articles describing the activities of integrated units include James L. Hicks, "Integration a Fact as We Fight Koreans," *Afro-American*, August 19, 1950, 1–2; and James L. Hicks, "Mixed Chutists [*sic*] Land in Korea," *Afro-American*, September 30, 1950, 1–2. The black press took notice of what many activists and soldiers considered to be an inordinate number of courts-martial of African American soldiers. Notably, editors with *The Crisis*, the magazine of the National Association for the Advancement of Colored People (NAACP), began condemning what they described as the "smearing [of] Negro GIs in Korea" in December 1950. The press challenged accusations that African American soldiers had run from their posts or ignored orders that increased in the last months of 1950. The high number of African American soldiers charged with misconduct caused Thurgood Marshall, special counsel of the NAACP, to launch an investigation into the conditions surrounding their arrests and prosecutions in military courts. In the report summarizing his findings, Marshall called for an end to Jim Crow policies in the army because they made African American soldiers vulnerable to unjust treatment. Although lawyers with the NAACP successfully advised and represented a number of accused soldiers, persistent allegations of African American soldiers' cowardice tempered celebrations of the army's integration. "Smearing Negro GIs in Korea," *The Crisis*, December 1950, 715; "Along the N.A.A.C.P. Battlefront," *The Crisis*, December 1950, 716–718; "Along the N.A.A.C.P. Battlefront," *The Crisis*, January 1951, 39; "Mr. Marshall Reports," *The Crisis*, March 1951, 180. For more on the accusations of incompetence against black soldiers and subsequent courts-martial, see Bowers et al., *Black Soldier, White Army*, 172–178, 185–189; Knauer, *Let Us Fight as Free Men*, 195–211; and Phillips, *War! What Is It Good For?*, 135–143.

64 Cumings, *Korea's Place in the Sun*, 278–288. For more on the Chinese entry into the Korean War, see Lowe, *The Korean War*, 41–47.

65 For more on origins of the rollback strategy, see Cumings, *Korea's Place in the Sun*, 275–298; and Lowe, *The Korean War*, 36–47.

66 James L. Hicks, "U.S. Army in Korea Lacked Radios and Rifles Too: No Need to Be Surprised at Early Dearth of Equipment for Winter," *Afro-American*, December 2, 1950, 15; Milton A. Smith, "Reds Inflicting Heavy Losses: 24th Forced to Give Up Earlier Gains, Enemy Gets Dropped Supplies," *Afro-American*, December 9, 1950, 1; Milton Smith, "Defeat in Korea Stunning to Yanks," *Afro-American*, December 16, 1950, 1; "Colonel Okays Integration: Mixed Second Division Units' Bravery Lauded," *Afro-American*, December 30, 1950, 1.

67 Charles Earnest Berry Collection, Veterans History Project.

68 Charles Brooks Collection (AFC/2001/001/10963), Veterans History Project, American Folklife Center, Library of Congress.

69 Joseph Crawford Collection (AFC/2001/001/65354), Veterans History Project, American Folklife Center, Library of Congress.

70 Alfred Lloyd Simpson Collection (AFC/2001/001/43905), Veterans History Project American Folklife Center, Library of Congress; Charles Bernard Rangel Collection, Veterans History Project; John Anderson Thomas Collection (AFC/2001/001/16416), Veterans History Project, American Folklife Center, Library of Congress; Robert White Collection (AFC/2001/001/10909), Veterans History Project, American Folklife Center, Library of Congress; and Bowers et al., *Black Soldier, White Army*, 199–218.

71 Morrow, *What's a Commie Ever Done to Black People?*, 15–19.

72 Ibid., 71, 87.

73 Phillips, *War! What Is It Good For?*, 135–135.

74 Knauer, *Let Us Fight as Free Men*, 137.

75 For more on black soldiers' responses to the violence of the Korean War and the inequalities they experienced in the military, see Phillips, *War! What Is It Good For?*, 12, 15–17, and 154–158; Green, *Black Yanks in the Pacific*, 124–129; and Knauer, *Let Us Fight as Free Men*, 143–153. Philips references the comments of Corporal George F. Baynham in his letter to the editor of the *Afro-American* when describing the ways some soldiers identified similarities in the oppression of African Americans in the US South and Koreans. George F. Baynham, "Hear Our Lord Amen," *Afro-American*, August 4, 1951, 4.

76 Von Eschen, *Race Against Empire*, 22–23.

77 Mullen, *Afro-Orientalism*, vx.

78 Ibid., 3.

79 Ibid., 12–31.

80 Von Eschen, *Race Against Empire*, 107.

81 Ibid., 123–124.

82 Green, *Black Yanks in the Pacific*, 124–129.

83 Farrar, *Baltimore Afro-American*, 11–12, 15, 21, and 187; and Broussard, *African American Foreign Correspondents*, 143, 152–153.

84 Jimmy Hicks, "Natives, Cows, Dogs, Chickens Live in Same Huts, Conditions Shocking," *Afro-American*, September 30, 1950, 12. Hicks also describes his

discomfort with the physical surroundings in "Korean Assignment No 'Bed of Roses': Too Much Lacking," *Afro-American*, July 29, 1950, 7.

85 Ralph Matthews, "Seoul Is Smelly, Dead—Matthews," *Afro-American*, August 11, 1951, 1.

86 Ralph Matthews, "Korean War National Tragedy: 212,554 Dead, Wounded 600,000 Homeless Wrecked," *Afro-American*, September 1, 1951, 14.

87 Ralph Matthews, "A Rejuvenated Metropolis: Seoul, Once Dead City, Outlives War's Ravages," *Afro-American*, September 1, 1951, 14.

88 Eugene Hill, Jr. Collection (AFC/2001/001/44094), Veterans History Project, American Folklife Center, Library of Congress.

89 Knauer, *Let Us Fight as Free Men*, 129–162. For more on civil rights strategies of the Cold War era, see Dudziak, *Cold War Civil Rights*, Plummer, *Rising Wind*; and Singh, *Black Is a Country*.

90 Earl D. Johnson, Memo, "Racial Segregation in FECOM," July 19, 1951, in *Blacks in the United States Armed Forces: Basic Documents*, vol. 12: *Integration*, ed. Morris J. MacGregor and Bernard C. Nalty (Wilmington, DE: Scholarly Resources., 1977), 197–198; Knauer, *Let Us Fight as Free Men*, 195–199, 209. Peace talks began in July 1951 but stalled in December 1951 over the issue of the repatriation of prisoners of war (POWs). For more on the status of POWs in Korean peace talk negotiations, see Lowe, *The Korean War*, 72–89; and Monica Kim, "Empire's Babel."

91 William Knox Collection (AFC/2001/001/05481), Veterans History Project, American Folklife Center, Library of Congress; Ralph Matthews, "GIs Welcome Integration, Don't Like Army Method," *Afro-American*, December 8, 1951, 14.

92 Broussard, *African American Foreign Correspondents*, 152–153.

93 Ralph Matthews Sr., "Men of War Become Life Savers: Soldiers from 23 States Build Playground in Korea," *Afro-American*, December 1, 1951, 14.

94 Pate, *From Orphan to Adoptee*, 29–30. For more on orphanages in Korea, see Hübinette, *Comforting an Orphaned Nation*, 38–41.

95 Pate, *From Orphan to Adoptee*, 32.

96 Ibid., 103–104.

97 Oh, *To Save the Children of Korea*, 57. Oh also includes statistics from UNKRA that placed the number of children in these facilities at 38,700. "Thoughtful Soldier Makes Orphans Happy," *Afro-American*, December 22, 1951, 2.

98 Ralph Matthews Sr., "89th Tankers Make War Orphans Happy: Chip in 9,000,000 Won from Their Army Pay, Give Up Candy Rations," *Afro-American*, November 3, 1951, 9.

99 Ralph Matthews, "Think of Christmas and Him," *Afro-American*, December 22, 1951, 14.

100 "Relief Packages Can Be Sent to Korea," *Afro Magazine*, February 8, 1952, 8.

101 Hosu Kim, *Birth Mothers*; Soh, *The Comfort Women*.

102 Soh, *The Comfort Women*, 7–20, 23–24, 211, and 117–127.

103 Moon, *Sex among Allies*, 27.

104 Soh, *The Comfort Women*, 212.

105 Moon, *Sex among Allies*, 72.

106 The scholarship on comfort women has exposed the ways Japanese officials and Korean officials, family members, and communities participated in systems that exploited large numbers of Korean women. For more on comfort women and the evolution of Japanese and Korean military prostitution, see Moon, *Sex among Allies*; and Yoshimi, *Comfort Women*.

107 Ralph Matthews, "How Sex Demoralized Our Army in Korea," *Afro-American*, August 5, 1950, 7.

108 Memo, "Marriages between American citizens and Korean citizens (nationals)," November 28, 1951, Records of the 8th Army AG, Record Group 338, Box 519, National Archives at College Park, College Park, MD (hereafter Archives II).

109 Zeiger, *Entangling Alliances*, 6, 131–132. The military enacted the policy giving commanding officers the final decision in a soldier's request to marry in 1942.

110 Zeiger, *Entangling Alliances*, 169; and Nakamura, "Families Precede Nation and Race?," 23–74. Although the 1947 amendment eliminated racial restrictions, it maintained time limitations and did not allow war brides from Japan and Korea to become US citizens. Japanese and Korean war brides would not be eligible for US citizenship until the passage of the 1952 McCarran-Walter Act (Immigration and Nationality Act of 1952). Although the McCarren-Walter Act maintained the national origins quotas that began in 1924 when Congress passed the Johnson-Reed Act (Immigration Act of 1924), it did eliminate the restrictions on Asian immigration that were a part of the 1924 Act.

111 Green, *Black Yanks in the Pacific*, 65.

112 Ibid., 72–77; Knauer, *Let Us Fight as Free Men*, 144–148.

113 For a comprehensive analysis of the systemic gender oppression that accompanies militarization see Enloe, *Bananas, Beaches, and Bases*, and Sturdevant and Stoltzfus, *Let the Good Times Roll*.

114 Green, *Black Yanks in the Pacific*, 80. For more on soldiers' marriages to Korean women, see Yuh, *Beyond the Shadow of Camptown*.

115 "Weary GIs Do Pusan Stomp," *Afro-American*, September 9, 1950, 19.

116 Joseph Crawford Collection, Veterans History Project.

117 Hicks, "Natives, Cows, Dogs, Chickens," 12.

118 Milton A. Smith, "Korean Belles 'No Trouble', Says Smith: VD Rate, Garlic Help Keep GIs 'Straight,'" *Afro-American*, December 16, 1950, 13.

119 James L. Hicks, "Japanese or American Girls: Which? Why?," *Afro-American*, October 7, 1950, 1–2.

120 Sidney Joulon, "On Romance in Japan: Sergeant Defends Soldiers' Actions," *Afro-American*, October 14, 1950, 4.

121 M. Cummings, "Advice for U.S. Gals," *Afro-American*, December 2, 1950, 4.

122 Frederick J. Bryant, "On GI's Behavior," *Afro-American*, November 4, 1950, 4.

123 James L. Hicks, "Many 24th Men Eye Brides in Japan," *Afro-American*, November 4, 1950, 1; James L. Hicks, "Officer Says Our Girls in Japan Not Attractive: Defends Morals of Native Women," *Afro-American*, November 25, 1950, 13. For more on

the legal, military, and social barriers to African American soldiers' marriages to Japanese women, see Green, *Black Yanks in the Pacific*, 60–71.

124 James Elmer Bishop Collection (AFC/2001/001/ 15442), Veterans History Project, American Folklife Center, Library of Congress; Eugene Hill Jr. Collection, Veterans History Project; and Morrow, *What's a Commie Ever Done to Black People?*, 32.

125 James Milton Harp Collection (AFC/2001/001/17213), Veterans History Project, American Folklife Center, Library of Congress.

126 Lawrence Penny Baltimore Collection (AFC/2001/001/16378), Veterans History Project, American Folklife Center, Library of Congress.

127 Plummer, "Brown Babies," 69–70. Also see Lee, "A Forgotten Legacy," 168–171. For more on the military's response to interracial intimacies and the German brown baby crisis, see Fehrenbach, *Race After Hitler*, 68–69.

128 Green, *Black Yanks in the Pacific*, 27–28.

129 James Elmer Bishop Collection, Veterans History Project.

130 Phillips, *War! What Is It Good For?*, 127.

131 For more on the consequences of African American soldiers' objectification of Asian women, see Green, *Black Yanks in the Pacific*, 52–86; and Knauer, *Let Us Fight as Free Men*, 153–159.

132 J. P. Spivey, "Girls in Korea Are Still Girls," *Afro-American*, June 2, 1951, 4.

133 Ralph Matthews, "Corrupt GIs Divert Food, Clothes; Every Native Wears a Part of Army Uniform; Black Market Thrives; Stealing Is Business; Pusan Stinks," *Afro-American*, September 15, 1951, 9.

134 Moon, *Sex among Allies*, 85–126. The army's attempts to control the spread of venereal diseases involved several levels of intervention. Education programs and medical inspections often proved insufficient regulation and the military had to coordinate with government and police officials in Japan and Korea to establish programs that targeted prostitutes and penalized sex workers more than soldiers. For more on regulatory methods and the effects they had on Korean sex workers, see Bowers et al., *Black Soldier, White Army*, 52–55; and Moon, *Sex among Allies*.

135 Moon, *Sex among Allies*, 27–28.

136 Matthews, "Corrupt GIs Divert Food, Clothes," *Afro-American*, September 15, 1951, 9.

137 Ralph Matthews, "UN Forces Save Thousands from Dope Dens Keep Virgil [*sic*] Spotting 'Junk,' Splotched Girls," *Afro-American*, October 6, 1951, 14. For more on the issue of drug addiction and soldiers in Japan and Korea, see Bowers et al., *Black Soldier, White Army*, 53–55, 264–265; and Green, *Black Yanks in the Pacific*, 118–119.

138 Kim, "Reparation Acts," 330.

139 For more on the discursive power of orientalism, see Mullen, *Afro-Orientalism*; and Said, *Orientalism*, 284–328. The 1882 Chinese Exclusion Act was the first US immigration restriction to target a specific nationality. It prohibited the immigration of Chinese laborers for ten years. Subsequent renewals closed the door to significant Chinese immigration until Congress repealed the Act in 1943, in part,

because the United States and China were allies during World War II. The US and Japanese governments worked together to limit the immigration of Japanese laborers with the 1908 Gentlemen's Agreement. The Agreement stipulated that the Japanese government would prevent immigrations of Japanese laborers to the United States by refusing to issue passports to individuals classified as a skilled or unskilled laborer. The Agreement did make provisions for family reunification that allowed Japanese laborers who had already entered the United States to bring their families. The 1924 Immigration Act would eliminate this provision, however. The Japanese officials also played a role in slowing migrations of Korean laborers to the States after Korea became a protectorate of Japan in 1905. The Japanese government successfully pressured the Korean government to prohibit Korean migrations to the States before Japan annexed Korea in 1910. Because the Philippines became a territory of the United States in 1898, migrants from that nation would not face these kinds of immigration restrictions until 1934. That year, Congress passed the Tydings-McDuffie Act, which recognized that nation's independence but severely limited the possibility for Filipinos to immigrate to the United States. For more on the history of Asian exclusion and opposition to exclusion, see Kurashige, *Two Faces of Exclusion*; Ngai, *Impossible Subjects*; Takaki, *Strangers from a Different Shore*; and Yang, *Asian Immigration*.

140 "Korean War Brought Soldiers New Deal," *Amsterdam News*, August 1, 1953, 1, 13; M. D. Cartwright, "What Korea Was About," *Amsterdam News*, August 8, 1953, 16; Alex L. Wilson, "Wilson Says Mixed Army Big Gain of Korean War," *Chicago Defender*, August 8, 1953, 1–2; "Truce Is Signed, Fighting Ends," *Afro-American*, August 1, 1953, 1; and "The Lesson of Korea," *Afro-American*, August 8, 1953, 4.

CHAPTER 2. THE NATIONAL URBAN LEAGUE AND THE FIGHT FOR US ADOPTION REFORM

1 For more on the evolution of adoption service delivery for African American clients in the United States, see Briggs, *Somebody's Children*; Franklin, *Ensuring Inequality*; Herman, *Kinship by Design*; Melosh, *Strangers and Kin*; and Solinger, *Wake Up Little Susie*. Sarah Potter offers a counter-example of the tendency of agencies to limit African Americans' adoption options that shows how local initiatives did increase adoptions among working-class African Americans. Potter, *Everybody Else*.

2 Weiss, *The National Urban League, 1910–1940*, 67.

3 Moore, *A Search for Equality*, 144–145; and Weiss, *The National Urban League*, 64–68.

4 Reed, *Not Alms but Opportunity*, 174.

5 Parris and Brooks, *Blacks in the City*, 352. For more on the National Urban League's origins and social work orientation, see Armfield, *Eugene Knickle Jones*; Reed, *Not Alms but Opportunity*; and Weiss, *The National Urban League, 1910–1940*, 71–79.

6 Moore, *A Search for Equality*, 48, 49–55.

7   Ibid., 150.

8   For more on the history of the Urban League's adoption project and its shift from efforts to increase African American adoptions to programs that experimented with the placement of African American children with white adoptive families, see Spence, "Whose Stereotypes and Racial Myths?."

9   Nelson C. Jackson, "The National Urban League's Project in Foster Home and Adoption Services," February 1, 1953, Box I: B19, Folder: Adoption Program, Reports and Statements, 1953–1961, National Urban League records, Manuscript Division, Library of Congress, Washington, DC (hereafter NUL records).

10 Eugene Beasley to Katherine F. Lenroot, April 6, 1950, Box 452, Folder 7-3-3-4-1, 1949–1952, Appeals from People Wishing Children for Adoptions, Records of the U.S. Children's Bureau, Record Group 102, National Archives II, College Park, MD (hereafter Children's Bureau records); Mrs. Albert Bashfield to Children's Bureau, January 25, 1949, Box 451, Folder: 7-3-3-4-1, 1949–1952, Appeals from People Wishing Children for Adoptions, Children's Bureau records; and Marion S. Goodwin to Doris Higgins, February 25, 1953, Box 685, Folder: December 1953, Adoption 1953–1956, Children's Bureau records.

11 Parris and Brooks, *Blacks in the City*, 353; Nelson C. Jackson, "The National Urban League's Project in Foster Home and Adoption Services," 1, and 2; and Fanshel, *A Study in Negro Adoption*, 10–13.

12 Bertha C. Reynolds, "A Way of Understanding an Approach to Case Work with Negro Families," *The Family* 12, no. 7 (November 1931): 203–208.

13 Leora L. Conner, "The Effects of Case Work Services on Socio-Political Factors in the Negros Life," *The Family* 22, no. 7 (November 1942): 243, 245.

14 Walter P. Townsend, "An Expanding Adoption Service for Negro Children," September 23, 1953, 5, Box I: B19, Folder: Adoption Program, Reports and Statements, 1953–1961, NUL Reports records.

15 Ibid., 11.

16 Townsend, "An Expanding Adoption Service for Negro Children," 6, 8.

17 Melosh, *Strangers and Kin*, 38.

18 Herman, *Kinship by Design*, 64–72, 155–191, 351.

19 Townsend, "An Expanding Adoption Service for Negro Children," 4, 7, 8.

20 "Services for Negro Unmarried Mothers, Their Children and or Adoptive Parents," December 7, 1951, Central File 1949–1952, Box 455, File 7-4-2-1, Unmarried Mothers, Children's Bureau records.

21 Solinger, *Wake Up Little Susie*, 51, 65–76, 161–164.

22 Mrs. Albert Bashfield to Children's Bureau, January 25, 1949, Box 452, Folder: 7-3-3-4-1, 1949–1952, Appeals from People Wishing Children for Adoptions, Children's Bureau records; Mrs. James Davis to Welfare folks, January 3, 1949, Box 452, Folder: 7-3-3-4-1, 1949–1952, Appeals from People Wishing Children for Adoptions, Children's Bureau records.

23 Mildred Arnold to Staff, Social Service Division, March 1949, Box 455, Folder: 7-4-1-2 Nonresident Unwed Mothers (Interstate Problems) 1949–1952, Children's

Bureau records; Mildred Arnold to Mrs. B. T. Henry, December 1, 1950, Box 451, Folder: 7-3-3-4-1, 1949–1952, Appeals from People Wishing Children for Adoptions, Children's Bureau records; and I. Evelyn Smith to Hollie L. Bryant, July 7, 1952, Box 451, Folder: 7-3-3-4-1, 1949–1952, Appeals from People Wishing Children for Adoptions, Children's Bureau records.

24 Nelson C. Jackson, "The National Urban League's Project in Foster Home and Adoption Services," 2–3, 4.

25 Forrester B. Washington, "Greetings," *Intake* 1, no. 1 (1936): 3, Atlanta University Center Robert W. Woodruff Library, Box: Atlanta University School of Social Work Newsletters, Folder: INTAKE, volume 1, no. 1, November 1936 (hereafter Atlanta University School of Social Work records); and Atlanta University School of Social Work Bulletin, 1949–1950, 13, Box Atlanta University School of Social Work Bulletin, 1927–1949, Folder: 1949–1950, Atlanta University School of Social Work records.

26 For more on the changing definitions of hard-to-place children, see Balcom, *Traffic in Babies*, 159–161, 196–203; and Herman, *Kinship by Design*, 196–201. Catherine E. Rymph notes that African American children were not counted among the hard-to-place for much of the first half of the twentieth century because most agencies did not provide adoption services to black clients. Rymph, *Raising Government Children*, 124.

27 Nelson C. Jackson, "The National Urban League's Project in Foster Home and Adoption Services."

28 Weiss, *The National Urban League, 1910–1940*, 85, 118.

29 Nelson C. Jackson, "The National Urban League's Project in Foster Home and Adoption Services, 5; and Weiss, *The National Urban League, 1910–1940*, 83, 88, 168.

30 Nelson C. Jackson, "Foster Home and Adoptive Services for Minority Children," n.d., 7–8, and 12, Box I: B19, Folder: Adoption Program, Reports and Statements, 1953–1961. In one case the Urban League was instrumental in securing $200,000.00 for community organization planning and recruitment of adoptive parents for minority children.

31 Nelson C. Jackson to Lester B. Granger, March 8, 1954, Box I: B19, Folder: 1953–1955, Adoption Program Correspondence and Memoranda (General), NUL Reports I records.

32 Annie Lee Sandusky to Maynard Catching, June 23, 1954, Box 685, Folder: April 1954, Children's Bureau records.

33 Nelson C. Jackson to Lester B. Granger, April 26, 1954, Box I: B 19, Folder: Adoption Program, Correspondence and Memo, 1953–1959, NUL records; Michael Schapiro to Nelson C. Jackson, May 10, 1954, Part I: Box I: B1, Folder: Correspondence and Memo (General), 1953–1959, NUL records; Schapiro included the following news clippings describing the Child Welfare League of America's plan: Joan Cook, "Broad Study of Adoption Field Planned," *New York Herald Tribune*, January 13, 1954; Dorothy Barclay, "League to Study Adoption Policies," *New York Times*, January 13, 1954.

34 Ashby U. Gaskins to Nelson C. Jackson, May 21, 1954, Box I: B 19, Folder: Adoption Program, Correspondence and Memoranda, 1953–1959, NUL records; Rose Graul to Lester B. Granger, May 5, 1954, Box I: B 19, Folder: Adoption Program, Correspondence and Memoranda, 1953–1959, NUL records; and Nelson C. Jackson to Rose Graul, June 3, 1954, Box I: B 19, Folder: Adoption Program, Correspondence and Memoranda, 1953–1959, NUL records.

35 Weiss, *The National Urban League, 1910–1940*, 216–218; and Nelson C. Jackson, "The National Urban League's Project in Foster Home and Adoption Services," 7 and 8.

36 Weiss, *The National Urban League, 1910–1940*, 74. Weis referenced, Robert L. Dexter, "The Negro in Social Work," *Survey*, 46, June 25, 1921, 439; and Lester B. Granger, "On Suggested Project in Foster Home and Adoption Services for Negro Children," June 4, 1954, Box I: B 19, Folder: Adoption Program, Correspondence and Memoranda, 1953–1959, NUL records.

37 Nelson C. Jackson to Rose Graul.

38 Lester B. Granger, "On Suggested Project in Foster Home and Adoption Services for Negro Children."

39 Nelson C. Jackson, "The National Urban League's Project in Foster Home and Adoption Services," 13, 15.

40 Fanshel, *A Study in Negro Adoption*, 14–17, 28, 46–47.

41 William S. Jackson, "Our Evolving Task in Adoption," March 26, 1958, 7 and 9, Part I: Box I: B1, Folder: Correspondence and Memo (General), 1956–1959, NUL records.

42 Ibid., 8–9.

43 Ibid., 10–11.

44 William S. Jackson, "Confidential Report to Study Committee," March 26, 1956, 14, Box I: B19, Folder: Adoption Program, Correspondence and Memoranda, 1953–1959, NUL records.

45 Nelson C. Jackson, "Community Action on Adoption," November 19, 1955, 3, Box I: B19, Folder: Adoption Program, Correspondence and Memoranda, 1953–1959, NUL records.

46 For more on the race and class dimensions of housing discrimination in the twentieth century, see Jackson, *Crabgrass Frontier*; Meyer, *As Long as They Don't Move Next Door*; and Self, *American Babylon*, 159–170.

47 Nelson C. Jackson, "Community Action on Adoption," 4.

48 Annie Lee Sandusky to Rev. Maynard Catching, June 23, 1954, Box 685 7-3-3-4, 1953–1954, Adoptions, Folder: April 1954, Children's Bureau records.

49 In a 1979 study, researcher Dawn Day demonstrates the prevalence of social workers' color preferences when placing children of color. For more on Day's analysis, see Day, *Adoption of Black Children*, 65.

50 William S. Jackson, "Confidential Report to Study Committee," 1.

51 Ibid., 1, 8, 9, 10.

52 Mrs. William Cunningham to Katherine F. Lenroot, March 9, 1949, Box 452, Folder 7-3-3-4-1, 1949–1952, Appeals from People Wishing Children for Adoptions;

and Mrs. Eugene Beasley to Katherine F. Lenroot, April 6, 1950, Box 452, Folder 7-3-3-4-1, 1949–1952, Appeals from People Wishing Children for Adoptions.

53 William S. Jackson, "Confidential Report to Study Committee," 11–12.

54 Ibid., 3, 4–5.

55 Ibid., 2, 4, 6–7.

56 William S. Jackson, "Our Evolving Task in Adoption," 11, 19.

57 William S. Jackson, "Confidential Report to Study Committee," 22.

58 Ibid., 18, 19, 23, 24.

59 Ibid., 19; and Nelson C. Jackson, "The National Urban League's Project in Foster Home and Adoption Services," 1; For more on the social workers' changing attitudes towards unwed mothers, see Kunzel, *Fallen Women, Problem Girls*; Rains, *Becoming an Unwed Mother*; Solinger, *Wake Up Little Susie*; Vincent, *Unmarried Mother*; and Young, *Out of Wedlock*.

60 Jackson's proposals highlight what social justice adoption reformers continue to promote. Dorothy Roberts's work in particular demonstrates the need for greater attention to the ways that social welfare reform and child welfare reform would reduce the need for adoption. For more on the contemporary issues of race and inequality that structure the nation's child welfare systems, see Roberts, *Shattered Bonds*.

61 William S. Jackson, "Our Evolving Task in Adoption," 14, 15, 19, 23, 24.

62 Ibid., 18.

63 Moore, *A Search for Equality*, 77. For more on the importance of Community Chests to the expansion of the Urban League Movement, see ibid., 56–58.

64 Ibid., 145, 182–185.

65 Mahlon T. Puryear to Nelson C. Jackson, October 3, 1956, Box I: B22, Folder: White Citizens Council Correspondence and Memoranda, 1954–1963, NUL records.

66 Anne Sweet to Nelson C. Jackson, January 16, 1957, Box I: B22, Folder: White Citizens Council Correspondence and Memoranda, 1956–1963, NUL records.

67 Nelson C. Jackson to Executive Secretaries of Local Affiliates, July 10, 1957, Box I: B22, Folder: White Citizens Council Correspondence and Memoranda, 1956–1963, NUL records.

68 Moore, *A Search for Equality*, 145.

69 Harry T. Alston to Jack [Nelson Jackson], October 7, 1956, Box I: B22, Folder: White Citizens Council Correspondence and Memoranda, 1956–1963, NUL records; and Clare Golden, Report of Field Visit, January 7, 1958, Box 674, Folder: 7-3-1-3, December 1957, 1953–1957 Interstate Placement, Non-Resident Problems, Juvenile Immigration, Transient Boys, Children's Bureau records.

70 Spence, "Whose Stereotypes and Racial Myths?," 145.

71 Ibid., 158, 160.

72 "Resolutions for the Delegate Assembly at the 1963 National Urban League Conference," August 1, 1963, Box 964, Folder: 0-2-9-1 1963–1966, Children's Bureau records.

73 Zitha R. Turitz, "Discussion with National Urban League of Revision of Adoption Standards," October 2, 1963, Box 13, Folder: 7-Standards-Adoption, 1957–1958, 1963–1965, Child Welfare League of America records, Social Welfare History Archives, University of Minnesota (hereafter CWLA records).

74 Guichard Parris, "Draft of a Paper Describing the Role of the National Urban League in the Development of its Adoption and Foster Care Programs," 1959, 31, Box I: B19, Folder: Adoption Program, Reports and Statements, 1953–1961, NUL records.

75 "Report of Adoption and Foster Care Activities of National Urban League Branch Offices," 1955, 1, 2, 5, 6, Box I: B 19, Folder: Adoption Program, Reports and Statements, 1953–1961, NUL records.

76 Anita Bellamy, "Report of Adoptions Project—1 January to 15 September 1960," 3, Box I: B30, Folder: Program Department, Affiliates File–Washington, DC Adoption Project, 1960, NUL records.

77 Bellamy, "Report of Adoptions Project—1 January to 15 September 1960," 4, 5; and Caroline F. Ware, "Report to Board," September 28, 1960, 1, 2, Box I: B30, Folder: Program Department, Affiliates File–Washington, DC Adoption Project, 1960, NUL records.

78 Bellamy, "Report of Adoptions Project—1 January to 15 September 1960," 6; and Ware, "Report to Board," 2.

79 Leila Calhoun Deasy and Olive Westbrooke Quinn, "The Urban Negro and Adoption of Children: A Preliminary Report on a Study of the Attitudes Toward and Experiences with Adoption of 484 Negro Adults in Baltimore, Maryland and Washington, D.C.," September 5, 1961, 1, Box I: B30, Folder: Program Department, Affiliates File–Washington, DC Adoption Project, NUL records.

80 Ibid., 6.

81 Ibid., 5.

82 William S. Jackson, "Confidential Report to Study Committee," 11.

83 Ibid., 8–9, 10, 11.

84 Townsend, "An Expanding Adoption Service for Negro Children," 1. For more on the NUL's efforts to increase African Americans' access to foster care, see Rymph, *Raising Government Children*, 125–130.

85 Rymph, *Raising Government Children*, 3, 6, 12–13, 20–23, 71–84.

86 Ibid., 64.

87 Ibid., 43–65.

88 Mink, *Wages of Motherhood*, 123–150.

89 Billingsley and Giovannoni, *Children of the Storm*, 70–79; and Rymph, *Raising Government Children*, 53–65.

90 Billingsley and Giovannoni, *Children of the Storm*, 86–97. For more on the role race played in child welfare reform efforts for African Americans, see Roberts, *Shattered Bonds*.

91 William S. Jackson, "Our Evolving Task in Adoption," 18; and Cernoria D. Johnson to Katherine B. Ottinger, March 26, 1964, Box 964, Folder 0-2-9-1, 1963–1966,

Children's Bureau records. For a discussion of the failure of NUL's Foster Home and Adoption Project with specific emphasis on its Kansas City, Missouri initiative, see Billingsley and Giovannoni, *Children of the Storm*, 139–173.

92 Nelson C. Jackson, "The National Urban League's Project in Foster Home and Adoption Services," 1.

93 Nelson C. Jackson to Dr. Ira DeA. Reid, December 16, 1955, Box I: B19, Folder: Adoption Program, Correspondence and Memoranda, 1953–1959, NUL records.

94 Rymph, *Raising Government Children*, 128.

95 William S. Jackson, "Confidential Report to Study Committee," 8.

96 Ibid.

97 Ibid.

98 Billingsley and Giovannoni, *Children of the Storm*, 141–143; and William S. Jackson, "Our Evolving Task in Adoption," 16.

99 Working Committee on Standards for Foster Family Care Meeting Notes, November 1956, Box 13, Folder: 5 Standards-Foster Care, 1957–1959, CWLA records; and *Child Welfare League of America Standards for Foster Family Care Service* (New York: Child Welfare League of America, 1959).

100 Dorothy Roberts argues compellingly and convincingly that adoption is not a solution to the nation's contemporary foster care challenges. She explains that many structural inequalities create the conditions under which minority children are separated from their families. Child welfare officials and politicians focus on family failings and not the problems that stem from poverty, and the lack of access to quality education and employment, which has informed child welfare policies that punish instead of help families in crisis. Indeed, Roberts demonstrates that for family preservation efforts to work, child welfare policies will have to undergo radical reform. Roberts, *Shattered Bonds*, 149–165.

101 Billingsley and Giovannoni, *Children of the Storm*, 94.

102 "A Program to Improve Foster Home and Adoptive Services for Negro Children," n.d., 1 and 10; and Nelson C. Jackson, "Foster Home and Adoptive Services for Minority Children," n.d., 12.

103 Annie Lee Davis Sandusky, "Today's Children Lost in Foster Care," May 15, 1961, Box 132, File 7-3-3-2 Today's Children Lost in Foster Care, Children's Bureau records.

104 Walter P. Townsend, "An Expanding Adoption Service for Negro Children," 10.

105 Fanshel and Shinn, *Dollars and Sense in the Foster Care of Children*, 6, 17, 21, 26.

106 "Intercountry Adoption Committee Meeting Minutes," December 13, 1957, Box 4, Folder: ISS 1957, ISS records.

107 Susan T. Pettiss, "Effect of Adoption of Foreign Children on U.S. Adoption Standards and Practices," May 15, 1958, Box 11, Folder: Children, Adoption Manual and Other Printed Material, ISS records. Pettiss's speech is also found in *Child Welfare*, July 1958, Box 59, Folder Study on Proxy Adoptions 1957–1958, CWLA records.

108 Billingsley and Giovannoni, *Children of the Storm*, 139–173.

CHAPTER 3. AFRICAN AMERICAN FAMILIES, KOREAN BLACK
CHILDREN, AND THE EVOLUTION OF TRANSNATIONAL RACE RESCUE

1 Helen Wilson to Augusta Mayerson, January 21, 1953, Box 35, Folder: Korea Correspondences, vol. I, ISS records.

2 D. S. Kim, "A Country Divided," 5–9; E. Kim, *Adopted Territory*, 47–48; and Hübinette, *Comforting an Orphaned Nation*, 38–39.

3 Augusta Mayerson to Helen Wilson, February 25, 1953, Box 35, Folder: Korea Correspondence vol. 1, ISS records.

4 According to Kimberly M. McKee, when the South Korean government created the nation's Family Law as a part of the Civil Code in 1948, it specified that husbands alone could add children to a family's registry. McKee, "Monetary Flows and the Movements of Children," 143–144.

5 Oh, *To Save the Children of Korea*, 66–67.

6 Ibid., 22–23; and "Procedures for Adoption of Korean Child," July 6, 1953, Box 35, Folder: Korea Correspondence, vol. 1, ISS records.

7 For more on the origins of and motivations behind Korean transnational adoption, see Briggs, "Mother, Child, Race, Nation"; Briggs, *Somebody's Children*; Choy, *Global Families*; Hübinette, *Comforting an Orphaned Nation*; E. Kim, *Adopted Territory*; Klein, *Cold War Orientalism*; Oh, *To Save the Children of Korea*; Pate, *From Orphan to Adoptee*; and Winslow, *The Best Possible Immigrants*.

8 "Korean Survey," vol. 2, no. 1, January 1953, Department of State General records, Record Group 59, Box 1, Folder: Korea—January through December [1953] #2, National Archives II, College Park, MD (hereafter Department of State records).

9 Helen Wilson to Augusta Mayerson, January 21, 1953, Box 35, Folder: Korea Correspondences, vol. I, ISS records; Augusta Mayerson to Helen Wilson, February 25, 1953, Box 35, Folder: Korean Correspondence vol. 1, ISS records.

10 Jane Russell Waterfield to Elizabeth H. Ross, September 11, 1953, Central File 1949–1952, Box 676, Folder 7-3-1-3, December 1953, 1953–1957 Interstate Placement, Non-Resident Problems, Juvenile Immigration, Transient Boys (Runaways, 7-1-1-6), Children's Bureau records. For more on Jane Russell Waterfield's involvement in international adoption, see Choy, *Global Families*, 100–103; and Moira J. Maguire, "Foreign Adoptions and the Evolution of Irish Adoption Policy, 1945–52," *Journal of Social History* 36, no. 2 (Winter 2002): 390–391, 393.

11 E. Nora Ryan to US Children's Bureau, February 3, 1953, Box 676, Folder 7-3-1-3 February 1955, 1953–1956 Interstate Placement, Non-Resident Problems, Juvenile Immigration, Transient Boys (Runaways, 7-1-1-6), Children's Bureau records.

12 I. Evelyn Smith To Dr. E. Nora Ryan, February 18, 1953, Box 676, Folder 7-3-1-3 February 1955, 1953–1956 Interstate Placement, Non-Resident Problems, Juvenile Immigration, Transient Boys (Runaways, 7-1-1-6), Children's Bureau records.

13 I. Evelyn Smith to Bernice E. Scroggie, June 18, 1953, Box 676, Folder 7-3-1-3 December 1953, 1953–1956 Interstate Placement, Non-Resident Problems, Juvenile Immigration, Transient Boys (Runaways, 7-1-1-6), Children's Bureau records.

14 "Voluntary Aid to Korean Children Headquarters, Eighth Army," January 19, 1954, Department of State General Records, East Asian Affairs Branch, Record Group 59, Box 5698, Decimal File 1950–54, 895B.49/1–1954, National Archives II, Baltimore, MD (Hereafter Department of State East Asian Affairs Branch records).

15 Thurston B. Morton to Senator Herbert Lehman, March 5, 1954, Box 1302, Decimal File 320.22/1–1854 to 325.84/1/350, 1950–1954, Department of State Records; and "Voluntary Aid to Korean Children Headquarters, Eighth Army," January 19, 1954, Box 5698, Decimal File 1950–54, 895B.49/1–1954, Department of State Records.

16 For more on the development and evolution of US-Korean relations, see Cumings, *Korea's Place in the Sun*; Cumings, *The Korean War*; Chae-Jin Lee, *A Troubled Peace*; and Moon, *Sex Among Allies*.

17 Memo, Jessup to Kotschnig, October 10, 1950, Box 1, Folder: Korea—January through December [1953] #2, Department of State records; and "Statement of Government Pledges and Contributions," December 31, 1954, Box 1281, Entry: CDF 1955–1959, United Nations, Department of State records. Kim, *The Unending Korean War*; and Seth, *A Concise History of Modern Korea*.

18 Memorandum of Conversation, "Entry of Korean War Orphans into the United States," July 17, 1953, Box 1, Folder: Korea—January through December [1953] #2, Department of State records.

19 For more on refugee legislation and immigration restrictions, see Bon Tempo, *Americans at the Gate*, 34–45; Daniels, *Coming to America*, 338–344; and Ngai, *Impossible Subjects*, 227–230.

20 Choy, *Global Families*, 78–79.

21 Winslow, *The Best Possible Immigrants*, 74–75. Arissa Oh explains that the orphan provisions of the 1957 Refugee-Escapee Act gave the attorney general jurisdiction over the orphan program. Oh, "From War Waif to Ideal Immigrant," 40.

22 Choy, *Global Families*, 78–79; E. Kim, *Adopted Territory*, 55–56; Oh, *To Save the Children of Korea*, 48–55, 148–151; Park Nelson, *Invisible Asians*, 52–58; Pate, *From Orphan to Adoptee*, 74–75, 107–108; and Winslow, *The Best Possible Immigrants*, 74–76, 96–98. Congress passed a number of orphan provisions in several Refugee Acts to facilitate the adoptions of Korean children after the RRA expired in December 1956. One significant Act was the 1957 Refugee-Escapee Act, which created a two-year window for an unlimited number of orphans age fourteen and younger to enter on non-quota visas. This Act also required adopting families to comply with their state's adoption regulations before finalizing a transnational adoption.

23 Hübinette, *Comforting an Orphaned Nation*, 38–44; Oh, *To Save the Children of Korea*, 57–63; Pate, *From Orphan to Adoptee*, 30–33; and Sarri, Baik, and Bombyk, "Goal Displacement and Dependency in South Korean-United States Intercountry Adoption," 89.

24 Hübinette, *Comforting an Orphaned Nation*, 46.

25 Sarri et al., "Goal Displacement and Dependency in South Korean-United States Intercountry Adoption," 92.

26 "Procedures for Adoption of Korean Child," July 6, 1953, Box 35, Folder: Korea
    Correspondence, vol. 1, ISS records; "Adoption Program-Korea: Descriptive Re-
    port," 1956, Box 35, Folder: Korea-Reports and Visits to Korea, 1956, ISS records;
    "Korean Legal Procedures Affecting Children Coming to the United States for
    Adoption," August 1958, Box 11, Folder: Miscellaneous Forms for Adoption Proce-
    dures, ISS records; and E. Kim, "The Origins of Korean Adoption," 11.
27 For a description of the early efforts of the South Korean government to pass an
    orphan adoption law, see Hübinette, *Comforting an Orphaned Nation*, 45–46,
    49–50; Oh, *To Save the Children of Korea*, 54–55; and Sarri et al., "Goal Displace-
    ment and Dependency in South Korean-United States Intercountry Adoption,"
    92–95.
28 Grace A. Reeder to I. Evelyn Smith, January 21, 1954, Box 676, Folder: 7-3-1-3 May
    1954, 1953–1956 Interstate Placement, Non-Resident Problems, Juvenile Immigra-
    tion, Transient Boys (Runaways 7-1-1-6), Children's Bureau records; I. Evelyn
    Smith to Grace A. Reeder, March 23, 1954, Box 676, Folder: 7-3-1-3 May 1954,
    1953–1956 Interstate Placement, Non-Resident Problems, Juvenile Immigration,
    Transient Boys (Runaways 7-1-1-6), Children's Bureau records.
29 Richard Steinman to Joseph H. Reid, January 13, 1954, Box 676, Folder: 7-3-1-3
    May 1954, 1953–1956 Interstate Placement, Non-Resident Problems, Juvenile Im-
    migration, Transient Boys (Runaways 7-1-1-6), Children's Bureau records.
30 Ibid.
31 Mrs. George [Grace] H. Rue to Bessie C. Irvin, n.d., Box 35, Folder: Korea Cor-
    respondence, vol. 1, ISS records.
32 Ibid.
33 Ellen Visser to Susan T. Pettiss, June 13, 1955, Box 35, Folder: ISS Branches Korea
    "RR-5" 1954–December 1955, ISS records.
34 Woo, "A New American Comes 'Home,'" 70. Woo notes that before 1955, the De-
    partment of the Army did not keep track of soldiers' requests for information about
    Korean transnational adoption. Some officials even deliberately slowed the process
    down when some soldiers did attempt to fulfill the requirements. Ibid., 66–67.
35 "Sergeant Wins Fight to Adopt Korean Lad," *Pacific Stars and Stripes*, October 18, 1953.
36 Examples of the *Pacific Stars and Stripes* coverage of Korean adoptions includes
    Cpl. Peter Steele Bixby, "No. 1 Sargy, Sambo Plan Life Together," *Pacific Stars
    and Stripes*, November 1, 1950, 2; "Sergeant Wins Fight to Adopt Korean Lad,"
    Pacific Stars and Stripes, October 18, 1953; "Korean Boy's Parents OK Adoption
    by Sergeant," *Pacific Stars and Stripes*, December 24, 1953, 7; "ROK-American
    Girl Gets Home in U.S.," *Pacific Stars and Stripes*, March 22, 1955, 11; "Air Force
    Couple Launches Operation Baby Lift," *Pacific Stars and Stripes*, May 5, 1956,
    11; and "U.S. Father in Korea Stymied on Adoptions," *Pacific Stars and Stripes*,
    January 29, 1956, 6.
37 "Summery Narrative Report to Reiger," December 20, 1955, Department of State
    General Records, Records of the Foreign Service Posts of the Department of State,
    Record Group 84, Box 4, File 350, National Archives II, Baltimore, MD.

38 Choy, *Global Families*, 23.

39 Ellen Visser to Susan T. Pettiss, June 13, 1955, Box 35, Folder: ISS–Branches Korea "RRA5" 1954–1955, ISS records; and Miss McKay to W. E. Kneeland, May 17, 1956, Box 11, Folder: Miscellaneous Forms for Adoption Proceedings, ISS records.

40 Steve Wareck, "Air Force Couple Launches Operation Baby Lift," *Pacific Stars and Stripes*, May 5, 1956, 11; "Airlift Speeds Adoption of Korean Orphans," *Pacific Stars and Stripes*, August 24, 1956, 10; "Suggestions to Those Who Inquire About Adoption of Orphans under the Refugee Relief Program," n.d., Box 674, Folder: 7-3-1-3 December 1957, 1953–1957 Interstate Placement, Non-Resident Problems, Juvenile Immigration, Transient Boys, Children's Bureau records; and "Pair Has Special Cargo-Korea Adoptees," *Pacific Stars and Stripes*, November 16, 1956, 14.

41 Major General Edward F. Witsell to Commanders-in-Chief and Commanding Generals, "Support of Legal Dependents," April 27, 1950, Records of the Eighth Army AG, Record Group 338, Box 464, Folder: 250.1 January–August 1950, National Archives II, College Park, MD (hereafter Eighth Army AG records).

42 Headquarters of Eighth Army, "Weekly Directive," May 6, 1950, Box 464, Folder: 250.1 January–August 1950, Eighth Army AG records; "Report of the Committee of Experts on the Recognition and Enforcement of Maintenance Obligations," March 18, 1954, Box 4, Folder: ISS 1954, ISS records; J. T. Kaigler, "Report of Character Guidance Activities Calendar Quarter Ending 30 September 1956," November 8, 1956, Records of the Office of the Chief of Chaplains, Record Group 247, 637, folder 000.3, National Archives II, College Park, MD; and Bruce E. Balding, "A Better Life," *Pacific Stars and Stripes*, April 16, 1956, 17.

43 Paul R. Cherney to Mrs. Morris Hadley, "Report on Visit to Korea, June 23 to July 9, 1965," July 20, 1965, Folder: Korea, Child Placement Service, General, 1964–1965, Box 35, ISS records; and "National Agency Information for the National Budget Committee," March 1954, Box 4, Folder: ISS 1954, ISS records.

44 For more on adoptions of Greek children following the Greek Civil War (1946–1949), see Winslow, *The Best Possible Immigrants*, 34–69.

45 "Tentative Procedural Outline," March 1954, Folder: Inter-country Adoptions Committee-ISS Reports, Box 3, ISS records; and National Agency Information for the National Budget Committee, March 1954, Box 4, Folder: ISS 1954, ISS records. The US Children's Bureau was also instrumental in establishing protocols for US international adoption programs. Officials with the Children's Bureau highlighted the history of their intercountry child welfare work in concert with ISS, the Catholic Committee for Refugees, and the United Hebrew Immigrant Aid Society, in Katherine B. Oettinger, "Statement before the Subcommittee on Immigration and Naturalisation [*sic*] Senate Committee on the Judiciary," May 20, 1959, Box 132, Folder 7-3-1-3, Children's Bureau records.

46 "Have Jacket Will Travel. . . . The Story of WAIF-ISS," n.d., Box 4, Folder: ISS 1957, ISS records; ISS Minutes of Board of Directors Meeting, September 23, 1954, Box 4, Folder: ISS 1954, ISS records.

47 Adrian Booth Brian to I. Evelyn Smith, December 2, 1953, Box 676, Folder: 7-3-1-3 December 1953–1956 Interstate Placement, Non-Resident Problems, Juvenile Immigration, Transient Boys, Children's Bureau records. Jane Russell Waterfield's description of the creation of WAIF-ISS is included in Jane Russell Waterfield and Susan T. Pettiss, "International Adoptions: Possibilities and Problems," *Summary of Proceedings: Officers, Committees (American Bar Association. Section of Family Law)* 1961: 15–27.

48 ISS Minutes of the Executive Committee, October 11, 1956, Box 4, Folder: ISS Material Received 1956, ISS records; ISS Minutes of Board of Directors Meeting, April 15, 1954, Box 4, Folder: ISS 1954, ISS records; ISS Minutes of Board of Directors Meeting, October 1, 1957, Box 4, Folder: ISS 1957, ISS records; and Florence Boester, "Summary Report of Initial Organization, ISS Delegation Korea," May 6, 1957, Box 4, Folder: ISS 1957, ISS records.

49 Susan Pettiss to Miss Eleanor Wright and Mary Vaughn, March 26, 1956, Folder: ISS Adoption1955–1958, Box 10, ISS records.

50 Ibid.

51 "ISS Program for Selection of Children for Adoption Under the Refugee Relief Act," June 21, 1954, Box 3, Folder: Intercountry Adoptions Committee-ISS Reports, ISS records; Margaret A. Valk, "Descriptive Report-Visit to Korea of November 21–30, 1956," December 1956, Box 35, Folder: Korea Reports and Visits to Korea, 1956, ISS records; and Ellen Visser to Susan T. Pettiss, January 15, 1955, Box 35, Folder: ISS Branches Korea "RR-5" 1954–December 1955, ISS records.

52 Ellen Visser to Susan T. Pettiss, January 15, 1955, Folder: ISS Branches, Korea "RRA-5" 1954–December1955, Box 35, ISS records.

53 Margaret A. Valk, "Descriptive Report—Visit to Korea of November 21–30, 1956," December 1956, Box 35, Folder: Korea Reports and Visits to Korea, 1956, ISS records.

54 Oh, *To Save the Children of Korea*, 90.

55 For more on Holt's role in Korean transnational adoption, see Choy, *Global Families*, 78–95; Hübinette, *Comforting an Orphaned Nation*, 47–49; Oh, *To Save the Children of Korea*, 8, 80–111; Pate, *From Orphan to Adoptee*, 101–125; and Winslow, *The Best Possible Immigrant*, 70–141.

56 Oh, *To Save the Children of Korea*, 91; and Pate, *From Orphan to Adoptee*, 103–107.

57 Oh, *To Save the Children of Korea*, 8.

58 Although Holt's adoption work in Korea led to the expansion of Korean transnational adoption, SooJin Pate argues convincingly for a reconceptualization of the origins of Korean adoption that addresses the complicated ways soldiers first performed the role of rescuing father that Holt's story depicts. Pate, *From Orphan to Adoptee*, 1–6.

59 Margaret A. Valk, "Descriptive Report-Visit to Korea of November 21–30, 1956," December 1956, Box 35, Folder: Korea Reports and Visits to Korea, 1956, ISS records. The rumor suggested that North Korean officials paid a youngster to kidnap a mixed-race child from an orphanage in South Korea. North Korean officials

then put the mixed-race child on display to shame South Koreans. Susan T. Pettiss to Lois McCarthy, May 1, 1957, Folder: Children, Adoption Plans of Racially Mixed Children, 1954–1965, Box 10, ISS records; and Oh, *To Save the Children of Korea*, 92–94.

60 Choy, *Global Families*, 81; Oh, *To Save the Children of Korea*, 92–95; and Winslow, *The Best Possible Immigrants*, 84, 86.

61 Richard L. Neuberger to Herbert C. Hoover, August 31, 1956, Folder: Korea General 1947–1960, Box 2, Department of State East Asian Affairs Branch records.

62 Hübinette references research conducted by sociologist Won Moo Hurh, who estimated that there were approximately 12,280 mixed-race born in Korea between 1950 and 1965: Hübinette, *Comforting an Orphaned Nation*, 42.

63 Pate, *From Orphan to Adoptee*, 29–30, 108; Hübinette, *Comforting an Orphaned Nation*, 38–40; and Oh, *To Save the Children of Korea*, 57–63.

64 I base these numbers on statistics found in Choy, *Adopted Territory*, 25; and Hübinette, *Comforting an Orphaned Nation*, 261.

65 Tobias Hübinette notes that 70–90 percent of the children placed between 1953 and 1959 were mixed-race Koreans, *Comforting an Orphaned Nation*, 48–49.

66 Choy, *Global Families*, 15–45; Hübinette, *Comforting an Orphaned Nation*, 52, 56; Oh, *To Save the Children of Korea*, 82.

67 Moon, *Sex Among Allies*, 35; For more on South Koreans' responses to African American soldiers and the presence of camp towns, see Yuh, *Beyond the Shadow of Camptown*, 27–28.

68 Margaret A. Valk, "Descriptive Report–Visit to Korea of November 21–30, 1956," December 1956, Box 35, Folder: Korea Reports and Visits to Korea, 1956, ISS records.

69 Paul R. Cherney, "Notes on Field Visit—ISS Korea Staff," July 12, 1962, 23, Box 35, Folder: Korea-General/Adoptions from 1961, Discard, ISS records.

70 Paul Cherney, "Notes on Field Visit—ISS Korea Staff," July 12, 1962, 18–19, Box 35, Folder: Korea–General/Adoptions from 1961, Discard, ISS records.

71 Paul Cherney, Report "Visit to Korea, June 23 to July 9, 1965," Box 35, Folder: Korea: Child Placement Service, General 1964–1965, ISS records.

72 H. Kim, *Birth Mothers*, 6–7.

73 Memo—"Picture of Child for Natural Mother," Elise L. Heller to Adoption Staff, August 14, 1967, Box 10, Folder: Adoption Correspondence, ISS records.

74 Susan T. Pettiss, February 10, 1956, Box 10, Folder: Children: Independent Adoption Schemes—World Vision, ISS records.

75 Fanshel, *A Study in Negro Adoption*; and Hill, *Informal Adoption*.

76 ISS cases, Box 79, Folder 57, ISS records.

77 ISS cases, Box 135, Folder 4, ISS records.

78 ISS cases, Box 91, Folder 35, ISS records.

79 "U.S. Father in Korea Stymied on Adoptions," *Pacific Stars and Stripes*, January 29, 1953, 6.

80 Margaret A. Valk, "Adjustment of Korean American Children and Their American Adoptive Homes," April 1957, Box 10, Folder: Adjustment of Korean American Children, ISS records.

81 ISS cases, Box 180, Folder 31, ISS records; and ISS cases, Box 81, Folder 13, ISS records.

82 Berebitsky, *Like Our Very Own*, 102–127.

83 ISS cases, Box 81, Folder 13, ISS records.

84 Ellen Visser to Susan T. Pettiss, June 13, 1955, Box 35, Folder: ISS–Branches Korea "RRA5" 1954–1955, ISS records; and "Laws Governing Adoptions by Aliens in Korea," July 31, 1954, Box 35, Folder: Korea–General/Adoptions, ISS records. The Advisory Committee on Voluntary Foreign Aid received the laws translated from Korean to English from the American Embassy in Seoul. The Ministry of Justice and the Korean Civil Assistance Command provided these laws to US officials.

85 "Procedures for Processing Foreign Children for Immigration and Adoption by American Citizens," n.d., Box 4, Folder: ISS 1957, ISS records; "Procedures for Adoption of Korean Children," July 6, 1953, Box 35, Folder: Korean Correspondence vol. 1, ISS records; and ISS Cases, Box 78, Folder 1, ISS records. The families who knew the adopted child used the DSR-5 form, and families who received a child picked by an adoption agency used the DSR-6.

86 ISS Cases, Box 139, Folder 30, ISS records.

87 ISS Cases, Box 183, Folder 20, ISS records.

88 ISS Cases, Box 128, Folder 2, ISS records.

89 ISS Cases, Box 19, Folder 65, ISS records. "Seaver" is not the family's real surname. I have used pseudonyms for all of the names of families whose cases I accessed through the ISS case records.

90 Ibid.

91 Green, *Black Yanks in the Pacific*, 47.

92 Ibid.

93 Ralph Matthews, "GI'S Ponder Peace Moves: Not All Anxious for War to Be Over," *Afro-American*, September 22, 1951, 8.

94 Ralph Matthews, "American Women in No Rush to Leave Japan: Matthews Finds Far East Happy Grounds for Women," *Afro-American*, August 25, 1951, 11. Brenda Gayle Plummer describes a similar pattern that existed in Germany during the post–World War II German occupation. African American women could hire German women to serve as their maids, which gave them a domestic status and position over white women that they could not have experienced in the States. Plummer, "Brown Babies," 78.

95 Mrs. Lester Hajacker to President Harry Truman, July 25, 1951, Box 451, Folder: 7-3-3-4-1, 1949–1952, Appeals from People Wishing Children for Adoptions, Children's Bureau records.

96 Gardner W. Munro to Paul Cherney, November 9, 1964, Box 35, Folder: Korea, Child Placement Service, General, 1964–1965, ISS records.

97 Clare Golden, Report of Field Visit, December 11–13, 1957, January 7, 1958, Box 674, Folder: 7-3-1-3 December 1957, 1953–1957 Interstate Placement, Non-Resident Problems, Juvenile Immigration, Transient Boys, Children's Bureau records; and Minutes of the Intercountry Adoption Committee Meeting, November 10, 1958, Box 59, Folder: Study on Proxy Adoptions, 1959–60, CWLA records.

98 Minutes of the Intercountry Adoption Committee Meeting, November 10, 1958, Box 59, Folder: Study on Proxy Adoptions, 1959–60, CWLA records.

99 George K. Wyman to Martha Eliot, February 25, 1955, Box 675, Folder: 7-3-1-3 October 1955, 1953–1957 Interstate Placement, Non-Resident Problems, Juvenile Immigrants, Transient Boys, Children's Bureau records; "Meeting to Back War Orphan Plan: Korea Proxy Method Proponents Will Protest Intervention," *Los Angeles Times*, April 27, 1955, Box 675, Folder: 7-3-1-3 October 1955, 1953–1957 Interstate Placement, Non-Resident Problems, Juvenile Immigrants, Transient Boys, Children's Bureau records. The documents describing the activities of the Hwangs incorrectly spell the name as Whong or Whang.

100 George K. Wyman to Martha Eliot, February 25, 1955, Box 675, Folder: 7-3-1-3 October 1955, 1953–1957 Interstate Placement, Non-Resident Problems, Juvenile Immigrants, Transient Boys, Children's Bureau records.

101 Ellen Visser to Susan T. Pettiss, June 13, 1955, Box 35, Folder: ISS Branches Korea "RR-5" 1954–December 1955, ISS records.

102 Ruth Graves to State Department of Social Welfare, Kansas City, January 22, 1957, Box 675, Folder 7-3-1-3 September 1957, 1953–1957 Interstate Placement, Non-Resident Problems, Juvenile Immigration Transient Boys, Children's Bureau records.

103 Ibid.

104 Dorothy W. Bradley to Anna E. Sundwall, June 27, 1957, Box 675, Folder 7-3-1-3 September 1957, 1953–1957 Interstate Placement, Non-Resident Problems, Juvenile Immigration Transient Boys, Children's Bureau records; and Ruth Graves to State Department of Social Welfare, Kansas City, January 22, 1957, Box 675, Folder 7-3-1-3 September 1957, 1953–1957 Interstate Placement, Non-Resident Problems, Juvenile Immigration Transient Boys, Children's Bureau records.

105 Ruth Graves to State Department of Social Welfare, Kansas City, January 22, 1957, Box 675, Folder 7-3-1-3 September 1957, 1953–1957 Interstate Placement, Non-Resident Problems, Juvenile Immigration Transient Boys, Children's Bureau records.

106 E. Kim, *Adopted Territory*, 60–69; and Oh, *To Save the Children of Korea*, 56.

107 ISS–Korea Branch to ISS–American Branch, September 17, 1957, Box 10, Folder: Children, Independent Adoption Schemes, Clemmons, Mrs. Leroy 1957, ISS records.

108 Anna E. Sundwall to Proctor Carter, November 10, 1958, Box 884, Folder: 7-3-1-3 September 1959 Non-Resident Problems (Include Juvenile Immigrant, Transient Boys), Children's Bureau records; and Anna E. Sundwall to Chief, Program Development Branch, February 5, 1959, Box 884, Folder: 7-3-1-3 September 1959 Non-Resident Problems (Include Juvenile Immigrant, Transient Boys), Children's Bureau records.

109 N. G. Walker to Patricia T. Schloesser, June 30, 1959, Box 884, Folder: 7-3-1-3 September 1959 Non-Resident Problems (Include Juvenile Immigrant, Transient

Boys), Children's Bureau records; Erwin W. Raetz to Kansas State Department of Welfare, January 17, 1959, Box 884, Folder: 7-3-1-3 September 1959 Non-Resident Problems (Include Juvenile Immigrant, Transient Boys), Children's Bureau records; and Josephine Thomas to Paul R. Shanahan, September 1959, Box 884, Folder: 7-3-1-3 September 1959 Non-Resident Problems (Include Juvenile Immigrant, Transient Boys), Children's Bureau records.

110 Choy, *Global Families*, 82–95; Park Nelson, *Invisible Asians*, 52–54; and Oh, *To Save the Children of Korea*, 52–53. For more on the passage of the Refugee Relief Act and the early years of the Refugee Relief Program, see Bon Tempo, *Americans at the Gate*, 45–59; Oh, *To Save the Children of Korea*, 148–151; Winslow, *The Best Possible Immigrants*, 71–75.

111 Mildred Arnold to Katherine B. Oettinger, June 16, 1958, Box 885, 7-3-1-3 1958–1962, Folder: 7-3-1-3 Non-Resident Problems, Children's Bureau records.

112 Susan Pettiss to Files, June 6, 1958, Box 10 Programs: Adoption, Folder: Children: Independent Adoption Schemes—1958–1959 vol. II, Holt, Harry, ISS records.

113 Mildred Arnold to Katherine B. Oettinger, June 16, 1958, Box 885, 7-3-1-3 1958–1962, Folder: 7-3-1-3 Non-Resident Problems, Children's Bureau records.

114 Tobias Hübinette explores the similarities between baby lifts and slavery's middle passage in "From Orphan Trains to Babylifts," 145.

115 Oh, *To Save the Children of Korea*, 82.

116 Harry Holt to Friends, December 27, 1956, Box 10, Folder: Children: Independent Adoption Schemes 1955–1957 vol. 1 Holt, Harry, ISS records.

117 Choy, *Global Families*, 81–89.

118 Arnold Lyslo to Susan T. Pettiss, December 27, 1958, Box 10, Children, Independent Adoption Schemes1958–1959 vol. II Holt, Harry, ISS record.

119 J. Morgan, "Adoption by Proxy: Red Tape Abolished in Case of Koreas," *Sepia*, July 1959.

120 Susan T. Pettiss, Memo, Files-Washington RRA-5, n.d., Box 10, Folder ISS Adoption 1955–1958 (continued), ISS records. For more on Harry Holt and the expansion of proxy adoptions in Korea, see Choy, *Global Families*, 78–95; Kim, *Adopted Territory*, 43–81; Park Nelson, *Invisible Asians*, 52–65; Oh, *To Save the Children of Korea*, 79–111; Winslow, *The Best Possible Immigrants*, 84–98.

121 Walter A. Heath to J. M. Wedmeyer, June 21, 1960, Box 884 7-3-1-3 1958–1962, Folder: 7-3-1-3 July 1960, Non-Resident Problems (Include Juvenile Immigrant, Transient Boys), Children's Bureau records. The names used in this section are pseudonyms and not the names of the families described in the case. This story is an example of the dangerous practice of rehoming that has received media attention in a number of outlandish cases. One particularly disturbing contemporary example involved an adoptive mother from Tennessee who sent the seven-year-old child she adopted from Russia back to that country on a plane alone. She sent a note with the child saying that he was "violent and troubled." "Adoptions from Russia plunged into Uncertainty," *Washington Post*, April 16, 2010.

122 Edith Stander to Walter A. Heath, May 24, 1960, Box 884 7-3-1-3 1958–1962, Folder: 7-3-1-3 July 1960, Non-Resident Problems (Include Juvenile Immigrant, Transient Boys), Children's Bureau records.

123 Jean Seldan to Verna E. Lauritzen, June 17, 1960, Box 884 7-3-1-3 1958–1962, Folder: 7-3-1-3 July 1960, Non-Resident Problems (Include Juvenile Immigrant, Transient Boys), Children's Bureau records.

124 The story of Edith Ott demonstrates the dangers of proxy adoption that inspired child welfare officials to denounce the practice. In 1957, Ott was indicted for the murder of her adopted Korean daughter, Mary Kay Ott. The twenty-two-month-old child suffered head trauma and died. For more on the Ott case, see Choy, *Global Families*, 93–94.

125 Herman, *Kinship by Design*, 218–222; Oh, *To Save the Children of Korea*, 146–151; and Winslow, *The Best Possible Immigrants*, 98–104.

126 Hübinette, *Comforting an Orphaned Nation*, 49–51. Oh explains that the passage of both the 1961 Orphan Adoption Special Law and Child Welfare Act was a consequence of the political upheaval that followed the overthrow of President Syngman Rhee's administration in 1961 by General Park Chung Hee, who became president of South Korea in 1963. Oh, *To Save the Children of Korea*, 54, 182. For more on General Park's role in developing the relationship between the expansion of Korean international adoption and South Korea's industrialization, see Oh, *To Save the Children of Korea*, 178–179.

127 Hübinette, *Comforting an Orphaned Nation*, 44–50; and Oh, *To Save the Children of Korea*, 182–183. General Park's administration allowed only four licensed agencies in South Korea to arrange out-of-country placements by 1970. Harry Holt's Holt Children's Services was one of those licensed agencies.

128 Pate, *From Orphan to Adoptee*, 108.

129 Oh, *To Save the Children of Korea*, 150.

130 Eleanor Lines to Lorraine Carroll, March 11, 1957, Box 10 Folder: Children-Independent Adoption Schemes 1955–1957, vol. 1, ISS records.

131 Margaret A. Valk, "Adjustment of Korean American Children," April 1957, Box 10, Folder: Adjustments of Korean American Children in Their Adoptive Homes, ISS records.

132 Eleanor Lines to Lorraine Carroll, March 11, 1957, Box 10 Folder: Children-Independent Adoption Schemes 1955–1957, vol. 1, ISS records.

133 "Intercountry Adoption Committee Meeting Minutes," December 13, 1957, Box 4, Folder: ISS 1957, ISS records.

134 Clare Golden, "Report of Field Visit," January 7, 1958, Box 674, Folder: 7-3-1-3 December 1957, 1953–1957 Interstate Placement, Non-Resident Problems, Juvenile Immigration, Transient Boys, Children's Bureau records.

CHAPTER 4. THE NEW FAMILY IDEAL FOR KOREAN
BLACK ADOPTION

1 ISS cases, Box 56, Folder 22, ISS records. The names used throughout this chapter are pseudonyms of the adoptive families whose records are a part of the ISS case records to ensure confidentiality. I also use "Mr." and "Mrs." throughout the text to distinguish between the husbands and wives.

2 Ibid.

3 Ibid.

4 For more on changes in adoption standards and ideas about matching in domestic and transnational adoption, see Balcom, *Traffic in Babies*; Herman, *Kinship by Design*; Melosh, *Strangers and Kin*; and Winslow, *The Best Possible Immigrants*.

5 Herman, *Kinship by Design*, 158.

6 Berebitsky, *Like Our Very Own*, 129.

7 E. Kim, *Adopted Territory*, 59.

8 Gordon, *Pitied but Not Entitled*, 37–43, 47–48, 87.

9 Jones, *Labor of Love, Labor of Sorrow*, 199.

10 White, *Too Heavy a Load*, 29; Gordon, *Pitied but Not Entitled,* 136–137, 144; and Jones, *Labor of Love, Labor of Sorrow*, 184–185.

11 Report, Fannie Wall Children's Home and Day Nursery, July 17, 1954, Records of the National Association of Colored Women's Clubs, 1895–1992, Microfilm Edition.

12 Gate City Day Nursery Pamphlet, Box 2, Folder 8: Gate City Day Nursery Assn., Frankie V. Adams Collection, Atlanta University Center Robert W. Woodruff Library, Atlanta GA.

13 Day, *The Adoption of Black Children*, 3–16; Jones, *Labor of Love, Labor of Sorrow*, 263, 271–272, 306; Kunzel, *Fallen Women, Problem Girls*; and Solinger, *Wake Up Little Susie*.

14 Economist Thomas N. Maloney compiled these statistics from the Integrated Public Use Microdata Series Census samples of the mean annual earnings of wage and salary workers. For more on African Americans' economic characteristics in the twentieth century, see Thomas N. Maloney, "African Americans in the Twentieth Century," http://eh.net/encyclopedia/article.

15 White, *Too Heavy a Load*, 160; Jones, *Labor of Love, Labor of Sorrow*, 262, 305; and Maloney, "African Americans in the Twentieth Century."

16 ISS Cases, Box 30, Folder 38, ISS records.

17 I. Evelyn Smith to Vivian Powell and Laurene Trent, April 2, 1953, Box 684, Folder: 7-3-3-4, May 11, 1956 1953–1957 Adoptions, Children's Bureau records.

18 ISS Cases, Box 57, Folder 31, ISS records; ISS Cases, Box 128, Folder 2, ISS records; and ISS Cases, Box 150, Folder 9, ISS records.

19 ISS Cases, Box 57, Folder 31, ISS records.

20 ISS Cases, Box 128, Folder 2, ISS records.

21 ISS Cases, Box 54, Folder 5, ISS records.

22 Ibid.
23 Ibid.
24 ISS Cases, Box 161, Folder 5, ISS records; and ISS Cases, Box 57, Folder 31, ISS records.
25 ISS Cases, Box 22, Folder 1, ISS records.
26 ISS Cases, Box 78, Folder 1, ISS records.
27 ISS Cases, Box 81, Folder 35, ISS records.
28 Bowlby, *Maternal Care and Mental Health*, 13, 73.
29 Fanshell and Shinn, *Dollars and Sense in the Foster Care of Children*, 1.
30 Collins, *Black Feminist Thought*, 188, 211.
31 Coontz, *The Way We Never Were*, 239–243.
32 "How Negro America Lives: The Jacksons of Bellerica," *Our World*, March 1954, 66; Nancy A. Walker, "The Ladies' Home Journal, 'How America Lives' and the Limits of Cultural Diversity," *Media History* 6, no. 2 (2000): 129–138.
33 Green, *Selling the Race*, 3.
34 "How Negro America Lives: The Jacksons of Billerica," 69.
35 Kozol, *Life's America*, 239–242.
36 "How Negro America Lives: The Jacksons of Billerica," 69.
37 Ibid., 66–73.
38 Ibid.
39 "How Negro America Lives: Keeping Up with the Joneses," *Our World*, June 1954, 58.
40 "How Negro America Lives: The Garretts of Montclair," *Our World*, July 1954, 70.
41 "How Negro America Lives: The Mischals of Cleveland," *Our World*, April 1954, 29.
42 How Negro America Lives: The Rhodens of Chicago," *Our World*, August 1954, 38.
43 Annie Lee Sandusky, "A Child Needs a Family—Preferably His Own," May 28, 1959, Box 132, Folder: 7-3-3-1, Children's Bureau records. For more on Sandusky's efforts to increase services to African American unwed mothers and children needing adoption, see Solinger, *Wake Up Little Susie*, 62–68.
44 ISS Cases, Box 102, Folder 13, ISS records.
45 ISS Cases, Box 58, Folder 10, ISS records.
46 Potter, *Everybody Else*, 91.
47 Collins, *Black Feminist Thought*, 178–183.
48 ISS Cases, Box 121, Folder 17, ISS records.
49 ISS Cases, Box 94, Folder 20, ISS records.
50 Bowlby, *Maternal Care and Mental Health*, 72–73.
51 Gordon, *Pitied but Not Entitled*, 113.
52 Potter, *Everybody Else*, 97–123.
53 For more on the activities of twentieth-century African American middle-class reformers and club women, see Shockley, *"We, Too, Are Americans"*; White, *Too Heavy A Load*; and Wolcott, *Remaking Respectability*.
54 For more on the Korean women's position in US-Korean foreign policy, see Moon, *Sex Among Allies*; and Yuh, *Beyond the Shadow of Camptown*.
55 ISS Cases, Box 78, Folder 1, ISS records.

56 ISS Cases, Box 192, Folder 4, ISS records.
57 ISS Cases, Box 158, Folder 18, ISS records.
58 ISS Cases, Box 150, Folder 9, ISS records.
59 Susan T. Pettiss, Memo to Files–Washington RRA–5, 1956; Box 10, Programs: Adoption; Folder: ISS Adoption 1955–1956 (continued), ISS records.
60 ISS Cases, Box 19, Folder 65, ISS records.
61 ISS Cases, Box 79, Folder 57, ISS records.
62 Susan T. Pettiss, Memo to Files–Washington RRA–5, 1956; Box 10, Programs: Adoption; Folder: ISS Adoption 1955–1956 (continued), ISS records; and ISS Cases, Box 91, Folder 35, ISS records.
63 ISS Cases, Box128, Folder 2, ISS records.
64 ISS Cases, Box 94, Folder 20, ISS records.
65 ISS Cases, Box 176, Folder 32, ISS records.
66 ISS Cases, Box 183, Folder 20, ISS records.
67 ISS Cases, Box 192, Folder 4, ISS records.
68 Pate, *From Orphan to Adoptee*, 102–103.
69 ISS Cases, Box 57, Folder 31, ISS records.
70 ISS Cases, Box 121, Folder 17, ISS records.
71 Marcelo and Lulu Calip to U.S. Refugee, August 18, 1955, Box 675, Folder: 7-3-1-3 April 1956 1953–1957 Interstate Placement, Non-Resident Problems, Juvenile Immigration, Transient Boys, Children's Bureau records; and Marcelo and Lulu Calip to Mr. Gula, August 14, 1956, Box 675, Folder: 7-3-1-3 April 1956, 1953–1957 Interstate Placement, Non-Resident Problems, Juvenile Immigration, Transient Boys, Children's Bureau records.
72 ISS Cases, Box 94, Folder 20, ISS records.
73 ISS Cases, Box 102, Folder 13, ISS records.
74 ISS Cases, Box 78, Folder 1, ISS records.
75 ISS Cases, Box 117, Folder 1, ISS records.
76 ISS Cases, Box 119, Folder 24, ISS records.
77 ISS Cases, Box 91, Folder 35, ISS records.
78 ISS Cases, Box 139, Folder 30, ISS records.
79 Park Nelson, *Invisible Asians*, 144. Park Nelson also provides a literature review of selected research on identity formation for transracially and transnationally adopted children produced in the 1970s to the present by child welfare professionals. Until the 1990s, these analyses reported largely positive conclusions regarding the outcomes for transracially and transnationally adopted children. However, adult adoptees and scholars have challenged these conclusions, noting that some researchers underreported issues of loss and difficult identity formation. For more on the critical assessments of transracial and transnational identity formation, see Park Nelson, *Invisible Asians*, 71–92; and Pate, *From Orphan to Adoptee*, 127–153.
80 Huh, "Korean Adopted Children's Ethnic Identity Formation," 81.
81 Ibid., 92–93.
82 Many scholars have evaluated the role that international scrutiny and criticism of US race relations played in advancing Civil Rights agendas in the United States,

including Borstelmann, *The Cold War and the Color Line*; Dudziak, *Cold War Civil Rights*; Brenda Gayle Plummer, *In Search of Power: African Americans in the Era of Decolonization, 1956–1974* (New York: Cambridge University Press, 2013); Plummer, *Rising Wind*; and Von Eschen, *Race Against Empire*.

83 Plummer, *Rising Wind*, 211.

84 Winslow, *The Best Possible Immigrants*, 80.

85 ISS Cases, Box 57, Folder 34, ISS records.

86 Daniel Jasper, Report, "Engaging North Korea: Recommendations from AFSC's 65 Years of Humanitarian Engagement on the Korean Peninsula," American Friends Service Committee, June 1, 2017 (https://www.afsc.org).

87 ISS Cases, Box 57, Folder 34, ISS records.

88 ISS Cases, Box 149, Folder 7, ISS records.

89 ISS Records, Box 184, Folder 39, ISS records.

90 ISS Cases, Box 171, Folder 1, ISS records.

91 ISS Cases, Box 191, Folder 16, ISS records.

92 ISS Cases, Box 117, Folder 20, ISS records.

93 Gary Brooten, "The Multiracial Family," *New York Times*, September 26, 1971, 78. Winslow also describes the media coverage of white families' transracial and/ or transnational adoptions from the 1950s to the 1970s that often framed their actions as politically and racially progressive acts. Winslow, *The Best Possible Immigrants*, 132–135.

CHAPTER 5. PEARL S. BUCK AND THE INSTITUTIONAL AND
RHETORICAL REFRAMING OF US AND KOREAN ADOPTION

1 Pearl S. Buck, "An Interview with My Adopted Daughter," *Cosmopolitan Magazine*, April 1946, 96.

2 Margaret Fischer, interview by Jane Rabb, May 26, 1978. Tape recording. Jane Rabb Collection, Lipscomb Library, Randolph College, Lynchburg, VA (hereafter JR collection).

3 Kozol, *Life's America*.

4 Conn, *Pearl S. Buck*.

5 Emily Cheng, "Pearl S. Buck's 'American Children': US Democracy, Adoption of the Amerasian Child, and the Occupation of Japan in *The Hidden Flower*," *Frontiers: A Journal of Women Studies* 35, no. 1 (2014): 182.

6 Briggs, *Somebody's Children*, 151.

7 Herman, *Kinship by Design*, 204.

8 Klein, *Cold War Orientalism*, 123, 135, 143–144, 178.

9 Ibid., 178.

10 Doctors diagnosed Carol with phenylketonuria disease (PKU), which caused severe mental disabilities. Conn, *Pearl S. Buck*, 71.

11 Ibid., 70–71, 80, 188, 328.

12 Identifying Robbie as Caucasian was culturally and legally significant. Although East Indians gained the legal classification Caucasian in the United States in the

first decade of the twentieth century, which allowed immigrants from India to naturalize, East Indians lost this status in 1917. The Immigration Act of 1917 created the Asiatic Barred Zone that restricted immigration from most Asian nations and called into question East Indians' access to citizenship in the United States. The 1923 Supreme Court decision in *U.S. v. Bhagat Singh Thind* made East Indians ineligible for citizenship. This restriction would remain in place until the 1952 McCarran-Walter Act eliminated racial restrictions. For a discussion of the changing categories of and legal significance of "Caucasian," see Sohoni, "Unsuitable Suitors."

13 Pearl S. Buck, "The Story of Welcome House," n.d., 1, Welcome House Scrap Book 2, Series 4, Record Group 1, Buck and Walsh Papers, Archives of Pearl S. Buck International, Perkasie, PA (hereafter PSB International records); Conn, *Pearl S Buck*, 312–313. Buck and her husband Richard Walsh acquired *ASIA* magazine in 1941, and they established the East West Association to encourage cultural sensitivity between US Americans and citizens of China, India, Japan, and other Asian nations.

14 Buck, "Notes on Welcome House," *Alumnae Bulletin* 49, no. 1 (November 1955): 34–35, Box 1, Folder: Letters, JR collection.

15 Lois Burpee, interview by Nora Stirling, February 24, 1976, Box 9, Folder: "Burpee, Lois (Mrs. David), Pennsylvania neighbor and Welcome House supporter," Nora Stirling Collection, Lipscomb Library, Randolph College, Lynchburg, VA (hereafter NS collection).

16 Mary G. Graves, interview by Nora Stirling, June 27, 1976, Box 10, Folder: Graves, Mary G., NS collection.

17 Herman, *Kinship by Design*, 45, 205–209.

18 Ibid., 199, 205–208. Herman notes that Judge Justine Wise Polier's father was the rabbinic leader Stephen Wise who co-founded the National Association for the Advancement of Colored People (NAACP). He and his wife, Louise Wise Waterman, encouraged Judge Wise's involvement in social justice and reform work. For more on the expanded role of white families in the adoptions of African American and Native American children and organized resistance to this shift, see Briggs, *Somebody's Children*, 28–93.

19 Klein, *Cold War Orientalism*, 143; Buck, "Notes on Welcome House," 34–35; Lois Burpee, interview by Nora Stirling; Mary G. Graves, interview by Nora Stirling, June 27, 1976, NS collection; Muriel Biester, interview by Nora Stirling, June 27, 1976, NS collection; Viola Yoder, interview by Nora Stirling, February 23, 1976, NS collection; Conn, *Pearl S. Buck*, 313, 314; and Margaret Fischer, interview by Jane Rabb. Christina Klein notes that author James A. Michener was a member of the board and he convinced Hammerstein to join, but Fischer does not mention Michener as a part of the first group to weigh in on Welcome House. Klein, *Cold War Orientalism*, 174. Buck biographer Peter Conn quotes Michener as saying that Buck "had no help from either Hammerstein or me when she started. She had a lot of help from us later when she had the wheels already moving." Conn, *Pearl S. Buck*, 314. But Michener had grown up in Doylestown and he did serve on the Welcome House board.

20 Lois Burpee, interview by Nora Stirling; Mary Graves, interview by Nora Stirling; Eve Eshleman, interview by Nora Stirling, August 27, 1976, Box 10, Folder: Eva S. Eshleman, NS collection; Mary Graves, interview by Nora Stirling; Conn, *Pearl S. Buck*, 338; and *Town Notes*, Bucks County, Pennsylvania, March 1, 1956. The *Town Notes* article stated that approximately 60 women were responsible for the operation of the shop.

21 Margaret Fischer, interview by Jane Rabb, May 26, 1978. Tape recording. Box 2, JR Collection; and Viola Yoder, interview by Nora Stirling, February 23, 1976, Box 9, Folder: Yoder, Viola Sell (Mrs. Lloyd), NS collection.

22 Viola Yoder, interview by Nora Stirling.

23 Dana Akins, Interview by Nora Stirling, March 27, 1976, Box 9, Folder: Akins, Dana, NS collection.

24 Buck, "Notes on Welcome House," 34–35, 36; Buck, *Children for Adoption*, 53–54, 70; and Buck, "The Story of Welcome House," 1–2.

25 "More Interest Seen in Adoption Problem," *New York Times*, June 2, 1950, 21.

26 Alice Hammerstein Mathais, interview by Nora Stirling, October 27, 1977, Box 10, Folder: Mathais, Alice, NS collection.

27 Muriel Biester, interview by Nora Stirling, Box 9, Folder: Biester, Muriel, NS collection; "Children Referred," *Welcome House Ledgers*.

28 For a discussion of changes in American families during the Cold War, see Kozol, *Life's America*; May, *Homeward Bound*; and Meyerwitz, *Not June Cleaver*.

29 "Children Referred," *Welcome House Ledgers*, 1–20.

30 Blackhawk, *Violence over the Land*; Brooks, *Captives and Cousins*; Gomez, *Exchanging Our Country Marks*; Gutiérrez, *When Jesus Came*; and Hogue, *Metis and the Medicine Line*. For more on the gender, race, and national hierarchies that structured social and sexual relations between colonizers and the colonized, see McClintock, *Imperial Leather*; and Stoler, *Carnal Knowledge and Imperial Power*.

31 Hodes, *White Women, Black Men*; Lui, *Chinatown Trunk Mystery*; and Teng, *Eurasian*.

32 Bailey and Farber, *The First Strange Place*; Kennedy, *Interracial Intimacies*; Pascoe, *What Comes Naturally*; and Wallenstein, *Tell the Court I Love My Wife*.

33 Muriel Biester, interview by Nora Stirling.

34 Lois Burpee, interview by Nora Stirling; and "Children Referred," *Welcome House Ledgers*.

35 Buck, "Notes on Welcome House," 36.

36 Alice Hammerstein Mathias, Interview by Nora Stirling.

37 Eva Eshleman, Interview by Nora Stirling, August 27, 1976, Box 10, Folder: "Eva S. Eshleman, PSB's French teacher, beginning in 1963; resident of Kutztown, PA," NS collection.

38 For more on the model minority stereotype, see Hsu, *The Good Immigrants*; J. Kim, *Ends of Empire*; Lee and Zhou, *The Asian American Achievement Paradox*; Park Nelson, *Invisible Asians*; and Takaki, *Strangers from a Different Shore*.

39 Choy, *Global Families*; Pate, *From Orphan to Adoptee*; Oh, *To Save the Children of Korea*; Winslow, *The Best Possible Immigrants*; and Woo, "A New American Comes 'Home.'"

40 Buck, "Notes on Welcome House," 34.
41 Pearl S. Buck, "Welcome House," *Reader's Digest*, July 1958, 46.
42 Rochelle Girson, "Welcome House," *Saturday Review*, July 26, 1952, 21.
43 Teng, *Eurasian*, 131.
44 Girson, "Welcome House," 21.
45 Pascoe, *What Comes Naturally*, 2–14; and Black, *War against the Weak*, 163–165. For more on miscegenation fears, see Kennedy, *Interracial Intimacies*, 18–19; and Spickard, *Mixed Blood*, 254.
46 Buck, "Notes on Welcome House," 37.
47 Viola Yoder, interview by Nora Stirling.
48 Buck, "Notes on Welcome House," 38.
49 Kennedy, *Interracial Intimacies*, 220; Pascoe, *What Comes Naturally*, 2–14; Romano, *Race Mixing*, 6–7; and Spickard, *Mixed Blood*, 254.
50 Buck, "Notes on Welcome House," 37.
51 Buck and Robeson, *American Argument*, 192.
52 For more eugenics, see Barkan, *Retreat of Scientific Racism*; and Alexandra Minna Stern, *Eugenic Nation*.
53 Kline, *Building a Better Race*, 2, 8–10, 20; Stern, *Eugenic Nation*, 4, 16–17, 18, 154; and Black, *War against the Weak*, 5, 23, 31, 378–391.
54 Buck, "Notes on Welcome House," 33.
55 Herman, *Kinship by Design*, 156–172; and Melosh, *Strangers and Kin*, 42–49.
56 Herman, *Kinship by Design*, 144.
57 Buck, "Notes on Welcome House," 35.
58 George D. Snell, "Hybrids and History: The Role of Race and Ethnic Crossing in Individual and National Achievement," *Quarterly Review of Biology* 26, no. 4 (December 1951): 331.
59 Buck, "Notes on Welcome House," 33.
60 Conn, *Pearl S. Buck*, 353. Sociologists also termed this type of selective race mixing "constructive miscegenation," and Teng explains that some theorists believed that only proximate racial groups produced superior offspring. Teng, *Eurasian*, 117–120.
61 Buck, *Children for Adoption*, 85.
62 Ibid., 90.
63 Buck, "Notes on Welcome House," 39.
64 For more on the activities of agencies experimenting with adoptions that placed children of color with white families, see Briggs, *Somebody's Children*, 35–37; and Herman, *Kinship by Design*, 204–215.
65 Buck, "Notes on Welcome House," 35.
66 Buck, "Notes on Welcome House," 38–39. Girson, "Welcome House," 21.
67 Buck, "The Story of the Welcome House," 2.
68 Choy, *Adopted Territory*, 22–45; and Oh, *To Save the Children of Korea*, 64–75.
69 Buck, "American Children: Alien by Birth," *Ladies' Home Journal*, November 1964, 40.
70 Buck, "The Children America Forgot," *Reader's Digest*, September 1967, 108–110.

71 Buck, "Welcome House," 47.
72 McKee, "Monetary Flows and the Movements of Children," 149.
73 Briggs, "Mother, Child, Race, Nation," 180–186.
74 Ibid., 181.
75 More examples of Buck's writings on Korean children include: Buck, "American Children: Alien by Birth," 39; "The Children American Forgot," *Reader's Digest*, September 1967, 109; and *Welcome Child*, 7.
76 Buck, "Should White Parents Adopt Brown Babies?" *Ebony*, June 1958, 26–28, 31.
77 Buck, "The Story of Welcome House," 1–2; Buck, *American Children*, 40; and Girson, "Welcome House," 21.
78 Conn, *Pearl S. Buck*, 151, 186, 232, 259, 265, 266, 356; and Pearl S. Buck, "Democracy and the Negro," *The Crisis*, December 1941, 376–377.
79 Ellen Visser to Susan T. Pettiss, January 15, 1955, Folder: ISS Branches, Korea "RRA-5" 1954–December 1955, Box 35, ISS records; Ellen Visser to Susan T. Pettiss, June 13, 1955, Folder: ISS Branches, Korea "RRA-5" 1954–December 1955, Box 35, ISS records; Descriptive Report–Visit to Korea of November 21–30, 1956, December 1956, Folder: Korea Reports and Visits to Korea, 1956, Box 35, ISS records.
80 I. Evelyn Smith to Elizabeth Parkhill, May 1952, Box 451, File 7-3-3-4-1, 194901952, Appeals from People Wishing Children for Adoptions, Children's Bureau records.
81 Mrs. George Berberian, Sr. to President Dwight Eisenhower, September 18, 1955, Box 684, File 7-3-3-4, Children's Bureau records.
82 Minutes of International Social Service National Advisory Council, October 1957, Box 4, Folder: ISS 1957, ISS records.
83 Agnes T. Miller to William T. Kirk, July 13, 1956, Box 23, Folder: Associations, Welcome House, 1955, ISS records. Buck, "Children Await You at Welcome House," *West Morris Star Journal*, August 6, 1970, listed the following fee scale: Yearly income of $3,999 = $150 fee; $4,000–$5,999 = $300; $6,000–$7,999 = $450; $8,000–$9,999 = $6,25; $10,000–$11,000 = $800; $12,000 and over = $1,000. These figures are also listed in the form "Costs Involved in Adoption through Welcome House."
84 Susan T. Pettiss to Mrs. Richard J. Walsh (Pearl S. Buck), May 10, 1957, Box 23, Folder: Associations Welcome House, 1955, ISS records.
85 Buck, "Should White Parents Adopt Brown Babies," 27–28.
86 Buck, *My Several Worlds*, 286–287.
87 Conn, *Pearl S. Buck*, 165–166.
88 Buck and Robeson, *American Argument*, 191–192.
89 Buck, *My Several Worlds*, 364, 365.
90 Buck, "Should White Parents Adopt Brown Babies," 31.
91 "Children Referred," *Welcome House Ledgers*, 2–27. There is a note in the ledger on page 13 for a similar case in 1955, involving a child identified as one quarter African American. This child's case was identified "rejected . . . not oriental Negro."
92 "Children Referred" *Welcome House Ledgers*.
93 Buck, "Unit Provokes Racial Adoptions," *Hartford Times*, April 21, 1958.

94 Minutes of the Children's Survey Committee, September 27, 1960, Box 32, Folder: PSB Correspondence, 1960 Korea, PSB International records. The committee's goal was to "obtain information in order to estimate the extent of needs existing among the socially, mentally and physically handicapped children in Korea, both full Korean and mixed blood children, so that individuals and agencies that are concerned about welfare of children in Korea may plan and serve them more intelligently by developing new services where needed." Report of the Children's Survey Committee, September 30, 1960, Box 32, Folder: PSB Correspondence, 1960 Korea, PSB International records; "Resume of the Development and Activities of the Children's Survey Committee," November 1960, Box 32, Folder: PSB Correspondence, 1960 Korea, PSB International records; and Hum Yun, to Pearl S. Buck, December 23, 1960, Box 32, Folder: PBS Correspondence, 1961 Korea, PSB International records.

95 Burpee, interview by Nora Stirling.

96 Conn, *Pearl S. Buck*, 312–314, 366.

97 Muriel Biester, interview by Nora Stirling; and Margaret Fischer, interview by Jane Rabb.

98 Conn, *Pearl S. Buck*, 207, 99–300.

99 Lois Burpee, interview by Nora Stirling; and Margaret Fischer, interview by Jane Rabb.

100 Conn, *Pearl S. Buck*, 354.

101 Sara Rowe, interview by Nora Stirling, December 7, 1976, Box 11, Folder: Rowe, Sarah L., NS collection.

102 Conn, *Pearl S. Buck*, 355–358.

103 Buck to Mrs. Lorene Reierson, March 21, 1961, 1, Box 38, Folder: PSB Correspondence—Pearl S. Buck Foundation, February–March 1966, PSB International records.

104 Conn, *Pearl S. Buck*, 354–376.

105 Pearl S. Buck Foundation Benefit Ball Program, 1965, Box 35, Folder: PSB Correspondence–1965–Pearl S. Buck Foundation, PSB International records.

106 Lillian W. Wolfson, interview by Nora Stirling, June 26, 1976, Box 12 Folder: Wolfson, Lillian E., NS collection.

107 Newsletter, Harrisburg Volunteer Chapter of Pearl S. Buck Foundation, December 8, 1967, Box 43, Folder: PSB Correspondence–1968–Pearl S. Buck Foundation January–February 1968, PSB International records.

108 Newsletter, Miami Volunteer Chapter of Pearl S. Buck Foundation, approx. 1968 Box 43, Folder: PSB Correspondence–1968–Pearl S. Buck Foundation January–February 1968, PSB International records.

109 "Benefit Ball Follows Premier of 'Pebbles,'" *New York Times*, December 21, 1966, 33.

110 Pearl S. Buck to Mrs. Hubert Humphrey, June 13, 1966, 2, Box 38, Folder: Correspondence–Pearl S. Buck Foundation, April–October 1966; and Pearl S. Buck to Secretary of Defense, Robert McNamara, February 16, 1968, 3, Box 43,

Folder: PSB Correspondence–1968–Pearl S. Buck Foundation January–February 1968, PSB International records.

111 Conn, Pearl. S. Buck, 352–355; and Buck to Mrs. Lorene Reierson, March 21, 1961, 3.

112 Pearl S. Buck to Dunn [sic] Gifford, c/o Senator Edward Kennedy, February 16, 1968, 2, Box 42, Folder: PSB Correspondence-1968 Pearl S. Buck Foundation, PSB International records.

113 Buck, "The Children America Forgot," 109.

114 Pearl S. Buck to Dunn [sic] Gifford, February 16, 1968, 2; and Pearl S. Buck to Lorene Reierson, March 21, 1966, 4.

115 Pearl S. Buck to Mrs. Harry Holt, March 21, 1966 and April 26, 1966, 2–3, Box 37, Folder: PSB Correspondence 1966, PSB International records; and Pearl S. Buck to Mrs. Hubert Humphrey, June 13, 1966, 2.

116 Choy, Global Families, 39.

117 Paul Cherney, "Report on Visit to Korea, June 23 to July 9, 1965," July 20, 1965, Folder: Korea, Child Placement Service, General, 1964–1965, Box 35, ISS records.

118 Choy, Global Families, 39.

119 Gardner Munro to Paul Cherney, 1964, Box 35, Folder: Korea, Child Placement Service, General, 1964–1965, ISS records; Paul Cherney, Report in Visit to Korea: June 23 to July 9, 1965, July 20, 1965, Box 35, Folder: Korea-Child Placement Service, General 1964–1965, ISS records; "The KAVA Resolution on Children with Racially Mixed Parentage," January 22, 1964, Box 35, Folder: Korea-Child Placement Service, General 1964–1965, ISS records; and Paul R. Cherney to Mrs. Morris Hadley, July 20, 1965, Box 35, Folder: Korea, Child Placement Service, General, 1964–1965, ISS records. George Whitener used his affiliation with the Presbyterian Church to promote this program, and ten mixed-race children entered an all-Korean middle school in 1964.

120 Pearl S. Buck to Dunn [sic] Gifford, c/o Senator Edward Kennedy, February 16, 1968, 2.

121 Buck, "The Children America Forgot," 108; Conn, Pearl S. Buck, 313.

122 Pearl S. Buck to Dunn [sic] Gifford, February 16, 1968, 2.

123 Pearl S. Buck to Donald P. Miller, January 29, 1968, 2, Box 43, Folder PSB Correspondence–1968, PSB Correspondence, PSB International records.

124 Lillian W. Wolfson, interview by Nora Stirling.

125 Pearl S. Buck to Secretary of Defense Robert McNamara, February 16, 1968, 2.

126 Conn, Pearl S. Buck, 359.

CONCLUSION

1 Hübinette, Comforting an Orphaned Nation, 71–75; and Oh, To Save the Children of Korea, 194–200.

2 Condit-Shrestha, "South Korea and Adoption's Ends; Hübinette, Comforting an Orphaned Nation, 49; and Oh, To Save the Children of Korea, 82.

3 Kim, Birth Mothers, 44.

4 Selman, "Intercountry Adoption: Research, Policy and Practice," 277–278.

5 Hübinette, *Comforting an Orphaned Nation*, 63.

6 Oh, *To Save the Children of Korea*, 82.

7 Ibid.

8 Hübinette, *Comforting an Orphaned Nation*, 49.

9 Sarri, Baik, and Bombyk, "Goal Displacement and Dependency in South Korean-United States Intercountry Adoption," 89.

10 Pate, *From Orphan to Adoptee*, 108.

11 Kim, *Adopted Territory*, 72; and Oh, *To Save the Children of Korea*, 191.

12 Moon, *Sex Among Allies*, 28.

13 Ibid., 58–67.

14 Lee, *A Troubled Peace*, 41, 68–70, 90.

15 Ibid., 134.

16 Ibid., 170.

17 Ibid., 256.

18 Moon, *Sex Among Allies*, 35–39, 48–56.

19 Ibid., 23.

20 Kim, *Birth Mothers*, 83; and Oh, *To Save the Children of Korea*, 190.

21 McKee, "Monetary Flows and the Movements of Children," 142.

22 Kim, *Birth Mothers*, 45.

23 McKee, "Monetary Flows and the Movements of Children," 144.

24 Ibid.

25 Hübinette, *Comforting an Orphaned Nation*, 68–69. Kim, *Adopted Territory*, 72. In 1968, the new director of CPS, Mr. Tahk, briefly took the agency back to its roots, to the dismay of ISS officials. At the March 12, 1968 ISS Board of Directors meeting, they complained that CPS was sending referrals for mixed-race Korean children only.

26 Ibid., 159.

27 Pate, *From Orphan to Adoptee*, 88.

28 Helen Wilson to Augusta Mayerson, January 21, 1953, Box 35, Folder: Korea Correspondences, vol. I, ISS records. Oh, *To Save the Children of Korea*, 195.

29 Memo, Ann Shyne to Professional Staff, April 15, 1971, Box 16, Folder 3: Adoption—General, 1970–72, CWLA records.

30 Rose M. Kreider and Elizabeth Raleigh, "A Nationally Representative Comparison of Black and White Adoptive Parents of Black Children" (SEHSD Working Paper #2017–10, American Sociology Association, Seattle, Washington, August 20–23, 2016).

31 Spence, "Whose Stereotypes and Racial Myths?," 143–146.

32 Briggs, *Somebody's Children*, 98. For a sobering critique of the contemporary challenges African American families face in US child welfare systems and the inequities of the MEPA-IEP, see Roberts, *Shattered Bonds*.

33 Day, *The Adoption of Black Children*, 30, 45, 47. For more on institutional barriers to adoptions involving African Americans, see Billingsley and Giovannoni, *Chil-*

dren of the Storm; Fogg-Davis, *The Ethics of Transracial Adoption*; and Herman, *Kinship by Design*, 198.

34 Herman, *Kinship by Design*, 229, 250. Rachel Rains Winslow notes that African American social workers played important roles in efforts to determine what was in the best interest of Vietnamese black children in the early 1970s. It is revealing that these professionals recommended that Vietnamese black children should remain with their mothers in Vietnam because it was evident that the mothers loved and were endeavoring to care for their children. Winslow, *The Best Possible Immigrants*, 157.

35 Pate, *From Orphan to Adoptee*, 119–120.

36 Oh, *To Save the Children of Korea*, 191–192, 195–200.

37 Ibid., 192.

38 Briggs, *Somebody's Children*; Kim, *Birth Mothers*; Trenka, Oparah, and Shin, *Outsiders Within*.

39 Moon, *Sex Among Allies*, 71–74.

40 Yuh, *Beyond the Shadow of Camptown*, 212–214.

41 Jerry Crow, "Ward Learned by Mom's Example," *Los Angeles Times*, February 4, 2006, http://articles.latimes.com.

42 Paul Wiseman, "Ward Spins Biracial Roots into Blessing," *USA Today*, April 10, 2006, http://usatoday30.usatoday.com.

43 James J. Na, "Hines Ward's Tale of American Transcendence," *Seattle Times*, May 17, 2006, http://old.seattletimes.com.

44 "Steelers' Ward Returns to South Korea," April 4, 2006, ESPN.com New Services, http://espn.go.com; For more on South Korean officials' efforts to address the complicated history of intercountry adoption, see Kim, *Adopted Territory*.

45 "Ward Ends Korean Visit with a Promise," April 12, 2006, TRIB Live, http://trib-live.com.

46 Kyung-Jin Lee, "An Adopter and the Ends of Adoption," 282–291; and Park Nelson, *Invisible Asians*, 189–193.

BIBLIOGRAPHY

ARCHIVES AND SPECIAL COLLECTIONS
Amistad Research Center, New Orleans, LA
Records of the Auxiliary to the National Medical Association
Archives of the Pearl S. Buck House, Pearl S. Buck International, Perkasie, PA
Papers of Pearl S. Buck, Record Group 1
Library of Congress, Manuscript Division, Washington, DC
Records of the National Urban League
Lipscomb Library, Randolph College, Lynchburg, VA
Jane Rabb Collection
Nora Stirling Collection
Manuscript, Archives, and Rare Book Library, Emory University, Atlanta, GA
Josephine Baker Collection
Robert W. Woodruff Library and Archives Research Center, Atlanta University, Atlanta, GA
Frankie V. Adams Collection
Atlanta University School of Social Work Vertical Files
Josephine Baker Vertical Files
Social Welfare History Archives, University of Minnesota, Minneapolis
International Social Service, Administrative Records
International Social Service, Case Records
Child Welfare League of America Records
Special Collections and Archives, Fisk University, Nashville, TN
Dorothy L. Brown Collection
Ophelia Settle Egypt Collection
United States National Archives and Records Administration, College Park, MD
US Department of State, Record Group 59
US Department of State, Foreign Posts, Record Group 84
US Children's Bureau, Record Group 102
West Virginia State Archives, Charleston, WV
Pearl S. Buck Vertical Surname File

NEWSPAPERS AND PERIODICALS
Baltimore Afro-American
Boston Globe
Chicago Defender

The Crisis
Ebony
Jet
New York Amsterdam News
New York Times
Our World
Pacific Stars and Stripes
Sepia

PUBLISHED BOOKS AND ARTICLES

Armfield, Felix L. *Eugene Knickle Jones: The National Urban League and Black Social Work, 1910–1940*. Urbana: University of Illinois Press, 2012.

Armstrong, Charles K. *The Koreas*. New York: Routledge, 2007.

Bailey, Beth L. and David Farber. *The First Strange Place: The Alchemy of Race and Sex in World War II Hawaii*. New York: Free Press, 1992.

Balcom, Karen. *Traffic in Babies: Cross-Border Adoption and Baby-Selling between the United States and Canada, 1930–1972*. Toronto: University of Toronto Press, 2011.

Bardaglio, Peter W. *Reconstructing the Household: Families, Sex, and the Law in the Nineteenth-Century South*. Chapel Hill: University of North Carolina Press, 1995.

Barkan, Elazar. *Retreat of Scientific Racism: Changing Concepts of Race in Britain and the United States Between the World Wars*. Cambridge, UK: University of Cambridge Press, 1992.

Bartholet, Elizabeth. *Nobody's Children: Abuse and Neglect, Foster Drift, and the Adoption Alternative*. Boston: Beacon Press, 1999.

Bell, Joyce M. *The Black Power Movement and American Social Work*. New York: Columbia University Press, 2014.

Berebitsky, Julie. *Like Our Very Own: Adoption and the Changing Culture of Motherhood 1851–1950*. Lawrence: University Press of Kansas, 2000.

Billingsley, Andrew and Jeanne M. Giovannoni. *Children of the Storm: Black Children and American Child Welfare*. New York: Harcourt, Brace, Jovanovich, 1972.

Black, Edwin. *War against the Weak: Eugenics and America's Campaign to Create a Master Race*. New York: Four Walls Eight Windows, 2003.

Blackhawk, Ned. *Violence over the Land: Indians and Empires in the Early American West*. Cambridge, MA: Harvard University Press, 2008.

Bon Tempo, Carl. *Americans at the Gate: The United States and Refugees during the Cold War*. Princeton, NJ: Princeton University Press, 2008.

Booker, Christopher B. *"I Will Wear No Chain!": A Social History of African American Males*. Westport, CT: Praeger, 2000.

Borstelmann, Thomas. *The Cold War and the Color Line: American Race Relations in the Global Arena*. Cambridge, MA: Harvard University Press, 2001.

Bowers, William T., William M. Hammond, and George L. MacGarrigle. *Black Soldier, White Army: The 24th Infantry Regiment in Korea*. Washington, DC: Center of Military History United States Army, 1996.

Bowlby, John. *Maternal Care and Mental Health*. Geneva: World Health Organization, 1951.

Briggs, Laure. "Mother, Child, Race, Nation: The Visual Iconography of Rescue and the Politics of Transnational and Transracial Adoption." *Gender and History* 15, no. 2 (2003): 179–200.

———. *Somebody's Children: The Politics of Transracial and Transnational Adoption*. Durham, NC: Duke University Press, 2012.

Brooks, James F. *Captives and Cousins: Slavery, Kinship, and Community in the Southwest Borderlands*. Chapel Hill: University of North Carolina Press, 2001.

Broussard, Jinx Coleman. *African American Foreign Correspondents: A History*. Baton Rouge: Louisiana State University Press, 2013.

Brown, Joseph E. *Black Soldier of Mercy*. Timberlake, NC: Righter Publishing, 2010.

Buck, Pearl S. *My Several Worlds*. New York: John Day, 1954.

———. *Welcome Child*. New York: John Day, 1963.

———. *Children for Adoption*. New York: Random House, 1964.

———. *Matthew, Mark, Luke, and John*. New York: John Day, 1966.

Buck, Pearl S. and Eslanda Goode Robeson. *American Argument*. New York: John Day, 1949.

Callahan, Cynthia. *Kin of Another Kind: Transracial Adoption in American Literature*. Ann Arbor: University of Michigan Press, 2010.

Carp, E. Wayne. *Family Matters: Secrecy and Disclosure in the History of Adoption*. Cambridge, MA: Harvard University Press, 1998.

———, ed. *Adoption in America: Historical Perspectives*. Ann Arbor: University of Michigan Press, 2002.

Chafe, William. *The Unfinished Journey: America Since World War II*. New York: Oxford University Press, 1986.

Choy, Catherine Ceniza. *Global Families: A History of Asian International Adoption in America*. New York: New York University Press, 2013.

Chung, David. *Syncretism: The Religious Context of Christian Beginnings in Korea*. Albany: State University of New York Press, 2001.

Clark, Donald N. "The Missionary Impact: Reflections on a Century of Korean-American Relations." *Korean Culture* 3, no. 2 (July 1982): 26–33.

Clemetson, Lynette and Ron Nixon. "Overcoming Adoption's Racial Barriers." *New York Times*, August 17, 2006. http://www.nytimes.com/.

Cohen, Lizabeth. *A Consumer's Republic: The Politics of Mass Consumption in Postwar America*. New York: Knopf, 2003.

Collins, Patricia Hill. *Black Feminist Thought: Knowledge, Consciousness, and the Politics of Empowerment*. New York: Routledge Classics, 2000.

Condit-Shrestha, Kelly. "South Korea and Adoption's Ends: Reexamining the Numbers and Historicizing Market Economies." *Adoption and Culture* 6, no. 2 (2018): 364–400.

Conn, Peter. *Pearl S. Buck: A Cultural Biography*. Cambridge, UK: Press Syndicate of the University of Cambridge Press, 1996.

Coontz, Stephanie. *The Way We Never Were: American Families and the Nostalgia Trap.* New York: Basic Books, 2000.

Cott, Nancy F. *The Bonds of Womanhood: "Women's Sphere" in New England, 1780–1835.* New Haven, CT: Yale University Press, 1977.

Cronon, E. David. *Black Moses: The Story of Marcus Garvey and the Universal Negro Improvement Association.* Madison: University of Wisconsin Press, 1955.

Cumings, Bruce. *The Origins of the Korean War: Liberation and the Emergence of Separate Regimes, 1945–1947.* Princeton, NJ: Princeton University Press, 1981.

———. *Korea's Place in the Sun: A Modern History.* New York: Norton, 2005.

———. *The Korean War: A History.* New York: Random House, 2010.

Daniel, Walter C. *Black Journals of the United States.* Westport, CT: Greenwood Press, 1982.

Daniels, Roger. *Coming to America: A History of Immigration and Ethnicity and America.* New York: Harper Collins, 1990.

Day, Dawn. *The Adoption of Black Children: Counteracting Institutional Discrimination.* Lexington, MD: Lexington Books, 1979.

Dinnerstein, Leonard and David M. Reimers. *Ethnic Americans: A History of Immigration and Assimilation.* New York: Columbia University Press, 2009.

Dorow, Sara K. *Transnational Adoption: A Cultural Economy of Race, Gender, and Kinship.* New York: New York University Press, 2006.

Dubinsky, Karen. *Babies without Borders: Adoption and Migration across the Americas.* New York: New York University Press, 2010.

Dudziak, Mary L. *Cold War Civil Rights: Race and the Image of American Democracy.* Princeton, NJ: Princeton University Press, 2000.

Eagles, Charles W. "Toward New Histories of the Civil Rights Era." *Journal of Southern History* 66 (November 2000): 815–848.

Elder, Glen, Jr. *Children of the Great Depression: Social Change in Life Experience.* Chicago: University of Chicago Press, 1974.

Enloe, Cynthia. *Bananas, Beaches, and Bases: Making Feminist Sense of International Politics.* Berkeley: University of California Press, 1990.

———. *Maneuvers: The International Politics of Militarizing Women's Lives.* Berkeley: University of California Press, 2000.

Estes, Steve. *I Am a Man: Race, Manhood, and the Civil Rights Movement.* Chapel Hill: University of North Carolina Press, 2005.

Fanshel, David. *A Study in Negro Adoption.* New York: Child Welfare League of America, 1957.

Fanshel, David and Eugene B. Shinn. *Dollars and Sense in the Foster Care of Children: A Look at Cost Factors.* New York: Child Welfare League of America, 1972.

Farrar, Jr., Hayward. *The Baltimore Afro-American, 1892–1950.* Westport, CT: Praeger, 1998.

Feffer, John. *North Korea, South Korea: US Policy at a Time of Crisis.* New York: Seven Stories Press, 2003.

Fehrenbach, Heide. *Race After Hitler: Black Occupation Children in Postwar Germany and America*. Princeton, NJ: Princeton University Press, 2005.

Fischer, Kristen. *Suspect Relations: Sex, Race, and Resistance in Colonial North Carolina*. Ithaca, NY: Cornell University Press, 2002.

Fogg-Davis, Hawley. *The Ethics of Transracial Adoption*. Ithaca, NY: Cornell University Press, 2002.

Foner, Jack D. *Blacks and the Military in American History*. New York: Praeger, 1974.

Franklin, Donna L. *Ensuring Inequality: The Structural Transformation of the African American Family*. New York: Oxford University Press, 1997.

Frazier, Edward Franklin. *The Negro Family in the United States*. New York: Dryden Press, 1948.

———. *Black Bourgeoisie*. Glencoe, IL: Free Press, 1957.

Gaines, Kevin. "The Historiography of the Struggle for Black Equality since 1945." In *A Companion to Post-1945 America*, edited by Jean-Christophe Agnew and Roy Resenzweig, 211–234. Malden, MA: Blackwell, 2002.

Garvey, Amy Jacques. "The Early Years of Marcus Garvey." In *Marcus Garvey and the Vision of Africa*, edited by John Henrik Clarke. New York: Random House, 1973.

Gilbert, James. *Men in the Middle: Searching for Masculinity in the 1950s*. Chicago: University of Chicago Press, 2005.

Gilmore, Glenda. *Gender and Jim Crow: Women and the Politics of White Supremacy in North Carolina, 1896–1920*. Chapel Hill: University of North Carolina Press, 1996.

Goldberg, Vicki. *The Power of Photography: How Photographs Changed Our Lives*. New York: Abbeville Publishing, 1993.

Gomez, Michael A. *Exchanging Our Country Marks: The Transformation of African Identities in the Colonial and Antebellum South*. Chapel Hill: University of North Carolina Press, 1998.

Gordon, Linda. *Pitied but Not Entitled: Single Mothers and the History of Welfare*. Cambridge, MA: Harvard University Press, 1994.

———. *The Great Arizona Orphan Abduction*. Cambridge, MA: Harvard University Press, 1999.

Green, Adam. *Selling the Race: Culture, Community, and Black Chicago, 1940–1955*. Chicago: University of Chicago Press, 2007.

Green, Michael Cullen. *Black Yanks in the Pacific: Race in the Making of American Military Empire after World War II*. Ithaca, NY: Cornell University Press, 2010.

Greene, Melissa Fay. "Do I Love Him Yet?." *Adoptive Families* 40 (September/October 2007): 40–43.

Guterl, Matthew Pratt. "Josephine Baker's 'Rainbow Tribe' Radical Motherhood in the South of France." *Journal of Women's History* 21, no. 4 (Winter 2009): 38–58.

Gutiérrez, Ramón A. *When Jesus Came, the Corn Mothers Went Away*. Redwood City, CA: Stanford University Press, 1991.

Gutman, Herbert. *The Black Family in Slavery and Freedom, 1750–1925*. New York: Pantheon Books, 1976.

Hall, Jacquelyn Dowd. "The Long Civil Rights Movement and the Political Uses of the Past." *Journal of American History* 91 (March 2005): 1233–1263.

Hanley, Charles J., Martha Mendoza, and Choe Sang-Hun. *The Bridge at No Gun Ri: A Hidden Nightmare from the Korean War*. New York: Holt Paperbacks, 2002.

Herman, Ellen. *Kinship by Design: A History of Adoption in the Modern United States*. Chicago: University of Chicago Press, 2008.

Hill, Robert. *Informal Adoption Among Black Families*. Washington, DC: National Urban League, 1977.

Hodes, Martha. *White Women, Black Men: Illicit Sex in the 19th-Century South*. New Haven, CT: Yale University Press, 1997.

Hogue, Michel. *Metis and the Medicine Line: Creating a Border and Dividing a People*. Chapel Hill: University of North Carolina Press, 2015.

Holloran, Peter C. *Boston's Wayward Children: Social Services for Homeless Children, 1830–1930*. Rutherford, NJ: Fairleigh Dickinson University Press, 1989.

Hübinette, Tobias. *Comforting an Orphaned Nation: Representations of International Adoption and Adopted Koreans in Korean Popular Culture*. Seoul: Jimoondang, 2005.

———. "From Orphan Trains to Babylifts: Colonial Trafficking, Empire Building, and Social Engineering." In *Outsiders Within: Writing on Transracial Adoption*, edited by Jane Jeong Trenka, Julia Chinyere Oparah, and Sun Yang Shin, 139–149. Cambridge, MA: South End Press, 2006.

Huebner, Andrew J. *The Warrior Image: Soldiers in American Culture from the Second World War to the Vietnam Era*. Chapel Hill: University of North Carolina Press, 2008.

Huh, Nam Soon. "Korean Adopted Children's Ethnic Identity Formation." In *International Korean Adoption: A Fifty-Year History of Policy and Practice*, edited by Kathleen Ja Sook Bergquist, M. Elizabeth Vonk, Dong Soo Kim, and Marvin E. Feit, 79–97. New York: Haworth Press, 2007.

Hsu, Madeline Y. *The Good Immigrants: How the Yellow Peril Became the Model Minority*. Princeton, NJ: Princeton University Press, 2015.

Jackson, Kenneth T. *Crabgrass Frontier: The Suburbanization of the United States*. New York: Oxford University Press, 1985.

Jacobs, Margaret D. *White Mother to a Dark Race: Settler Colonialism, Maternalism, and the Removal of Indigenous Children in the American West and Australia, 1880–1940*. Lincoln: University of Nebraska Press, 2009.

Jacobson, Matthew. *Whiteness of a Different Color: European Immigrants and the Alchemy of Race*. Cambridge, MA: Harvard University Press, 1998.

Johnson, John H. with Lerone Bennett, Jr. *Succeeding Against the Odds*. New York: Warner Books, 1989.

Jones, Jacqueline. *Labor of Love, Labor of Sorrow: Black Women, Work, and the Family from Slavery to the Present*. New York: Vintage Books, 1985.

Jules-Rosette, Bennetta. *Josephine Baker in Art and Life: The Icon and the Image*. Urbana: University of Illinois Press, 2007.

Kellogg, Charles Flint. *NAACP: A History of the National Association for the Advancement of Colored People, Volume I, 1909–1920*. Baltimore, MD: Johns Hopkins University Press, 1967.

Kennedy, Randall. *Interracial Intimacies: Sex, Marriage, Identity, and Adoption*. New York: Pantheon Books, 2003.

Kim, Dong-Choon. *The Unending Korean War: A Social History*, translated by Sung-ok Kim. Larkspur, CA: Tamal Vista Publications, 2009.

Kim, Dong Soo. "A Country Divided: Contextualizing Adoption from a Korean Perspective." In *International Korean Adoption: A Fifty-Year History of Policy and Practice*, edited by Kathleen Ja Sook Bergquist, M. Elizabeth Vonk, Dong Soo Kim, and Marvin E. Feit, 3–23. New York: Haworth Press, 2007.

Kim, Eleana J. "Wedding Citizenship and Culture: Korean Adoptees and the Global Family of Korea." In *Cultures of Transnational Adoption*, edited by Toby Alice Volkman, 49–80. Durham, NC: Duke University Press, 2005.

———. "The Origins of Korean Adoption: Cold War Geopolitics and Intimate Diplomacy." In *Working Paper Series (WP 09–09), US-Korea Institute at SAIS*, 3–26. Baltimore, MD: Johns Hopkins University Press, 2009.

———. *Adopted Territory: Transnational Korean Adoptees and the Politics of Belonging*. Durham, NC: Duke University Press, 2010.

Kim, Hosu. *Birth Mothers and Transracial Adoption Practice in South Korea: Virtual Mothering*. New York: Palgrave Macmillan, 2016.

———. "Reparation Acts, Korean Birth Mothers Travel the Road from Reunion to Redress." *Adoption and Culture* 6, no. 2 (2018): 316–335.

Kim, Jae Ran. "Scattered Seeds: The Christian Influence on Korean Adoption." In *Outsiders Within: Writing on Transracial Adoption*, edited by Jane Jeong Trenka, Julia Chinyere Oparah, and Sun Yang Shin, 151–162. Cambridge, MA: South End Press, 2006.

Kim, Jodi. *Ends of Empire: Asian American Critique and the Cold War*. Minneapolis: University of Minnesota Press, 2010.

Kim, Monica. "Empire's Babel: US Military Interrogation Rooms of the Korean War." *History of the Present: A Journal of Critical History* 3, no. 1 (Spring 2013): 1–28.

Klein, Christina. "Family Ties and Political Obligation: The Discourse of Adoption and the Cold War Commitment to Asia." In *Cold War Constructions: The Political Culture of United States Imperialism, 1945–1966*, edited by Christina Appy, 35–66. Amherst: University of Massachusetts Press, 2000.

———. *Cold War Orientalism: Asia in the Middlebrow Imagination, 1945–1961*. Berkeley: University of California Press, 2003.

Kline, Wendy. *Building a Better Race: Gender, Sexuality, and Eugenics from the Turn of the Century to the Baby Boom*. Berkeley: University of California Press, 2001.

Knauer, Christine. *Let Us Fight as Free Men: Black Soldiers and Civil Rights*. Philadelphia: University of Pennsylvania Press, 2014.

Kozol, Wendy. *Life's America: Family and Nation in Postwar Photojournalism*. Philadelphia: Temple University Press, 1994.

Kunzel, Regina. *Fallen Women, Problem Girls: Unmarried Mothers and the Professionalization of Social Work, 1890–1945.* New Haven, CT: Yale University Press, 1993.

Kurashige, Lon. *Two Faces of Exclusion: The Untold History of Anti-Asian Racism in the United States.* Chapel Hill: University of North Carolina Press, 2016.

Kwak, Tae-Hwan, John Chay, Soon Sung Cho, and Shannon McCune, eds. *U.S.-Korean Relations, 1882–1982.* Seoul: Kyungnam University Press, 1983.

Lee, Chae-Jin. *A Troubled Peace: U.S. Policy and the Two Koreas.* Baltimore, MD: Johns Hopkins University Press, 2006.

Lee, James Kyung-Jin. "An Adopter and the Ends of Adoption." *Adoption and Culture* 6, no. 2 (2018): 282–291.

Lee, Jennifer and Min Zhou. *The Asian American Achievement Paradox.* New York: Russell Sage Foundation, 2015.

Lee, Sabine. "A Forgotten Legacy of the Second World War: GI Children in Post-War Britain and Germany." *Contemporary European History* 20, no. 2 (May 2011): 157–181.

Lee, Yur-Bok and Wayne Patterson, eds. *One Hundred Years of Korean-American Relations, 1882–1982.* Tuscaloosa: University of Alabama Press, 1986.

Lowe, Peter. *The Korean War.* New York: St. Martin's Press, 2000.

Lui, Mary Ting Yi. *Chinatown Trunk Mystery: Murder, Miscegenation, and Other Dangerous Encounters in Turn-of-the-Century New York City.* Princeton, NJ: Princeton University Press, 2007.

May, Elaine Tyler. *Homeward Bound: American Families in the Cold War Era.* New York: Basic Books, 1988.

———. *Barren in the Promised Land: Childless Americans and the Pursuit of Happiness.* New York: Basic Books, 1995.

McClintock, Anne. *Imperial Leather: Race, Gender, and Sexuality in the Colonial Contest.* New York: Routledge, 1995.

McKee, Kimberly D. "Monetary Flows and the Movements of Children: The Transnational Adoption Industrial Complex." *Journal of Korean Studies* 21, no. 1 (2016): 137–178.

Melosh, Barbara. *Strangers and Kin: The American Way of Adoption.* Cambridge, MA: Harvard University Press, 2002.

Meyer, Stephen Grant. *As Long as They Don't Move Next Door: Segregation and Racial Conflict in American Neighborhoods.* Lanham, MD: Rowman & Littlefield, 2000.

Meyerwitz, Joanne. *Not June Cleaver: Women and Gender in Postwar America, 1945–1960.* Philadelphia: Temple University Press, 1994.

Millett, Allan R. *The War for Korea, 1950–1951.* Lawrence: University Press of Kansas, 2010.

Mink, Gwendolyn. *The Wages of Motherhood: Inequality in the Welfare State, 1917–1942.* Ithaca, NY: Cornell University Press, 1995.

Mintz, Steven and Susan Kellogg. *Domestic Revolutions: A Social History of American Family Life.* New York: Free Press, 1988.

Moon, Katharine H. S. *Sex Among Allies: Military Prostitution in U.S.-Korea Relations.* New York: Columbia University Press, 1997.

Moore, Jesse Thomas. *A Search for Equality: The National Urban League, 1910–1961.* University Park: Pennsylvania State University Press, 1981.

Morrow, Curtis James. *What's a Commie Ever Done to Black People?: A Korean War Memoir of Fighting in the U.S. Army's Last All Negro Unit.* Jefferson, NC: McFarland and Company, 1997.

Mullen, Bill V. *Afro-Orientalism.* Minneapolis: University of Minnesota Press, 2004.

Nakamura, Masako. "Families Precede Nation and Race?: Marriage, Migration, and Integration of Japanese War Brides after World War II." Dissertation, University of Minnesota, 2010.

Nelson, Claudia. *Little Strangers: Portrayals of Adoption and Foster Care in America, 1850–1929.* Bloomington: Indiana University Press, 2003.

Newman, Mark. *The Civil Rights Movement.* Westport, CT: Praeger, 2004.

Ngai, Mae M. *Impossible Subjects: Illegal Aliens and the Making of Modern America.* Princeton, NJ: Princeton University Press, 2004.

Oh, Arissa. "From War Waif to Ideal Immigrant: The Cold War Transformation of the Korean Orphan." *Journal of American Ethnic History* 31, no. 4 (Summer 2012): 34–55.

———. *To Save the Children of Korea: The Cold War Origins of International Adoption.* Redwood City, CA: Stanford University Press, 2015.

Palmer, John D. *The Dance of Identities: Korean Adoptees and Their Journey towards Empowerment.* Honolulu: University of Hawai'i Press, 2011.

Park Nelson, Kim. *Invisible Asians: Korean American Adoptees, Asian American Experiences, and Racial Exceptionalism.* New Brunswick, NJ: Rutgers University Press, 2016.

Parris, Guichard and Lester Brooks. *Blacks in the City: A History of the National Urban League.* Boston: Little, Brown, 1971.

Pascoe, Peggy. *What Comes Naturally: Miscegenation Law and the Making of Race in America.* New York: Oxford University Press, 2009.

Pate, SooJin. *From Orphan to Adoptee: U.S. Empire and Genealogies of Korean Adoption.* Minneapolis: University of Minnesota Press, 2014.

Patterson, James. *Freedom Is Not Enough: The Moynihan Report and America's Struggle over Black Family Life—from LBJ to Obama.* New York: Basic Books, 2010.

Phillips, Kimberly L. *War! What Is It Good For?: Black Freedom Struggles and the U.S. Military from World War II to Iraq.* Chapel Hill: University of North Carolina Press, 2012.

Plummer, Brenda Gayle. *Rising Wind: Black Americans and U.S. Foreign Affairs, 1935–1960.* Chapel Hill: University of North Carolina Press, 1996.

———. ed. *Window on Freedom: Race, Civil Rights, and Foreign Affairs, 1945–1988.* Chapel Hill: University of North Carolina Press, 2003.

———. *In Search of Power: African Americans in the Era of Decolonization, 1956–1974.* New York: Cambridge University Press, 2013.

Porter, Susan L. "A Good Home: Indenture and Adoption in Nineteenth-Century Orphanages." In *Adoption in America: Historical Perspectives*, edited by E. Wayne Carp, 27–50. Ann Arbor: University of Michigan Press, 2004.

Potter, Sarah. *Everybody Else: Adoption and the Politics of Domestic Diversity in Postwar America*. Athens: University of Georgia Press, 2014.

Rains, Prudence Mors. *Becoming an Unwed Mother: A Sociological Account*. Chicago: Aldine-Atherton Press, 1971.

Reed, Touré F. *Not Alms but Opportunity: The Urban League and the Politics of Racial Uplift, 1910–1950*. Chapel Hill: University of North Carolina Press, 2008.

Reid-Merritt, Patricia. *Righteous Self Determination: The Black Social Work Movement in America*. New York: Black Classic Press, 2010.

Rishell, Lyle. *With a Black Platoon in Combat: A Year in Korea*. College Station: Texas A & M University Press, 1993.

Roberts, Dorothy. *Shattered Bonds: The Color of Child Welfare*. New York: Basic Books, 2002.

———. "Adoption Risks and Racial Realities in the United States." In *Outsiders Within: Writing on Transracial Adoption*, edited by Jane Jeong Trenka, Julia Chinyere Oparah, and Sun Yang Shin, 49–56. Cambridge, MA: South End Press, 2006.

Roberts, Gene and Hank Klibanoff. *The Race Beat: The Press, The Civil Rights Struggle, and the Awakening of a Nation*. New York: Vintage Books, 2006.

Romano, Renee C. *Race Mixing: Black-White Marriage in Postwar America*. Cambridge, MA: Harvard University Press, 2003.

Rosenberg, Rosalind. *Beyond Separate Spheres: Intellectual Roots of Modern Feminism*. New Haven, CT: Yale University Press, 1982.

Rymph, Catherine E. *Raising Government Children: A History of Foster Care and the American Welfare State*. Chapel Hill: University of North Carolina Press, 2017.

Said, Edward W. *Orientalism*. New York: Vintage Books, 1979.

Sarri, Rosemary C., Yenoak Baik, and Marti Bombyk. "Goal Displacement and Dependence in South Korean-United States Intercountry Adoption." *Children and Youth Services Review* 20, no. 1/2 (1998): 87–114.

Self, Robert O. *American Babylon: Race and the Struggle for Postwar Oakland*. Princeton, NJ: Princeton University Press, 2003.

Seligmann, Linda J. *Broken Links, Enduring Ties: American Adoption Across Race, Class, and Nation*. Stanford, CA: Stanford University Press, 2013.

Selman, Peter. "Intercountry Adoption: Research, Policy and Practice." In *The Child Placement Handbook: Research, Policy and Practice*, edited by Gillian Schofield and John Simmonds, 276–303. London: British Association for Adoption and Fostering, 2009.

Seth, Michael J. *A Concise History of Modern Korea: From the Late Nineteenth Century to the Present*. Lanham, MD: Rowman & Littlefield, 2010.

Shah, Nayan. *Contagious Divides: Epidemics and Race in San Francisco's Chinatown*. Berkeley: University of California Press, 2001.

Sheldon, Robert L. *Daybreak in Korea*. Nashville, TN: Southern Publishing Association, 1965.

Shockley, Megan Taylor. *"We, Too, Are Americans": African American Women in Detroit and Richmond, 1940–54*. Urbana: University of Illinois Press, 2004.

Simon, Rita J., Howard Alstein, and Marygold S. Melli. *The Case for Transracial Adoption*. Washington, DC: American University Press, 1994.

Singh, Nikhil Pal. *Black Is a Country: Race and the Unfinished Struggle for Democracy.* Cambridge, MA: Harvard University Press, 2004.

Sitkoff, Harvard. *A New Deal for Blacks: The Emergence of Civil Rights as a National Issue.* New York: Oxford University Press, 1978.

Soh, C. Sarah. *The Comfort Women: Sexual Violence and Postcolonial Memory in Korea and Japan.* Chicago: University of Chicago Press, 2009.

Sohoni, Deenesh. "Unsuitable Suitors: Anti-Miscegenation Laws, Naturalization Laws, and the Construction of Asian Identities." *Law and Society Review* 41, no. 3 (2007): 587–618.

Solinger, Rickie. *Wake Up Little Susie: Single Pregnancy and Race before* Roe v. Wade. New York: Routledge, 1992.

Spence, Martine T. "Whose Stereotypes and Racial Myths? The National Urban League and the 1950s Roots of Color-Blind Adoption Policy." *Women, Gender, and Families of Color* 1:2 (Fall 2013): 143–179.

Spickard, Paul R. *Mixed Blood: Intermarriage and Ethnic Identity in Twentieth-Century America.* Madison: University of Wisconsin Press, 1989.

Stern, Alexandra Minna. *Eugenic Nation: Faults and Frontiers of Better Breeding in Modern America.* Berkeley: University of California Press, 2005.

Stoler, Ann Laura. *Carnal Knowledge and Imperial Power: Race and the Intimate in Colonial Rule.* Berkeley: University of California Press, 2002.

Strong, Lester. "Josephine Baker's Hungry Heart." *Gay and Lesbian Review* (September–October 2006). http://www.glreview.com.

Sturdevant, Saundra Pollack and Brenda Stoltzfus. *Let the Good Times Roll: Prostitution in the U.S. Military in Asia.* New York: New Press, 1993.

Takaki, Ronald. *Strangers from a Different Shore: A History of Asian Americans.* Boston: Little, Brown, 1989.

Teng, Emma Jinhaua. *Eurasian: Mixed Identities in the United States, China, and Hong Kong, 1842–1943.* Berkeley: University of California Press, 2013.

Trenka, Jane Jeong. *The Language of Blood: A Memoir.* St. Paul, MN: Borealis Books, 2003.

Trenka, Jane Jeong, Chinyere Oparah, and Sun Yung Shin, eds. *Outsiders Within: Writing on Transracial Adoption.* Cambridge, MA: South End Press, 2006.

Vincent, Clark E. *Unmarried Mother.* New York: Free Press of Glencoe, 1961.

Volkman, Toby Alice. *Cultures of Transnational Adoption.* Durham, NC: Duke University Press, 2005.

Von Eschen, Penny. *Race Against Empire: Black Americans and Anticolonialism, 1937–1957.* Ithaca, NY: Cornell University Press, 1997.

———. *Satchmo Blows Up the World: Jazz Ambassadors Play the Cold War.* Cambridge, MA: Harvard University Press, 2004.

Walker, Juliet E. K. "The Promised Land: The Chicago Defender and the Black Press in Illinois, 1862–1970." In *The Black Press in the Middle West, 1865–1985*, edited by Henry Lewis Suggs, 8–50. Westport, CT: Greenwood Press, 1996.

Wallenstein, Peter. *Tell the Court I Love My Wife: Race, Marriage, and Law—An American History.* New York: Palgrave Macmillan, 2004.

Weiss, Nancy J. "From Black Separatism to Interracial Cooperation: The Origins of Organized Efforts for Racial Advancement, 1890–1920." In *Twentieth-Century America: Recent Interpretations,* 2nd edition, edited by Barton J. Bernstein and Allen J. Matusow. New York: Harcourt Brace Jovanovich, 1972.

———. *The National Urban League, 1910–1940.* New York: Oxford University Press, 1974.

Welter, Barbara. *Dimity Convictions: The American Women in the Nineteenth Century.* Athens: Ohio University Press, 1976.

Wexler, Laura. *Tender Violence: Domestic Visions in an Age of U.S. Imperialism.* Chapel Hill: University of North Carolina Press, 2000.

Whang, Pom-Ju. *50-year History of Holt Children's Services, Inc.* Seoul: Holt Children's Service, 2005.

White, Deborah Gray. *Too Heavy a Load: Black Women in Defense of Themselves.* New York: Norton, 1999.

Winslow, Rachel Rains. *The Best Possible Immigrants: International Adoption and the American Family.* Philadelphia: University of Pennsylvania Press, 2017.

Wolott, Victoria W. *Remaking Respectability: African-American Women in Interwar Detroit.* Chapel Hill: University of North Carolina Press, 2001.

Wolseley, Roland E. *The Black Press, U.S.A.* Ames: Iowa State University Press, 1971.

Woo, Susie. "A New American Comes 'Home'": Race, Nation, and the Immigration of Korean War Adoptees, 'GI Babies,' and Brides." Dissertation, Yale University, 2010.

Woodson, Robert. *Black Hostages of the Child Welfare System: Strategies for True Reform.* Washington, DC: Heritage Foundation, 1991.

Wu, Ellen D. *The Color of Success: Asian Americans and the Origins of the Model Minority.* Princeton, NJ: Princeton University Press, 2014.

Yang, Philip Q. *Asian Immigration to the United States.* Cambridge, UK: Polity Press, 2011.

Yoshimi, Yoshiaki. *Comfort Women: Sexual Slavery in the Japanese Military During World War II.* New York: Columbia University Press, 2001.

Young, Leontine R. *Out of Wedlock: A Study of the Problems of the Unmarried Mother and Her Child.* New York: McGraw-Hill, 1954.

Yuh, Ji-Yeon. *Beyond the Shadow of Camptown: Korean Military Brides in America.* New York: New York University Press, 2002.

Yung, Judy. *Unbound Feet: A Social History of Chinese Women in San Francisco.* Berkeley: University of California Press, 1995.

Zeiger, Susan. *Entangling Alliances: Foreign War Brides and American Soldiers in the Twentieth Century.* New York: New York University Press, 2010.

INDEX

Adopt-A-Child, 79–80; "At Home" program, 81–82; color consciousness and adoption, 83–86, 255n49; housing reform, 82–83; placement and referral outcomes, 88

adoption as rescue, 4–7, 11, 106; 123; African Americans' narratives of rescue and responsibility, 23, 16, 116, 140–141, 147–148; Pearl S. Buck's evolving rescue narrative of hybrid superiority, 189, 203, 206–207, 216–218, 220; Harry Holt's religious justification for, 121, 122; soldiers' understanding of, 116

African Americans: adoptions of Korean black children, 11–13, 157–159; adoptions of WWII brown babies, 11–12; economic barriers to Korean adoption, 81–82, 129, 155, 157, 158; informal adoptions (US), 1, 8–9, 69, 94, 95, 126–127, 167; formal adoptions (US), 9, 13, 95–96, 100–101, 228

African American adoptive mothers: child welfare professionals' negative assessments of, 156, paid labor as a barrier to adoption, 96, 152, 156; social workers' evaluations of gender conformity of, 159–161; successful pairing of paid labor and parenting, 167–168

African American children: adoptability of, 74; as "hard-to-place," 102, 193, 254n26

African American soldiers: acts of violence against Korean civilians, 26–27; care of mascots, 30–32, 46; casualties during the Korean War, 37, 244n19; child-centered humanitarianism, 22, 37, 42; civil rights activism, 40; courts martial during the Korean War, 37, 45, 247n63; drug use and addiction, 57–58; and the nuclear family ideal, 130-135; single biological fathers rejected as Korean adoption candidates, 127–128; social and sexual relationships with Korean Women, 48, 51–57; social and sexual relationships with Japanese women, 51, 54; support of Korean orphanages, 32–33, 46–47; support of Japanese orphanages, 46

The Afro-American (newspaper), 23, 35, 45; critique of segregation, 35–36; defense of African American soldiers' wartime social and sexual relationships abroad, 48–49, 51–52, 56–57; defense of African American soldiers' manhood, 24, 30–31; on the Korean War, 35, 45, 48, 59–60

Afro-Orientalism: Pearl S. Buck's Afro-Orientalism, 208–209; African American soldiers' responses to, 40, 41, 51, 248n75; deployed by African Americans, 58–59; promotion by black intellectuals, 40

Aid to Dependent Children (ADC), 97, 153

Akins, Dana, 195

American-Korean Foundation (AKF), 108; assistance to ISS Korea branch, 120

Armed Forces Assistance to Korea, 46

ABOUT THE AUTHOR

Kori A. Graves is Assistant Professor in the Department of History at the University at Albany, State University of New York.